THE ATOM OF DELIGHT

THE ATOM OF DELIGHT

NEIL M. GUNN

Introduction by
JOHN PICK
Foreword by
DAIRMID GUNN

With an afterword by
ALAN SPENCE

Polygon
EDINBURGH

Foreword © Dairmid Gunn 1986
Introduction © John Pick 1986
Afterword © Alan Spence 1989
Atom of Delight © The Neil Gunn Estate

First published in Great Britain by
Faber and Faber, 1956
Reprinted by Polygon 1986, 1989, 1993
22 George Square, Edinburgh

Printed in Great Britain
by Redwood Press Ltd,
Melksham, Wiltshire

The publisher acknowledges subsidy from the
Scottish Arts Council towards the publication
of this volume.

Gunn, Neil M.
The atom of delight
1. Gunn, Neil —
    Biography
2. Authors, Scottish —
    20th century — Biography
1. Title
823'.912 PR6013.U64Z/

ISBN 0 7486 6155 7

Contents

Foreword

The Atom of Delight was Neil Gunn's last book and marked the end of a long and creative period of work that saw the publication of twenty novels. *The Grey Coast* appeared in 1926 and the last novel, *The Other Landscape*, in 1954. The very title *The Other Landscape* carries a symbolic overtone — that of Gunn's lifelong concern with the relationship between local reality and transcendent meaning. Gunn saw everyday reality in the Highlands of Scotland as something charged with symbolic significance. In each of his novels there is an element of search for what has been variously termed as wholeness, integration, delight or, simply, self. The way for the search was prepared by a prolonged and intense backward gaze at roots, origin and source.

This book has been called a spiritual autobiography. It certainly does not fit the idea of a conventional autobiography based on external facts of a public or private life. If it is to be called an autobiography at all, it is because it does contain circumstances and things that shaped a life. Also within it are incidents and places that appear in his novels and stories. This prompted John Pick and Francis Hart in their excellent biography of Gunn, *A Highland Life*, to write of it: "The book is reflective philosophy rather than autobiography. He could only write autobiography in fiction and fictional autobiography at that." The biographers' analysis could be applied, at least in part, to Marcel Proust, the French author to whom Gunn alludes in *The Atom of Delight*. Proust maintained that any worthwhile novel expressed the author's hidden self and explored memories of his own past. This theory was borne out by Gunn in his novels and is explicitly declared by him in the dedication to his brother John in a brilliant early novel, *Highland River*, which anticipates and prepares the way for his final work. "Some of the characters may have strayed in from *Morning Tide* under different names. I cannot explain this odd behaviour — apart from the old desire to be in on the hunt in any disguise." With *Morning Tide* such an archetypal novel of family life (and strongly influenced by Gunn's childhood experiences) the last phrase of the dedication could be considered the key to most of the author's work.

For Gunn there were two selves, the social self that presented itself to the world and the second self or inner core, which, like a proposition from Euclid, was autonomous and given. The inner core, the circle round himself, was precious to Gunn and nothing was more abhorrent or terrifying to him than its being threatened. Arthur Koestler's *Darkness at Noon*, written in the 1930s, made an immense impression on him. He was profoundly disturbed by the possibilities of psychiatric torture as practised in the modern police state. Some years later when prompted to write a novel with immediate relevance to the dark years straddling 1940 he came up with his anti-Utopian work, *The Green Isle of the Great Deep*. The novel illustrates the failures of the totalitarian state and its machinery of control over the individual to destroy minds alive to the values and experience that provide meaning. It concentrated Gunn's thinking on the importance of wholeness and spiritual integrity in a world increasingly dominated by materialism and the utilitarian philosophy of the greatest happiness for the greatest number.

In the early 1950s John Pick sent Gunn a copy of Eugen Herrigel's *Zen in the Art of Archery*. It was received with delight. Here was a centuries old tradition of exploration of a region remarkably similar to that which had fascinated Gunn throughout his creative life. The parallels between his own work and that of an alien tradition thrilled Gunn and caused him to plunge into the study of Zen Buddhism. Indeed the Eastern philosophy had a noticeable influence on the structure of *The Atom of Delight*. Gunn, however, never claimed to be an authority on Zen; he simply asserted that he felt at home with the exponents of Zen. He disliked the label mystic, with which he had been tagged, because of its unfortunate connotation of woolliness of thought and lack of clarity. For him, with his vision of light, the balance between intellectual and intuitive functions was all important. Reason had never to be abandoned — only kept in its place. After all, the atom of delight or, in Zen terms, the moment of Satori, was when a heightened awareness was achieved by the understanding going beyond the boundaries of conscious and limited intellect. The autobiography vividly depicts Gunn's two worlds — the everyday world to which he was bound by habit and fear and the world that lay beyond this, the other landscape or the landscape of delight. As a poetic novelist, Gunn in this autobiography and in all his works wanted to be seen not standing for, but amidst his words. John Pick and Francis Hart sum up most beautifully the wonder of the autobiography in a sentence from *A Highland Life*: "Once you accept *The Atom of Delight* in its own terms and live in its world, it is wise, enlivening, humorous and full of golden light." To that I have nothing to add.

29th June 1985   DAIRMID GUNN

Introduction

Neil Gunn was a deeply serious writer who liked to treat literature as a game, pretending that each book might be his last. He wrote to Nan Shepherd "I am not really a literary man ... for I don't know that one ever wants to have an understanding with anything so much as with life", and to Naomi Mitchison "Unless we're concerned with life in its vivid living moments, we should take to pamphlets". He was after the salmon of wisdom, but to satisfy him it had to be a real salmon in the pool. His books combine emotional and intellectual energy to an unusual degree and he wanted his readers to share not only his concern with the texture and vitality of experience but also his concern with its essence. It is not surprising that some of his novels aroused confusion and discomfort.

His last novel, *The Other Landscape* (1954), was ambitious and difficult to categorise and it was not understood. The misunderstandings saddened him and made him feel, not for the first time, that the fifties' climate of anxiety, cold war and despair was inimical to his most fundamental aims. Why were writers like John Cowper Powys and L. H. Myers, whose attention was always directed upon the meanings and value of human life, and for whose work he felt an affectionate admiration, universally ignored, while those who dealt in darkness and negation were awarded both praise and scrutiny?

Novels grow in a mind ready to nurture any fiction-seed which may alight there. After the critical cold shoulder turned to *The Other Landscape* Neil Gunn lost the urge to grow plants from fiction-seed. It was not encouraging when old friends felt as baffled as the critics. He wrote:

> Have just got a letter from Maurice Walsh, thanking me for my new book (*The Other Landscape*), and regretting that it will make no money. He struggled valiantly to find out what a lot of it was about. I suppose he's dead right. . . . Haven't written anything for a long time, and I'm afraid it will be a long time before I do.

His wife Daisy began to feel that the time might be too long. "He's not really happy without a book to write," she said. "Why don't *you* think of something?" This was a job to approach with caution. Any lure would need to be as subtly designed and as neatly tied as a trout fly, and I was no fly fisherman. Novels were 'out', and he shied away both from the abstract and the directly personal. What was left? It was a relief when he wrote:

> The point to which I took very great exception in your letter was that which suggested (1) I should begin to do some work on (2) of all things, wise insights and wisdoms. Apart from destroying my somnolent ease, what on earth do you mean? All I know in that way could be shoved down on two pages. And yet into me you put the gnawing bug. . . .

Of course the book he eventually produced is as different from my tentative notions as a butterfly from a chrysalis. Here is his account of work in progress, which shows his rich enjoyment in the chase:

> Yes, you've set me going, so I hope you're in as many difficulties, incredulities, absurdities, nonsensicalities and impossibilities. . . . But assuming the thing will have a shape it will be an autobiography, a detective story, a Freudian analysis (of Freud), a spoon for physics, a critical commentary on Yeats, Proust, Wordsworth, Rilke, and Uncle Tom Eliot, a high dive and a long swim into anthropology, poaching, church attendance and sucking eggs, and a way of using these in a sustained, convoluting, forward-and-backward search, with a ruthless precision in the complexities of expression, into the nature of delight. Now you've got it — without the short story which I'm planting in the middle of the plot like a flower pot (for something must be plain). And the title, the one and only certainty so far, *The Atom of Delight*. . . . I shan't be surprised if its half-concealed logic works up into a simple, naive philosophic system, and you know how a system chokes the wisdom you are always prepared to salute. Though I'll do my best with camouflage. . . .

This, as is usual with Neil Gunn, both reveals and conceals what he is about. It gives the impression that the book will be a kind of wandering at random through the realms of possibility. In fact there is nothing random about it. He always knew both in life and in literature exactly what he was doing, it was a form like that of a plant, grown from within itself. Throughout *The Atom of Delight* he knows where he is going and how he intends to get there, and if he dances off down byways he always returns to the road bearing gifts.

He had begun to reflect on his own life and to seek in memory those experiences which illuminate the rest — the moments of awakening, recognition and wonder. His intention was to recreate events and meditate on their implications and significance. Because some of the incidents are of a kind used again and again in the novels, to go back to the novels after reading *The Atom of Delight* is to find them enriched in a hundred unexpected ways. He writes, "What has autobiography to do with the atom of delight? It provides the atom. Any other way of providing it would be an imaginary way. That might save the face of the self but the self could never then say: It happened."

Throughout the book ideas draw their nourishment from the vivid freshness of the scenes described: the secret pandrop sucked in church; the cow "sleek, with sides bulging like a great cask"; the night expedition in the bush-haunted strath; "plump blaeberries with their misty bloom"; the tailor conducting his own song with a bottle; the arrow piercing the dumb man's hat — all these feed us with light.

Those who read only for such scenes may see the argument as an interruption, but the "interruptions" are essential to the story. Those who like an argument to be conducted formally within strict categories may resent the fact that themes appear and retire like themes in music, and in their resentment fail to see that the reasoning is close and the summaries concise and pointed. The book is like a voice in conversation, and wanders, juggles, balances, and threads a way through thoughts and memories as conversation does.

It is worth looking at Gunn's own account more carefully. He talks of "a ruthless precision in the complexities of expression", yet it is often said that *The Atom of Delight* tends towards the vague and elusive. There is indeed much in the book that is elusive but nothing at all that is vague. An examination, for example, of the drastic limitation of human nature inherent in the doctrines of behaviourism ends with the phrase "Pavlov did not succeed in producing the gayest of dogs", which not only sums up the argument but opens the mind to the possibility that joy may be as close to the essence of life as is salivation at the prospect of food.

Again, a formal philosopher could not improve upon "If life-mind is a function of matter then it would seem that the capacity of matter to function in this way must be latent within it", while it does not need a philosopher to appreciate the exactness of this description: "The sea was so full that it sighed. On the other side of the harbour entrance the small wave ran along the wooden piles of the breakwater, lipping them; and beyond, on the shingly beach, it broke in a small edging of white lace that shone before the bubbles died." He is justified, I think, in claiming precision of utterance.

The short story which he "plants in the middle" is an account of the boy's wild, secret struggle to catch a salmon bare-handed, another version of which appears in *Highland River*. Of course the story as told in *The Atom* is as much fiction as the story in *Highland River* — or, to put it another way, both are equally true. To recreate an incident from memory is necessarily to imagine it. Is he then importing into childhood an element of adult experience? He is returning with the most scrupulous attention to incidents in childhood and youth in order to discover their essential nature, and his reflections are those of a man in his sixties.

"I shan't be surprised if its half-concealed logic works up into a simple, naive philosophic system. . . . Though I'll do my best with camouflage" is accurate enough, for the argument does indeed develop into a not-so-simple, not-so-naive philosophic system, tied closely to the experiences on which it is based, and entirely free from jargon. Then why the camouflage? Because to lay claim to the creation of a system is to invite that destructive analysis which it is the mission of the book to make irrelevant; because too much definition and abstraction destroy the explorer's fun; because insight always comes upon its discoveries "by the way"; and because he takes a positive pleasure in being evasive.

This evasiveness produces peculiarities in the way the story is told. The fact that the central figure — who is, after all, Neil Gunn himself — is referred to as "the boy" gives to the account an oddly generalised air, and leads to some strange circumlocutions: "Will worked in the Admiralty and the other in the Home Office . . .". It takes us a moment to realise that this "other" is the author wearing a disguise. But the convention achieves two things: it increases the sense of objectivity, and prevents the hunter from becoming the hunted. He writes of the boy "putting a circle" round himself, so that he is protected "not only from the good intentions of his elders but also from whatever adult evil was let loose among them". "You merely turned your eyes away and, in the face of persistence, went anonymous." In his maturity Neil Gunn was warm, courteous and full of humour, prepared to accept with patience the unpleasant manifestations of others; but he allowed no trespass on his freedom and could withdraw into cold detachment should a persistent stranger cross invisible boundaries. This detachment proved more effective than anger and resentment, for to express negative emotion is to "give yourself away", and to "give yourself away" is to waste the energy on which creative work depends. His feelings were passionate and went deep, as the novels show; indeed they often tremble with emotional intensity and move on the edge of darkness. In contrast, when addressing the reader directly he fills his scenes with vitality while retaining a decent reticence.

This leads us to the question: is it legitimate to present your life as a subject for reflection if you are not prepared to present it whole, to give us the mean, vain and murky moments, of which adolescence is so full, as well as the moments of freedom and grace? All that Gunn says, for example, about the seamier side of his time in London is: "There were spells as dreary as the streets, anxieties and frets and miseries and fears and conflicts and temptations and illicit desires and obsessive sex and the rest. The old bundle of faggots." Nothing here is made explicit, nothing is brought alive. What darkness there is in the book is almost metaphysical — the boy's sudden fear of the formless night, and an attack on the mature man by a disintegrating force like "black electricity". Some readers may feel that he is evading them, refusing to grant them his trust.

I do not think this suspicion is justified. The job undertaken in *The Atom* is to discover where light is to be found, for when light is found it becomes possible to accept the dark. Gunn claims the source of delight in realisation of a "second self" which comes into its own when the everyday self is momentarily forgotten, by-passed or laid aside. Once it is understood that this hidden self, this witness able to attend with fresh awareness to all that lives and moves, is real and permanent, then freedom becomes possible, and shames, miseries and humiliations fall into place. "The second self is not an assumption. It is the fount from which assumptions proceed." To concentrate on the posturings and tribulations of the first self would be to distort the intention of the book.

This leads us directly to the argument, which rests solidly on delight as a creative experience and on that discovery of the second self, and from there develops its own logic. The discovery is simple, clear and sharp, there is nothing esoteric or mysterious about it. We find the source of delight and then forget we have found it, for the very thing it is most important to remember is the easiest to forget. I once asked a group of women whose insight I had learned to trust, each to relate an experience which they had found to be of great personal significance, stipulating that they should ignore those events normally prejudged as necessarily important — marriage, the birth of a child, the death of parents and so on — and rely on what now occurred to them spontaneously. One after another they began to recall some incident on the face of it merely accidental and "by the way" — "I was sitting in a meadow and saw the sun shining on the grasses and heard a bee buzz past and it all seemed wonderful". That kind of thing. These stories brought to mind an experience of my own. I was about five years old and playing some game like hide-and-seek. I ran under a wooden house built of pillars and lay alone in the deep cool shadow looking out at the sharp brilliance of sunlight. The tension of the game was gone and a kind of suspended wonder took its place. I felt: "This shade! That light! And here *I* am!"

Neil Gunn tried to communicate these moments often enough in his novels, particularly *The Well at the World's End*, but in *The Atom of Delight* he went further, he sought to explain them, and his account of "the boy in the stream" is personal, detailed, specific and central to the meaning of the book.

> The shallow river flowed around and past with its variety of lulling monotonous sounds; a soft wind, warmed by the sun, came upstream and murmured in my ears as it continually slipped from my face. . . .
>
> Then the next thing happened, and happened, so far as I can remember, for the first time. I have tried but can find no simpler way of expressing what happened by saying: *I came upon myself sitting there*.

> Within the mood of content, as I have tried to recreate it, was the self
> and this self was me.
>
> The state of content deepened wonderfully and everything was
> embraced in it.
>
> There was no 'losing' of the self in the sense that there was a blank from
> which I awoke or came to. The self may have thinned away — it did — but
> so delightfully that it also remained at the centre in a continuous and
> perfectly natural way. And then within this amplitude the self as it were
> became aware of seeing itself, not as an 'I' or an 'ego' but rather as a
> stranger it had come upon and was even a little shy of.

At this crucial point in the story "the boy" becomes "I" and we
are accepted fully into the author's trust.

Nor is this all. Activity produces its own realisation of the
"second self", when the player "in form" unerringly hits the
target or moves to the right place at the right time more swiftly
than thought can direct, so that the first self is lost in a realisation
of unity. It is as an object lesson in the meaning of this experience
that Gunn gives his account of Eugen Herrigel's *Zen in the Art of
Archery*. Since this seminal book of 1953 'Zen in the Art' of all and
anything has become an intellectual fashion, but Herrigel's initial
account remains unique for its simplicity of presentation and its
exactness of understanding.

The Atom of Delight takes us only — with a few events
imported from a later time — up to the writer's eighteenth year.
I do not believe that Gunn meant to limit his reflections to scenes
from childhood and youth. I think it was his (concealed)
intention to deal with adult life in a second volume. But he never
did so. He said once, "When I finished *The Atom of Delight* I felt
that was the end of my youth and now I'd really get down to
it. . . . But the energy wasn't there. You need to be able to
concentrate and I couldn't manage it." He was not referring only
to writing, but to *doing*, to making discoveries in the mind.
Despite the death of his wife and his own debilitating illness he
remained open, alert and full of understanding, and although he
wrote little he gave much.

It was a continuing source of wonder and interest to him that
letters arrived from far and near expressing gratitude and
affection for *The Atom of Delight*. It is one of those rare books
which appeals to individuals as having been written for each of
them alone, speaking directly to their condition and enabling

them to realise something they have always known and inexplicably lost. The book begins with the words "Often when looking for a thing I find something else". You may come to feel this as you read; nothing could be more rewarding.

21 July 1985. J. B. PICK

Chapter 1

By the Way

Often when looking for a thing I find something else. I knew what I was looking for, but what I find is surprising. At once some part of life is resurrected; persons move about, I see their faces, the place, almost the air of that forgotten time. Yes, it was like that! for now in some mysterious way the happenings, the arrested moments are cleansed. Outlines are clear; the expression in the eyes, caught out of a myriad of expressions, is the lasting, the essential one; clothes, colour; the leaves on the tree, the sky; not the scent, perhaps, but the freshness of the scent. Now there is no confusion. This is how it was; if love, it was wonderful; if tragedy, it is accepted at last. I inhabit that place and judge no more.

Sometimes, of course, it is not like that for what is found opens no door. At once I think of a small key in the bottom of an old gladstone bag. I have not seen it for a few years, but I remember coming across it after a house flitting when I was searching for something quite other. I tried it in the lock of the gladstone bag but it did not fit. It went into the hole but would turn neither way. Obviously it was the key of some other bag, but strive as I would to remember it, I couldn't. Yet if only it were possible, I fancied, to turn the key in the vanished suitcase, I should discover particular moments, scenes, incidents, names, in that distant period of my teens lodged half in London and half in Edinburgh. Vaguely through my mind go privacies; the corridors, the doors, to rooms in different lodgings; this youth and that girl; streets at all times but particularly at night; flares over stalls in side streets where ripe fruits from Covent Garden are sold cheap — a penny a pound for plums, twopence for strawberries — because in their luscious condition they could not hold together for another day; the adult life, the fantastic, the perverted human stories. . . . But for all these the small key means nothing in particular.

In that early age one quoted Omar Khayyam or other favourite poet without discomfort. "There was a Door to which I found no Key" could roll off the tongue — and off the mind — in a happy fatalism that was enriched by the picture of the poet-philosopher sitting under the bough with a loaf of bread, a flask of wine, a book of verse — and thou. The whole came to a conclusion not with thin sounds like *Finis* or *The End*, but with *Tamám Shud*. "Tamám Shud!" and the book whuffed shut not with a whimper but a bang. The small key is still up aloft in the rather battered gladstone bag, whose cheeks have fallen in, though it still sits on its own bottom, if somewhat awry, like one of Omar's pots.

Sitting on, I begin to perceive that research into lost times is a search for delights, for the particular moment, the arrested scene, that holds a significance difficult to define; but not at all vague; vivid, fine with a delight that words blur; as the word significance blurs the clear *this is it*.

What is this delight in its own moment, beyond considerations of thought, morals, politics, religion? Is it possible to hunt it out, to see how it happens, to realize how and when it comes about? And in the process to avoid as far as possible abstract words, as a naked boy avoids obstacles in his way when hunting a salmon in a pool?

I shall come upon the naked boy plunging after his salmon in a pool, for if the hunt is to be real it will have to be founded on actual experience. Clearly in the pursuit of the atom of delight autobiography must provide the atom. Any other way of providing it would be an imagined way. That might save the face of the self but the self could never then say: It happened to me. Presently, then, we shall follow a small boy in a Highland strath having his thrilling adventures, adventures that took him into depths where he caught a glimpse of fish even more evasive than salmon.

But every game hunt requires some preliminary reflections on the terrain, the aids and obstacles on the way, what destroys the scent or diverts the wind. Such reflections, indeed, can have a special kind of delight for every hunter who is sure that the quarry exists. Assuming our hunt has still got its quarry, delight, how do we pick up its spoor?

First, then, though the general direction, as in any sport, is forward, clues can be picked up by a cast back. But the backward cast becomes entirely nostalgic unless the clues are used in an actual hunt today and tomorrow. In what follows, this is never forgotten.

The second reflection, born from experience, is that in this hunt, more than in any other, the spoor is picked up by chance, often when least expected, and the quarry is come upon not by design so much as by the way; much as, in the simple matter of taking a holiday, a person knows that he needs a stroke of good luck to make it outstanding; for circumstances, the unknown, cannot be compelled into a pattern beforehand. Indeed he may find himself deceived by the setting and its personnel to the point of being so bored, frustrated, that he thinks: Never again!

But should he stumble into the game that is miraculously waiting for him, he knows *this is it*. Here is the circle and he finds himself in it. What luck! The whole of him comes together and, by coming together, expands. Even his dullest cell seems to grow radioactive and communicate delight in a way that had always been in him, he feels — given the chance.

His experience is rare, no doubt, and therefore memorable. But that makes no difference to the fact that he has had it. And it remains as simple and real as that, having tasted a strawberry, he knows he has tasted it — munch and juice and swallow — and not all the king's men with all the king's inexhaustible variety of regulations and prohibitions drawn by all the king's horses, mechanical, atomic and all, can wash the taste away; not anyhow until the brain itself is washed, and even then the impression, the impress on some grey substratum, remains. That can be rubbed out only by killing.

The difference between "by the way" and "on the way" may be the difference between not having any kind of philosophy and having one. To be "on the way" is to have an idea of what Eastern thought calls the Way. But whether there is such a Way or not, there can be no doubt at all about "by the way". What happens by the way is not a matter of philosophy but of life, of universal experience. One can of course attempt to analyse it, to fit it into this system of thought or that, but by its very nature it is bound to cause a diversion in the neatly fitted jigsaw. In the end the diversion becomes the deviation that wrecks the system.

No wonder those who create systems fear it like the devil. This simple atom of longing, of delight, carries a high explosive potential. It is verbally miscalled from "the irrational" to "heresy". It has been hanged, drawn and quartered, burnt at the stake, gassed, and shot in the back of the neck. Then up it pops when least expected; with a smile, too, that is a whole dawn of wonder — if persecution hasn't got its claws in too deep; and, if so, at least persecution is then seen for what it is — senseless, futile, the bloody destroyer.

So in the hunt one has to keep an eye open for the chance clue. Not that the eye will always spot it; or, rather, the eye may see it but will consider it of no value because it is outside the pattern of what is expected. Afterwards, perhaps in the moment of defeat, comes the reflection: If only I had realized. . . .

But clues are for the hunt, and the quarry here is delight. How to get an early glimpse of the quarry? For it has an atom in its core that is even more elusive than those atoms hunted by physicists. A few simple words may be said about physicists, but for our immediate purpose there are game-book records already in existence. These records, sometimes called literature, not only cover the territory but on occasion flush the quarry itself. However, let it be clear that clues and glimpses from such quarters will be accepted only as aids in the hunt. No reflections will be considered of value unless they stem from experience. Always, first: it happened.

So in this preliminary survey of the ground let me make it a personal matter straight away by saying that recently, quite by chance, I was handed a novel to read, and let me add at the same time that if a book or two is examined at any length in the course of this narrative it is not in any attempt to distinguish them in their excellence from other books but in their aptitude for the hunt.

The novel is called *The Near and the Far*, by L. H. Myers. The setting is India in the sixteenth century, the canvas very wide, the characterization extremely diverse, and thought ranges from darkest superstition to the creation of a synthetic religion by the mighty emperor, Akbar. One does not think of it as an ambitious creation because it is controlled in all its parts by an easy mastery. Anyhow, as a setting it is of a piece, and its range over human motive is certainly broad.

But as I read I find that at long or short intervals a pencil line has been drawn in the margin by the owner of the book against certain sentences or passages. At once this arrests the eye as any peephole might or unblinded window at night. The feeling of an invasion of privacy is at once oddly uncomfortable and fascinating. For any such marking is primarily a give-away of the mind that moved the pencil. So this is what the marker is like in her inmost recesses! As it happens, these are passages I might have marked myself, and I read them over again with the peculiar pleasure of discovery, the delight that momentarily withdraws from the book and enjoys itself. Emperors and gurus, slaves and mad elephants, are gone with the sixteenth century. To pick up by chance so rare a community of understanding!

Then the mind takes the next step, to the author, for he wrote the lines. So he is like that! Apart from the elephants and emperors, the setting and the décor, this is where he gives himself away; though I am not deceived by this phrase, for quite simply now I realize that this is what he has in him to give, that finally it is of the nature of all he has to give.

That other readers might have made other markings, or been so unimpressed as to make no markings at all, has no relevance for our particular experience. This happened to us. General criticism is in a world apart, like the swinging monkeys in the forests.

Those few marked passages were more than spotlights on a stage. Indeed the stage could have done without them and the action remained quite clear. They were spotlights on something other, and they gave the whole a special significance, perhaps the only lasting significance. But this is difficult territory and for the moment all that need be said is that the passages were come upon unexpectedly, by the way. And if anything need be added about the author, even by way of a guess, it is that they came to him unexpectedly too, when the mysterious inner worker, on his own, distils for himself his own blessed drop.

Chapter 2

The Atom

The moment of happiness in life which comes not to order but unexpectedly. But is happiness quite the word, or even delight? Sometimes the moment seems one of insight from which the emotional tone or colour comes away. Think of a note of music struck in an absolute silence and of the ear listening to the overtones. Now "insight" is not enough. No word is ever quite enough, not in this kind of hunt. For instance, the sudden note of music does something to the silence of which one had become unaware; it arrests the silence, brings awareness of it, and by so doing defines it for the listening ear. It is an insight into the silence. It cleanses the moment, and through the clarity one's listening ascends with the overtones, while one's being remains at the centre of the experience, in that tranced condition not yet capable of saying, "My God, that was wonderful!" So the insight is into something more than the silence, it is an apprehension of other factors, even of that other kind of silence into which the ascending overtones finally vanish. Yet this whole complex, unanalysable because inexhaustible, is a moment of simple experience that happens to everyone. If so many words seem to obscure so simple an affair, blame the words, but hang on to the happening.

Hang on to the hunt, however elusive the quarry may be. And this elusiveness can become very annoying, even irritating, like midges or clegs that bite in the undergrowth. And the bites breed questions; one in particular: Is it worth it? Now, at this time of day?

The question grows more solemn as it spreads out until it includes the whole world, with big cold wars and small hot ones and scientists estimating just how many atomic bombs of a given kind would require to be dropped in a specified pattern to destroy all life on earth. Here is the stupendous fact, the big bang, and there is nothing elusive about it.

But the hunt for the big bang has been the most pertinacious exercise in elusiveness man has ever undertaken, from the first Greek thoughts about an atom to the last piece of research into its sub-nuclear contents. A hunt for something so infinitesimal, so evasive, that its very "existence" was a hypothesis. So small still that it cannot be seen, can never be seen, yet can be deduced from indications and intimations, "waves" in a tide that taken at the flood by some egomaniac may lead to human annihilation. As simple and stark as that, this hunt into the infinitesimals of matter, this long, devoted, marvellous effort to arrest and study the invisibly elusive. And it went on in its own world, as different from the world of clamour and war as a monastery from a stock exchange.

But I need not wade into heavy water over this, if already the thought has been born that nothing, no happening, no insight, in the realm of mind may be so small as to be insignificant, unexplosive. The thought has to be regarded coolly, without personal taint, for being humble about it, or "amused", is as absurd as being obsessed.

So if the physical atom is held to have a recognizable or consistent pattern, what about the atom of mind? Are there many mental atoms of varying constitution? Are they even more elusive than their material counterparts? Would it be possible so to follow one up that it might be cornered, even caught and made use of, much as the physicist has cornered and used his? Psychics and physics sound oddly companionable terms for warriors. Indeed their friendship has long been known to philosophers as Duality.

Happily we are concerned here neither with philosophies nor with physics, so let us get back to the question whether the hunt is worth while. It would appear, then, that its elementary or elusive nature need not be against it. This is something to have got hold of.

Having mentioned the novel, let me look at it next as a literary form on the odd chance of catching glimpses of further clues; and here some indication of direction may be given by those intelligent critics who have been saying that the novel has had its day, that it is now a threshing of threshed straw, a heap of human gossip that has been flailed over and over until hardly an oat of new interest or significance is left to chew.

Certainly some atom is being very elusive when a reader, having finished a novel, exclaims, "What a waste of time!" Clearly he might have found something more interesting — or less boring — in life itself. This feeling, if acute, may awake the thought that a chunk of life has literally been lost during the reading, and lost for ever. He suddenly has the sensation of himself within the dead blank of the lost time.

The book is tossed aside. He gets up and moves about, like an animal disturbed in its wood by it hardly knows what. The sensation of meeting his shadow in that blank hinterland can be an intimate and disconcerting experience.

But there are many kinds of novels. The kind that sets out to give a picture of human beings in their social and economic setting may, if it is sufficiently large and complicated, be so "like the thing" that it attains the verisimilitude of "a slice of life". The details are accurate, the way the factory, the department, the farm, the prison, the ship, the military headquarters is run is flawless. But a documentary film or a television camera can do this kind of projection with a greater verisimilitude, particularly for those with a weak visualizing faculty.

In the novel of high adventure, how can any fiction hope to compete in the realm of the fantastic and ghastly with what has been, and is, happening in the world of our day? Here, if anywhere, what is wanted even as pure thrill is an account of the real thing by the person who has done it.

Similarly, however brilliant an artist's technical accomplishment he would find it difficult, in the effort to achieve sheer "likeness", to compete with the colour photograph. Painting and sculpture have long recognized this. The painted trees we hang on our walls nowadays still remind us of trees, if sometimes only just.

For many, therefore, the record of sheer likeness, of truth to the facts, is not enough. Facts are not enough, and unless one actually needs a diet of them, can be very dull; anyway, they can be got from all kinds of reliable sources or presented accurately by appropriate mechanisms.

What is missing, then? Perhaps the characters have not been

brought to life; they are dummies, types. Despite the often immense skill devoted to building up their various parts (appearance, speech, action), the sum of their parts remains void as a ventriloquist's doll. But is this always a sufficient answer? For consider what happens when we are presented with a real-life adventure, written by the man who had the adventure but who, as sometimes happens, is an unskilled worker in words. The very clichés he uses, the "wooden" descriptions, the "dumb" reactions, contrive to enhance the authenticity of the blood-curdling yarn. Then let us be told that we have been hoaxed, that what we have read is a piece of fiction by a journalist who knows his readers as his onions.

When the sands shift so uncertainly underfoot where is the firm ground? Can we find what no hoax can play tricks with or analysis explain away?

To revert to that novel of old India. Before a woman goes to the trouble of getting a pencil, often for her an elusive implement, and marking a passage so that it may readily be found again, the passage must have conveyed some kind of insight that irradiated the mind not only with understanding but with the delight of understanding. The exact nature of the insight or understanding will be considered later. But, for the moment, here is the atom of delight in action and it has the effect of irradiating the mind with the kind of light in which the mind sees or discovers itself. That *I* should find *this* within *me*! It is an astonishing discovery that cannot be explained away any more than can the taste of a strawberry.

And the discovery does not stop there for, as has been said, the irradiation extends to the author of the book and discovers his mind; and then to the whole book, the characters, the plot or drama, the descriptions of scenery, the mad elephants and the swinging monkeys, all of whom and of which are given a vivid particularity, a new significance, that may be enhanced still further, at any moment, *by a new discovery*.

As a matter of curiosity, I asked her about her manner of reading the book. For one might suppose that such a book would be gulped like a thriller. But this had not been the case; in fact, the very opposite. As a busy housewife she had reserved it for reading in bed at night. "And it did not keep you awake?" "No. I read on till I come to some special bit. Then I put it away with a feeling of joy, knowing I would come back to it. I did not want it to be finished."

Clearly this reader has not grown tired of one particular novel; in short, for her the novel in its traditional form could provide the atom of delight. For her, the novel that was "a waste of time" was the novel that did not provide it. And for her this exhausted the whole debate on the novel as a literary form.

If this may seem an over-simplification of a very intricate affair, still I would suggest that it is of the nature of a solid foothold in the sally of discovery.

For we know, of course, that the novel has been changing, as social life has been changing. New techniques have been applied. Whether inside a novel or inside a factory new technical devices can, for example, quicken the tempo of production. What was cumbersome and slow becomes streamlined and swift. The old novelist and his reader would be bewildered by a fantastic juggling with time and place which has become a commonplace to the novelist and reader of today. I listen to a programme on the radio and am prepared by the interposition of a bar or two of music or a momentary fade-out for a jump in place from Paris to Peru or in time from James Joyce to Lao Tsu. The flashback as a device in story-telling is understood instantly by the dullest cinema addict. A new technique may initially bewilder, but if it is apt to its purpose it is accepted in a remarkably short time. Indeed as a novelty, even as an "obscurity", it has its devotees from the first moment. As a fact of human experience, this is known to anthropologists who have done field work among primitive tribes. When a daring innovator slipped off her grass girdle and tied a slip of cheap cotton print in its place, watching eyes goggled. My word! The "new Paris model" is an old excitement.

But the coloured slip of cotton did not alter the fundamentals. Despite the streamlining and the space-time juggling, the jet aircraft and the wireless, even the grass and the cotton and the stream of consciousness without commas, the gestation of a human being still takes nine months. The gestation of a new insight is of this order of creation, not of the order of a technical device. Technical devices may assist the labour of creation, verbal streamlining may appear to ease the birth of an insight, but the techniques required for the gestation of the insight in a man's mind or spirit are different from, if not quite opposed to, all that is invented in the realm of applied mechanics, whether in the factory or the studio.

The passage may vary with the marker, but every passage has this in common that it is an unexpected discovery, a revelation that irradiates life with delight.

Much of this may seem obvious. I hope so because it may permit one further step before we come on the boy racing through his strath, and, if only to illustrate the elusive nature of what I am after, let it be a rather difficult or debatable one.

Keats wrote: "Beauty is truth, truth beauty." Assuming one were given to this practice of marking passages, would one mark that passage? For my own part, I doubt it. If I did draw a light line in the margin it might assume the vague shape of a question mark, implying that truth and beauty can hardly be lumped together like that in a positively didactic statement. Austere metaphysicians have pooh-poohed the statement. In short, the atom of irritation interferes in that field where the atom of delight should have complete sway. Yet the passage as a poetic statement arrests; indeed among professional critics it has done quite a lot of arrestment. What then is so undefined or uncertain about it that it should act upon us in this way?

Now for the physicists who have a habit of appearing these days as hot news in the daily press, along with such simplified explanations of how an atom behaves, particularly in its more ferocious moments, that many of us fancy we are getting the hang of the thing. Out of such deep knowledge, let me try to draw a stroke or two that may have some bearing on the poet's statement.

In the comfortable old days of the classical mechanics you hit a billiard ball with the confidence that could predict its velocity and position at any subsequent point. At least a scientist could, in the sense that he could "work it out". Force and matter were then considered two very different things. But when the scientist in recent years got into the atomic underworld and started playing billiards with electrons he found that he couldn't plot the new balls in the old way. The nearer he got, for example, to pinpointing the position of the electron the further away he got from computing its velocity, and vice versa. That there was this "uncertainty relation", about which he would never be able to do anything, shocked him into what one distinguished physicist called a "soul-searching analysis", for he had to go on to realize that force and matter were no longer two things in themselves but two aspects of a something that contained them both. Behind the apparent duality was a profound unity. Similarly, when he began having a close look at the set-up of the electrons, he found himself discovering particles in this experiment, and waves in that. But one thing cannot be two different things? Possibly not, but one thing can show two different aspects of itself; and so we grope again towards accepting waves and particles as two aspects of a unity. The two aspects are not contradictory or self-cancelling, but complementary. Hence a new doctrine of complementarity among reflective physicists.

How now about Keats?

What we are given in his case are (1) a pursuit and apprehension of beauty so intense that its evocation may be marked in innumerable passages of his poetry and (2) a capacity for observation so precise that he can follow, for example, the flight of a nightingale, while that bird is in song, into a countryside realistically complete to its inmost recesses where the light is observed to take on a beechen-green tone and the shadows are for all practical purposes numberless.

When a poet thus equipped sets off after beauty and truth a certain or partial merging of the two becomes inevitable. That is not begging the question because we see it happening. The graph of the bird's flight becomes a thing of beauty. . . .

Then comes the last question. Did Keats in a memorable pursuit, in a super sally, so apprehend beauty and truth that they merged completely? If we take truth and beauty not as absolutes but as aspects, were they seen by the poet for one bright instant in the lineaments of their unity?

But that presupposes we have some warrant for taking them as aspects. Have we? Let us get down to earth again. We have gathered that particles and waves are different aspects of some kind of electronic unity that contains them both. Leaving the infinitely small, we find ourselves being told the same kind of story about the infinitely big. For Newton, space was an absolute

and time was an absolute. They were not aspects. But probing
continued and presently when Einstein began playing billiards
with stars he found that these two absolutes rather stood in the
way of explaining certain strange workings of the universe; but
they got out of his way and fell into line when he regarded them
not as absolutes but as aspects of a four-dimensional continuum,
of a unity that contained them both.

Let us take one further step and ask: has any scientist ever had
any kind of vision of this four-dimensional time-space
continuum? I am assured that there are those who have had "a
glimpse".

Did Keats have his "glimpse"?

My marginal pencil-wriggle with its uncertain shape of a
question mark would be read by an adequate critic as denoting
that I was "troubled", that I had not had "the glimpse" myself but
that I had had a vague intimation of it or I should have made no
mark at all. As for the inadequate critic — the critic who has not
had the glimpse — what he has to say can manifestly have no
relevance in this region of experience. When the glimpse is the
touchstone anything less is nothing.

It is a fascinating region where all kinds of odd juxtapositions
take place not only with a refreshing novelty but with at times a
rare assurance. I am only too aware of having appeared to drag
oddments of physics into the region in an effort to give the atom
of delight respectable company; or even, in the case of Keats, of
having used the physicist to substantiate the poet. But in this
region I am happy to discover that such a proceeding is perfectly
natural. It really has nothing to do with me or my desires at all.
Poetry is there and physics is there. And at once the exhilarating
question asks itself: are they absolutes or two aspects of a unity
behind?

That might well seem a high falutin question thrown at the
moon were it not for the word "exhilarating". From experience I
have discovered that where the exhilarating is, unity is round
about. Let us give the matter one extra probe. We all know that a
poet can become exhilarated in the exercise of his art. What about
a physicist? Or, to get at the irreducible basis of physics, what
about mathematics and the mathematician?

Pythagoras some 2,500 years ago was not only "the father of

mathematics" according to modern scientists but also a mystic. Discussing this rare conjunction, Bertrand Russell writes of "the intoxicating delight of sudden understanding that mathematics gives, from time to time, to those who love it. . . ."

I may now say with good face that a poet can get intoxicated too.

One final tidying-up comment on those "marked passages". After all, there is such a welter of them, with each reader marking his or her own in such profusion of mood and personal idiosyncracy, that we might despair of finding any direction or guiding principle among them. But we need not despair because in the literatures of the past time has done the winnowing work for us, as it will with the literatures of the present. Out of the welter the best is selected, whether from poetry, prose or recorded talk, the passages which contain the essence of that which moves or delights us in its most memorable form.

Chapter 3

Off and Away

From such high-flying over the terrain, let me get down to *living* passages, as in boyhood, the body, the senses, where delights are first come upon and mental complexity is a burden. Get rid of the burden, drop the shackles and run.

How often as a boy I did just that! To run until you forgot what you were running from, until the running itself became an exhilaration that flew until the wind of your speed brought water to your eyes and your toes touched the ground so lightly that with the very smallest of extra aids they could have skimmed it. When the Greeks carved their figure of Hermes, the swift messenger of the gods, they put a *small* wing on each sandal.

The slowing-up, the gasping, the return of the body's weight, the glance over each shoulder, and "I'm off!" has become "I'm away!"

I was away to the Strath.

In the Highlands of Scotland a strath is a small glen. For a small boy — a boy up to ten or twelve years of age — a strath is ideal in size, because its physical features are not so vast or extensive but they can be encompassed on foot yet are extensive or "far off" enough never to be exhausted in interest or wonder or the unexpected. A glen can be too big, its mountainous sides too high, its cataracts or river too fierce or deep to cross, its distances too bare and forbidding for a small boy to know with any intimacy more than his own home part of it. Our Strath we knew through-out its length — or very nearly. To walk its full length to the river source — always called the Waterhead — was the ultimate adventure and the thought of it inhabited the mind with a peculiar strangeness. Unlike the old lady who did not believe that Jerusalem was on this earth, we believed the Waterhead was — but only just, so we could laugh at the old lady very loudly in our appreciation of the joke. For a small boy three miles up a strath and three miles back, with loiterings and deviations, was a very long journey, indeed a whole day's adventure, with a meal missed and a hunger that made a leanness of the belly that could be felt inside. And outside, too, by one's own hand, or by the hand of a companion invited to "have a feel". We were given to "proving" things in this empirical way.

These first two or three miles were the rich ones. After that the trees thinned, the strath grew shallower, and glimpses of the moor were caught. It was a vast moor, austere as a desert, and the farthest rim of the horizon lit itself on the far edge of the world. Leftward the ridges of near hills shut off the mountains beyond, and somewhere in that country where moor and mountains met the river had its source. But the rich part was so infinitely varied in attraction that only in odd moments did we think, or dream, of one day setting out for the Waterhead.

It would be difficult even to make a list of individual attractions, for any one item had in the matter of place, quantity and quality a very intricate pattern, so that within a given or general attraction there were particular attractions, and for us, ah! it was the particular that mattered.

Take hazel nuts. Hazel trees grew at haphazard or in congested clumps throughout the whole area, on the river flats and on the steep slopes or braes, not so numerous as the birches, but more numerous than rowans (mountain ash), alders, oaks or other stunted varieties of trees that so often seemed to exist singly and did not interest us because we did not need them for any purpose. We hardly even noticed them, until they became particularly striking, like a rowan laden with a heavy crop of blood-red berries.

As there are varieties of apples so, for us, there were varieties in nuts. We could tell them at a glance by size and colour, just as one distinguishes a Cox's Orange Pippin from a Mackintosh Red. The glance, the appearance, told the invisible but all-important thing: the taste , the flavour. I do not know if a description of the taste of an Orange Pippin has ever been caught in a phrase but we had our phrase for the corresponding nut (which was not unlike the pippin in colouring) and it was "a whisky taste". That none of us may ever have tasted whisky was no matter. Our elders had, as we so very well knew, and possibly in some backward reach of time one elder, the days being dry, had chewed this particular nut and found within its slipping flavours the memory of a more ardent taste.

But apart from the different varieties or kinds, a knowledge of the places where they grew and spots where maturity came early, there was always the chance that in this strath of continuous exploration you would come on one particular tree where all the excellences were gathered together. And it happened.

The glance, the wonder, the doubt, the climbing, the cluster. You put your finger on the tip of the nut and it runs over in its sheath. Ripe! You turn it right over and out. Its bottom is dark brown. Not only brown but with a peculiar suggestion of greyness like a bloom. This is it! It must be! . . . *It is!* And the teeth you had all but shoved into your skull in cracking it settle back again.

Your pockets are already full of good enough nuts, selected nuts. You empty first one, and then another, throwing their contents away. Here and there along the wood you hear a shout, but instead of answering you grow quieter, more careful in your movements towards the topmost slender branch, where two or three clusters, like miniature nests of coloured birds, sing silently in the sun.

You climb down at last, quietly slip away from the tree until you reach the common path. Only then do you shout. And when in due course comparisons are made, the crackings and the tastings are over, and you are asked, "Where is the tree?", you smile. Ah!

But in addition to hazel nuts there were many fruits in their season. When I wrote that word "bloom" I thought of blaeberries. A big plump blaeberry with a misty bloom makes a wonderful conjunction with a hungry mouth. One by one at first; then the gathering of a handful, the tilted head, the open mouth, the slow crush, the pulping, the swirl of juices about the gums, the bathing of the uvula in the rich swallow, the lingering, the delicious aftermath; never savoured too long for savouring's sake, however, because other hands are too busy with the best.

Boys are prepared to investigate all edible things with a certain dispassion, beyond the prime need of filling the belly. We distinguished for example, between two pods of the wild violet before we split them with a thumb nail and exposed their tiny seeds, like seed pearls. There were those of us who said we could tell the difference in taste between the two kinds. If the seeds had a taste at all it must have been in some neutral or debatable region, but at least we attempted to investigate that region — while we ate the seeds. From the luscious sweetness of blaeberries and wild bees' honey, through neutrality, to the piercing face-contorting sourness of one quick chew-and-spit of the common sorrel, the Strath contrived to produce by way of the mouth many interesting and arresting moments.

Chapter 4

The Nut and the Stone

I can't remember now how I got on to the boulder in the river but I was there. It was a large flattish boulder and I was sitting on it with my legs stuck out in front at the angle which is wide enough both to give complete comfort and to crack nuts within it. I had picked a stone from the bed of the stream and was using it as a cracking hammer. This stone was about the size of my fist and a nice skill was required in its manipulation, for if its flat hitting surface developed the least tilt in its attack, the nut shot away from the impact with an astonishing speed. If to counter this impish trait I brought the stone down too heavily I merely smashed the nut, making an inedible hash of shell and kernel. Now no boulder or hammer-stone in nature is ever quite flat so some uncertainty as to the parallelism of the two surfaces at the point and moment of impact must remain. To offset that I found a small groove in the boulder. "Ah! that will hold you." And it did. Perhaps the Old Stone Age lasted so vast a time not because its people hadn't the brains to think of dressing the stone but because they used their brains to find the groove in the boulder.

The second satisfaction in this simple operation lay in the skill with which, time after time, I brought about precisely that extent of fracturing of the shell which permitted the easy withdrawal of an intact kernel. This satisfaction was definitely conscious.

The removal of the kernel from its shell to the mouth requires no particular skill in a boy, so the third conscious satisfaction was in the chewing. And what a chewing was there! The crack, the cross-section crushing, the tiny evasive splinters which the tongue hunts from between the teeth, the flattening of the last nodule, the mash, the mashing of the mash, until with the help of a generous spittle the whole attains that degree of liquidity which frees to the full the ultimate flavours, the quintessence of the whisky taste.

To ruminate, says a dictionary, is "to chew the cud: to meditate". As I sat on that boulder, staring downstream, my automatic jaws, in action so like a cud-chewing cow's, induced a state of content, which, far-sighted like the cow's saw nothing and, if meditative, meditated on nothing. The shallow river flowed around and past with its variety of lulling monotonous sounds; a soft wind, warmed by the sun, came upstream and murmured in my ears as it continuously slipped from my face. As I say, how I got there I do not remember. I do not even remember whether anyone had been with me on that expedition, much less what anxieties might have to be resolved with "excuses" when I got home. I was just there.

Then the next thing happened, and happened, so far as I can remember, for the first time. I have tried hard but can find no simpler way of expressing what happened than by saying: *I came upon myself sitting there.*

Within the mood of content, as I have tried to recreate it, was this self and the self was me.

The state of content deepened wonderfully and everything around was embraced in it.

There was no "losing" of the self in the sense that there was a blank from which I awoke or came to. The self may have thinned away — it did — but so delightfully that it also remained at the centre in a continuous and perfectly natural way. And then within this amplitude the self as it were became aware of seeing itself, not as an "I" or an "ego" but rather as a stranger it had come upon and was even a little shy of.

Transitory, evanescent — no doubt, but the scene comes back across half a century, vivid to the crack in the boulder that held the nut.

For the moment I leave it there and return to exploring the Strath.

Chapter 5

On the Hunt

Such boyish adventures as I have touched upon were yet as nothing to another kind of adventure which absorbed us to the last cells in our bodies. We were hunters, and we hunted in the primeval way. In comparison gathering nuts was a pastime, free and airy, weaving its paths among the autumn colours, heated in moments of rivalry, cunning, collapsing in laughter; it was safe, it was secure; there was no one to say, "These are my trees: get out!" The trees were there, like the earth and the sky.

But to hunt a salmon from a pool or any kind of game from its lair, that was forbidden, and the forbiddenness, coming from the adult world, held awful consequences. The primordial thrill of the hunt could be heightened to an almost unbearable degree by the imminence of this danger — the invisible presence with an all-seeing eye.

To the boy of the Stone Ages the invisible presence might have been a sabre-toothed tiger, but even if the tiger saw him, he would have had at his back or up a tree some recognized way of escape, the traditional sporting chance; for us it was enough if the gamekeeper saw us, at that moment we were done for.

The boy's world was entirely different from the adult's world. The grown man was a tall being moving amid the work and arrangements of life and death. For the boy, the funeral cortège passed, the school was left behind, the church door was shut — "I'm off!" — and he was into his own intense world. He could not see behind the gamekeeper's stern face; could not understand himself as the sort of "nuisance" that though unable to do much harm had better be discouraged early. When penalties were threatened, they became terrible in their ultimate obscure workings. "Shame on the home" . . . "prison" . . . and that awful unfinished sentence, "If this happens again. . . ."

It happened again. The persistence, the sheer courage, was so notable that it must have been in the blood out of an immense ancestry. It was, of course. If man has been on this earth for about a million years, only the last six thousand or so have been what we call civilized. For a stretch of time inconceivable to the mind he was a hunter. That this has conditioned the cells in his body and most of them in his head may be taken as biologically reasonable. Out of his hunting came the first arts and crafts: his shaped flints, his barbed bone spears, his paintings on the walls of prehistoric caves of animals remarkable to us still for a scarcely contained power. That these paintings were not intended altogether to be what we call works of art, that they served some higher purpose of compulsive magic in connection with the hunt, may be taken as fairly certain; as certain, say, as the compulsive magic in the sunflowers of Van Gogh or the apples of Cézanne which draw dollars from pockets that may happily be deep enough. In the latter case the nature of the compelling magic may be difficult to search out; in the former case, less difficult; but that in both cases the essence of the magic is the same may be the kind of discovery a man makes when he ends up coming upon himself as a prehistoric boy in a modern strath.

But the general situation in this matter of hunting in our Strath was a little more complicated than I have indicated. It was even more complicated than some of our psychological efforts to deduce God from the nature of the father. A father certainly had the authority and power to forbid, to deny, to punish. But so had the schoolmaster. So had the bearded minister of the church. So had the gamekeeper. But whereas we could dodge with certainty the father, the schoolmaster and the minister, we could not so dodge the gamekeeper because he alone had the truly terrible attribute of being both invisible and omnipresent. We never saw a god come out of a cloud, but we saw a gamekeeper come out of a clump of trees; and at a crucial moment, had the awful matter of choice been possible, we might have taken a chance on the unknown god.

If only complication stopped there! But the boy's world is contained by the adult world, and to this matter of hunting there was among adults a certain two-faced or ambivalent attitude. From the beginnings of their human history the Highlands have been a hunting ground. With their deer forests, grouse moors and salmon rivers they still are. Until comparatively recent times the Highlander had three freedoms: to take a salmon from the river, to take a deer from the hill, and to distil his drop of whisky from his own barley, without payment or tax. He has never quite forgotten that, hence the ambivalent attitude. The boy has not "worked all this out"; political, legal and moral aspects are of the adult world; but he knows the attitude at a glance. Just as he knows there is only one final question: "Did anyone see you?" And if he can answer "No", then his triumph as a skilful hunter is complete.

How complete may be better understood if it is remembered that in any Highland community the majority were crofters, mostly poor crofters — I am thinking back to my boyhood — and their simple diet could be monotonous. Yet in their own country they were the heirs of all the ages, and quite literally, in this matter of the hunting instinct, of the ages that went back to the Old Stone one. So when the boy presents his salmon more than one instinct is stirred. From an old cured herring, stiff with brine, to a fresh-run silver-scaled salmon is a gleaming change. An old Irishman once told me that in his part of the world the saying for a beautiful and reckless extravagance ran: "To hell with poverty, let us kill a hen!" But a hen — anyone can kill an old barn-door hen — and be one hen the less. But a salmon out of the blue, out of a legend that has come true — ah!

In a general way, then, hunting was forbidden. No parents would ask a child to hunt. It was wrong. The boy knew this. But he knew also that it wasn't quite so wrong if he wasn't caught. At a deeper level there was an older right.

I have no desire for further complications. I would gladly avoid them if I could. Yet they have to be indicated if only to suggest that delight did not drop into an open mouth. Wishful thinking was of no use to a boy unless followed by the act. Action was all, and the more complicated the thicket it had to thread the sharper the senses grew, with instincts ever ready to slip the leash that was finer than a hair.

For no one knew better than the boy that "It's the unexpected that happens!" And he used the phrase with the echo in it of an adult reflection. During the action he had his own hushed version: "You never know!" Two boys on a salmon hunt pause on the way to a pool and one says, "I think we should have look at the small pool over yonder." "What's the good of looking in that pool?" "You never know." And the trees listen with them to this one mysterious certainty.

Two was perhaps the ideal number on such an expedition, for then the acting, the scoffing, the facetiousness, the latent rivalries, that assail boys' relationships simply fall away and two become themselves in a rare companionship. Now things can be said that could never be said with others there. And these things are seldom if ever personal in the sense of emotional; on the contrary they are objective, moving at a little distance in an air of wonder, like a story — as it so often was — of an adventure in this same Strath told by a grown man. "Wasn't it queer?" "Yes it was. Queer, wasn't it?" "Yes. As Dougal said, it's the queer thing that happens." "Well, I'll tell you a queerer thing, and it's as sure as I'm sitting here and I'll tell you why. . . ." And so their conversation would go on until they found themselves sitting there and decided it was good — but maybe better if they now moved on, for if anyone had been about he would have shown himself by this time. . . .

Where there are two one can depend on the other; as the number increases the one gets drawn more and more into the interdependence of the many, until finally the "queer" gets lost in the general action. The utmost, the unique, expression of the queer always comes through the one. "There I was in that place and not a soul within miles. . . ." At once the listener can identify himself with the "I" as he never could with the many. A story is a story with its fascination and its thrills, irrespective of number, but that solitary "I" touches the quick.

To get the full impact of all elements, within and without, one had to be alone. So one did not want to be alone. But it happened, for the cunning that sought to achieve the glorious "I'm off!" didn't always come off.

Perhaps the simplest way to give some sort of pattern to this boyish complexity, to evoke it in action, would be by telling the story of what once happened when my companion did not turn up at the appointed spot and I went on alone, doing my own scouting, fearfully aware that I was by myself, but going on, and on, assuring myself that at least no one could do anything to me until he found me doing something, with every sense heightened to that pitch where even familiar bends or trees or boulders took on a look of extraordinary stillness or expectancy. Yet they didn't turn me back, neither here nor at the next bend, for not a soul did I see, nor hear a sound I couldn't account for. When surprised rabbits scurried off it meant no one had recently passed this way. When I flushed a couple of peewits and they took the air, screaming in a way that could be heard a mile off, I had thoughts that wouldn't have done them any good. And of course a curlew had to join in, and he could be heard two miles off. Where this actually happened was the only place from which I could be seen by anyone at a considerable distance, for it was the bare top of one of two precipices which made a deep river gorge. But I was soon over that crest and down to river level. The peewits settled, the curlew's whistle had fallen over the rim of the world, and all was quiet once more. And so I came in time to the special pool.

Looking at what followed, I now see not "myself" but the boy I was. An objective account might therefore come nearer a true reconstruction of what happened, for "I" is troublesome at the best of times and "the boy" moves out there in front of me. I can see his hair, the colour of his eyes, and the water running from his hair into his eyes. So let it be in the form of a short story, with the main incidents guaranteed and their sequence a matter of memory doing her best.

Chapter 6

The Boy and the Salmon

With his head tilted back to keep the water from lapping into his mouth, the boy feels for the bottom of the pool, and the big toe of his right foot comes gently against a surface that yields. As his eyes widen so does his mouth, and the water laps in. Choking and threshing the surface he rolls over, reaches blindly overhand, kicks hard and grounds on the edge of the pool, where his body goes into a slow convulsive squirm in its desperate effort to spew water and suck air at the same time. When it seems everything is coming up, a little breath gets down. As the gasping lessens, he draws out of the pool like an otter and subsides among the stones and gravel.

But the glisten of the incredible in his eyes does not lessen. The choking struggle had hardly interfered with it. Now the glisten holds and he listens. From the hazel tree at the neck of the pool, over on the other side where he has left his clothes, a cock chaffinch gives an angry *spink! spink!* But from the hillside above it a willow wren's song comes tumbling down over leafy branches in sunny ease. Its carefree warmth in that world of its own, which is also the watching world, is reassuring. Letting out the gasp he has held in, he lifts his head slowly and his eyes rove over the willow wren's trees, and round, and down to the river, and up the river to the bend where it disappears two hundred yards away, and still farther round until he is looking over his shoulder across the flat ground that runs back for a short distance to the other wooded slope of the winding Strath. No one. Not a suspicious movement of a branch. Nothing against a skyline. Nothing.

But even if there is an invisible someone, what of it? He has done nothing. They cannot collar him for doing nothing. So he gets up, his naked body clothed in this innocence, and doesn't even swim back the way he had come, but walks up round the edge, stooping and slipping awkwardly, as if his innocence for all the world had made a girl of him, as if the stones really hurt his feet, until he reaches the narrow neck of the pool. Here the gush of water is strong and his difficulty in crossing is laughable. But he gets across and on to the rock ledge beside his clothes under the shadow of the hazel tree, and in an instant his innocence vanishes.

That feel on his big toe, that slippery yielding as the salmon took the caress! He looks at his big toe. On its own it comes apart from the other toes and gives a small crack. The salmon liked the feel of his toe. Its body had given slightly, not lain over but yielded, as a dog to a hand it likes. And his touch had been light as a feather because the buoyant water had bobbed him off.

That nothing like this has ever happened to him before makes no difference. He *knows* it was a salmon. The feel of all the trout he ever guddled is in his fingers. He smothers the last cough from a harsh windpipe to listen.

The pool is as naked as himself, lying out there for anyone to watch. And he knows a lot about the pool because he has been here before; and once, unforgettably, with an elder brother and Angus. They are four to five years older and therefore almost like grown men, so when a brother as old as that, instead of threatening you with a cuff that will flatten you, says, "Come on!" red are the letters of that day.

In the preliminary talk, while they had been sitting and waiting for the feel of safety, his brother had pointed out the four spots in the pool where a salmon would lie. Two of them were invisible because of the brown tinge in the hill water that went black in the depths; one could not be seen unless you had a cat's eyes; and the fourth was so obvious that no salmon ever lay in it unless he had been finally scared out of the other three or was just in it like a miracle. When they had told him all this, with innumerable and amusing embellishments from the past, his brother sent him up through the trees to the crest in order to watch the moor road and to listen. Secretly he had hated going, because he wanted to see the salmon being caught; but he had hated it worse because he was terrified he could not watch well enough, particularly when he found that from the crest he could not see the pool for the trees.

But now he is alone, and when he doesn't know what to do, and tries to make his toe crack for something to do, it won't do it. For he knows quite well he can only make a fool of himself for nothing, because he hasn't a gaff. His brother and Angus always take a gaff; at least they take a big hook in a nest of stout string, and it's as easy as winking to draw it from an inside pocket and whip it to a straight hazel wand cut and trimmed on the spot. Then one goes into action in a deadly way, and the end of that way is never to be in a hurry putting the hook down, down, into the water. "Supposing," his brother had demonstrated, "your bare foot is the salmon." Down went the hook so slowly that by the time its remorseless point had come under the sole, the foot, taking no chances, had jerked away. His brother had laughed.

The boy's big toe suddenly cracks on its own. His mother, who often takes his side, says it is because he is growing too fast. But oh, supposing, just supposing, he could land that salmon now, wouldn't his brother have the laugh turned on him? And Angus, too? Wouldn't it be great? It would be that marvellous it would be — it would be — he cannot think of any adequate end to the marvel except the end of the world, and that isn't in the same class. What's the end of the world!

The absurd thought of it lifts him to his feet and he looks far and near; then he looks at the pool. It's bigger than a big floor, and in the two-thirds of it that could drown him he can't see the bottom. His features quicken with a touch of the wild, of the hawk's look, then go smooth with innocence as he strolls down the river, threading his way between the birches, flecks of light and shadow moving in a stream over his slim naked body. Fifty yards down he stops; through the listening that does not appear to be listening a hand goes out slowly to a leaf, nips off the leaf, brings its tip to teeth that tentatively nibble, while the eyes move slowly without movement of the head. He drops the leaf, climbs half way up the slope, and pauses again. Then quite suddenly he begins running back along the slope through the trees until he comes above the pool, but now he does not stop, he keeps going until he overshoots the pool below and commands the ground beyond. This pause is a dead stop whose final moment is a listening so intense that it would hear the sound beyond sound. His body thins away; he is not here but everywhere, along the near slope, by the grey face of the sheer rock over the next pool, within the quiet woods, under the summer sun, while he is standing there, his lips apart. Then he turns back to the pool and, without a splash, swims to the spot.

But this time he cannot find the spot — or else the salmon is gone. He spits out the water and tries again. His big toe hits the top of the concealed boulder a real crack. Near it! So he fills his lungs, breasts forward a few inches, throws his head back and thrusts down with all his pith at where the fish should be beside the boulder. He hits, and the underworld goes into revolution between his legs in an explosion that whirls and wallops and sucks his head clean under.

Luckily his lungs are so full that they can only let air out, and he breathes somehow by the verge, and looks between his legs to see that everything is all there. Everything is, so he tries to vomit, as though a flick of water has got past his wind. That awful explosive moment of panic fear! The two sides of his empty stomach come together and open his mouth in a final yaw. Then he feels better and examines his big toe. It moves silently, but it moves. Panic ebbs and the glisten is back in his eyes. "Yon frightened him!" The glisten all but smiles as he looks around and down himself to his toes. The big toe reaches out in a searching waggle. There are no scales between his legs. And, higher up, the nose of the torpedo had missed. Wasn't that the great luck? His great thankfulness induces a small upsurge of confidence and as he walks to the neck of the pool he almost wonders what he had been timid about before. For after all what was he doing but having a bathe? There was no law against that. It wasn't a sin. Anyone could bathe. He even stands and scans the bottom of the pool where it is visible. And when he gets back to his clothes he decides that the salmon might now very well be in the lie that needed a cat's eyes.

The long narrow ledge of rock a few inches above the water just accommodated his body at full stretch. He lowers his face on to the surface of the water until with forehead and one open hand he parts the flecks of foam that come from the gush in the pool's throat and so makes a small wavering window to peer down through. The underworld comes alive in golden motes and twists and shadows. The salmon's world. But amid the flicker and rush and vanishing shadows he sees nothing solid or stable. He lifts his head back, blows the water from his nostrils and rests, for it is a great strain hanging over from no proper grip.

But he is bitterly disappointed because he knows he can't *see*, for his brother had said to him, "Keep looking down, and you'll see a black shadow moving very slightly among the brown glistens close by the rock. It looks no bigger than a two-pound seatrout but if it's not a salmon of twelve pounds I'll eat my bonnet." But he couldn't see it, and his brother asked him if it's blind he was. This has made him secretly miserable for days and even doubt his whole future.

Now his brows gather; and he hangs over, and gets his eyes in the water and stares down until his body quivers from the breathless strain. All in a moment he sees the black shadow. He had been staring at it. It's there!

He lay back on the ledge and gulped. He had seen the shadow!

Now he is back by his clothes under the hazel tree. For what next? What to do? Would he fly home and get hold of his brother and tell him he had seen the shadow as sure as death? For what could he do, what could anyone do, without a hook to gaff the shadow? Nothing.

All the same he doesn't go. It's his shadow. Besides, his brother mightn't be home till late. Then comes the whisper from the boy who had seen the shadow in a far back age.

The first stone won't budge, but the second one just does, and when he gets it out of the pool's throat, he lifts it against his stomach and staggers with it to the narrow ledge.

It is flat with an edge that cuts through his fingers, but he lowers it carefully. This time his nose isn't three seconds in the water when he sees the shadow. He makes a wet mark on the ledge above the nose of the shadow. On his knees he draws the stone to the mark and eases it over. Its full weight all but has him in by the head. He holds on. He lowers away, the sharp edge downwards, another inch — one more — and he lets go. A moment of utter stillness, then a yard in front of his eyes the surface boils fiercely in blue and silver with a lash of a mighty tail that spits froth in his face.

The size of the fish and its strength are fearsome, but he is watching the pool. A swirl in the shallows at the tail-end where the salmon turns; the wave-swirls die out and all is as before.

The gulps come as if he had run a great race and, fear or no fear, down the pool he goes, wades the shallows at the foot, peering into the water, reaches the other side and comes up on the submerged flagstone with the clear miraculous lie. No fish there. Beneath the ledge, no shadow. Nowhere. So it must be the fourth, black, deep lie.

Within a couple of minutes he is heaving stones over that lie. They hit the surface with whacks that could be heard at horizons. They spout fountains in the air. Let them! A man cannot do something and not do it. Heave them in! That'll shift him! His recklessness is terrible and glorious. For at last he is committed.

How many hours he hunted the salmon on that summer day he could afterwards only guess, his absorption was so utterly complete. The water streaming down his face troubled him no more than it troubled an otter. Fear almost left him, except for the queer primitive fear that the salmon might boil up again between his legs. But even that didn't stop his big toe. And once when he nearly drowned himself the panic quickly passed and he felt the better for it, more confident.

But inevitably the time came when he could not find the salmon anywhere, when he was beaten. His teeth, he was astonished to find, chattered from the cold. He was tired. The magic faded as if the sun had gone in. He could hardly drag himself along the stones towards the neck of the pool, for now he would dress and go home.

He reaches the neck and is stepping in when he sees something green and solid where the water rushes by a slab of rock. The tail, the back fin, the head, wavering green in the flickering rush. Not two feet deep. Eighteen inches. The sudden flush from his thudding heart darkens his sight. He begins to quiver all over in a sickening weakness. The salmon will never wait. It will never wait! What can he do?

But his mind may cry as it likes, his body makes no mistake. Slowly, very slowly, it squats. His eyes never leave the water-screened fish. His hands grope for a lump of rock and drag it between his knees; very slowly he rises to his full height, pushes a foot forward, anchors it in the rush, slithers the other foot forward and feels for a firm hold; but the stones are slippery, he cannot quite get balance, his legs are too far apart, he sways; his mind gets the better of him: Now! Heave it at him now or you'll slip! He both heaves and slips, the missile falls short, and the salmon passes under as his body hits the water full length.

Sitting in the stream he cries aloud, and the heat of tears is behind his eyes. He tries to wipe his eyes in his rage but his right arm won't work. He has probably broken it. What next? For if only, if only, he had taken time *he could have killed the salmon*.

Compared with that, what was his arm? What was his bottom? Never would he get a chance like that again, never until kingdom come.

As he wriggles out of the water he slips again and, by trying to save his arm, only knocks his head on a granite boulder. But what does any part of him matter now? On the ledge his arm gets needles and pins, so it must have been the funny bone. It isn't funny. For if only he had taken time, inch by inch, the stone at the ready, inch by inch, like a Redskin, like his brother with the hook, he could have landed the stone on the salmon's nape and finished him. He would have killed the salmon.

His hand picks up his shirt and throws it down. His foot all but kicks his shorts anywhere. He doesn't care whether the black shadow is there or not. He starts off down the pool and wades across, missing nothing. He comes up on the submerged flagstone with its outer upright edge towards the pool — the miraculous lie — in no more than two feet of water. From the bottom end of it a narrow green fringe, shot through with sunlight, is just visible and wavers very slightly.

The miracle is too much for the boy; his heart goes clean across him and his knees weaken. He backs somehow and sits down. The face lifts and looks about his world. Two willow-wrens are singing, and a thrush far away. In that immemorial world he is small and vulnerable, with a heart beating sickeningly in the centre of what can do nothing.

Then he begins to do it, on all fours, with the slow motion of a stalking cat, until the green fringe is there again, the end of the salmon's tail. The rest of the fish is hidden from him by the flagstone, but when he gets abreast of the outer upright edge of the flagstone he will see the whole fish lying alongside it, so his approach must keep out of sight of the salmon's eye.

First he sees the tail, the whole tail, then the narrow wrist beyond, then the swell of the body to the dorsal fin — but he stops there and slowly draws back, for the upright edge of the flagstone has an outward tilt that protects the salmon's head. No one can drop a rock straight down on it. The fish is safe.

The Stone Age isn't much use now. Dropping a stone on a salmon's tail — one might as well drop salt. The tail . . . just the tail. . . . He thinks about it. For he knows things about a salmon's tail, and the first is that all its strength is in it. It's his tail that makes him leap waterfalls. Without his tail he wouldn't be able even to swim straight, if swim at all, not to speak of a torpedo. Hence it follows that if you can stop his tail from working you have him! To prove it: it's well known to everyone who knows anything that you can play a salmon on a line until you bring him close in and then all you have to do is bend down and grip him round the wrist, just above the tail, and lift him straight out. It's well known. "Tailing."

His approach to the tail leaves his stomach behind, for now he must get into position without letting the eye of the salmon see him. Flat open, his left hand steals forward towards the fringe, reaches it, inches in between it and the flagstone, until the fringe touches his wrist like a butterfly's wing, touches and untouches, as if the fish is troubled in his memories. At the touch he goes blind but he does not grab. He waits. Then out goes the other hand, for if in the case of a grown man one hand is enough then two should be ample for a boy. The strength may be in the tail but it cannot be used until the tail waggles. If the narrow wrist above the tail is grabbed from both sides as in a vice in the one instant, then the waggle wouldn't get a chance to start, and so the salmon would be helpless. At school, arithmetical reasoning is the boy's strength.

The fingers of his right hand begin to curve round the outside of the fringe. Would the salmon's outer eye see them? It's inch by inch now if ever it was. But his body, slewed towards the bank to keep away from the eye, develops a kink. The reach is going to be a little too far, but he daren't move his knees now so he increases the kink. When the hands are dead opposite they leap at each other and lock on the small of the tail.

The shoulders aren't yanked out of him and the pool isn't lifted into one mighty bucketful and smashed in his face but that is what

it feels like. He flounders and spews water for that's all that will
come up. But his head is up, his eyes sweeping the pool, and they
see a remarkable thing, they see a bow wave going down that pool
with the speed of a demented torpedo. Nor does the wave stop
and swirl round in the shallows, it goes on. He sees the dorsal fin.
The salmon is leaving the pool!

Forgetting he is in two feet of water he begins to run, pitches
headlong, and reaches out, overhand, underhand, and kicking in
a new complicated "crawl" that none the less grounds him in the
shallows, where he gets up and falls twice before he is on to the
dry stones and off.

The salmon is having a stormy passage because the river is at
summer level, spread out into small shallow pools, with
innumerable tails and necks and, everywhere, great boulders and
flagstones. In his haste, as though pursued by the father and
mother of all otters, the fish runs aground on a sloping flagstone,
wallops loudly, and is off; but the boy sees him, comes abreast of
him, skipping from one stone to another with a speed that had he
gone by the head might well have finished him.

Wading in, he heaves a stone that just misses, but it turns the
salmon. The fish can go faster up than down but blind speed is his
danger, for if he doesn't take the deepest runnel he will shore up
and flounder. The boy turns him again, and loses him, and finds
him in a small pool, where they come to close quarters. But as he
heaves his large stone he slips, goes headlong in front of the
salmon, and the salmon rams him in the navel. He embraces the
fish, but the great brute goes out at his chin like a greased thunder-
bolt. After that the boy goes berserk.

The end comes when he lands his heavy missile fair on the nape
where the otter bites, for the salmon, losing all sense of direction
now, tears through the shallows to one side and beaches himself
a full yard beyond the water's edge, there to wallop the stones
with the sounds of two immense butter-clappers. With his body
the boy blockades him, and in time wedges his head and kills him,
then lies beside him until his gasping lungs ease and he can see
properly.

But he doesn't see properly until the fish is lying on mossy
grass under a hazel tree. Then realization of what he has done
breaks on him. It is a cock fish, deep at the shoulders, marvel-

lously shaped, grace with power, perfect and magnificent. It is the biggest salmon he has ever seen. Wonder is in his adoration. He wipes some fine gravel off the silver. The incredible is true.

In a narrow crevice beneath an outcrop of grey lichened rock, he hides his salmon, plucked ferns above and below, and loose stones in front, so that no one passing would ever suspect the marvel within.

Perhaps the incredible in the true puts him a little beside himself, for as he walks back towards the pool and his clothes a delicious languor assails his body, and nature gets translated, too, so that the sunlight, the leaves, the pink roses of a wild briar — particularly the wide-open pink roses — seem to stop and look in a strange unforgettable way as he goes by, the shyness of adoration upon him.

Chapter 7

In the Dark

And then there is the night, the darkness; the preliminary comings and goings, followed by the setting out through the night to bring back the salmon. For of course it could never be done in daylight. Supposing you met the gamekeeper with the "evidence" on your back? Supposing, for that matter, you met anyone? Of all things that waggle, including the salmon's tail, the tongue is the most agile and its ripples reach farther than any ripple in a pool; from one ear to another, until there is not an ear left. And what then? Not to mention "next time"? For it wouldn't be much use saying you were just going for a walk next time. Who ever went "just for a walk" anyway? No one in the whole place. It was silly.

There are things that have to be kept dark, dark as the night.

"Mind," says his elder brother when he had got the whole story, "not a word to a soul till I come back."

"Where are you going?"

"Never mind. Wait for me — but not a word!" And off his brother goes.

But though he has the vague feeling that he had won the right now to go everywhere with his brother, he is not too disappointed because of the warmth that remains behind from the telling of the story. His brother had been that astonished! "I can't believe it!" he had said. He was great, his brother! There was nothing he didn't know, even if in school he hadn't been very good at his sums. But what's sums? Anyone could do sums if he just thought. But his brother had taken him through the story in a way that missed nothing, especially how things happened. That time when he had seen the salmon water-screened in the neck of the pool —

"I know," said his brother, nodding. "The stones are that

slippery yonder: you put out your foot to find a steady place and you can't find it, and your legs get too wide, with the water pushing at them. No wonder you missed him."

"It couldn't have been by much."

"I bet you fell on your nose then!"

"I did! Clean by the head. I got an awful knock."

"Did you? where?"

"Ach, just only my arm."

"Show me."

And though he tried to make light of it, his arm had to be bared, and then — for there might have been nothing — there was a blue mark. It was there.

"Boy, you've been in the wars!"

"Ach, I never hardly felt it."

"I bet you got needles and pins."

"I did!"

They both laughed. It was wonderful. In fact the only thing in the whole world that hadn't been so wonderful was the bit about the tail.

"Did you think you could hold him by the tail?" his brother had asked.

"As if I could!" It was laughable.

His brother said nothing, only there was a certain light in his eye, and as the boy glanced away from the light, he said, "Even *you* couldn't hold him by the tail. Could you?"

"Not when he's fresh. You have got to play him stiff before you can do that, and even then the tail is slippery. You have to have a big strong hand for that."

"Couldn't you take both your two hands?"

"Not if you're holding a rod or line with one." But the light in the eye broke into a smile, even if it didn't laugh yet.

"Oh, I knew fine I could never hold him. I just thought I would give him an awful fright."

"You did!" His brother laughed. "After all that had gone before, you certainly put the wind up him!" He was full of fun and pleasure. "And that was the thing to do — for it made him leave the pool."

"Of course," said the boy, with the flash of understanding that made light of arithmetical problems. "That was the only thing to do in the circumstances, wasn't it?"

"In the circumstances, yes." His brother, who was sitting on a bank, kicked his heels.

But by the time the rest of the story was told the tail was forgotten and his brother said, "Boy, it's great! I can hardly believe it."

"You could do it easy."

"Not at your age."

"But if you had been — like me —"

"I never did it anyway — not in a pool like yon — and that's proof."

It is difficult to get past proof. And he could see by the way he went into the house, and out, and in again, that his mother began suspecting something, so he stayed out. His younger brother was inclined to hang about him, too, until he told him to run off and play with other little boys, and when threats weren't enough, he chased him off. As you grow up you have to deal very firmly with the young, especially after you have first succeeded in making them suspect there's something strange and wonderful somewhere if they only knew.

It was nearly dusk before his elder brother appeared in the offing and beckoned with his head. He followed him past the outhouses and into the birch wood, and there was Angus.

"Boy," said Angus, "what's this I'm hearing?"

"What?" said the boy.

"And you had only your naked hands. Not even a pinch of salt to put on his tail."

"I hadn't your hook whatever!"

"Good, though!" And the laughter started.

All through his adventure he had to go again, and they revelled in it like connoisseurs, until companionship grew warm and rare and the boy could almost laugh at himself, for he knew they were proud of him, especially his brother, who had therefore to salt the pride now and then if only to bring out its savour.

The companionship is extraordinarily real for the boy. Nothing else could ever be so real as this, so rare and so fine. It is outside as well as inside, like the air, like breath.

"Do you think we should take him with us?" asks his brother.

"Why not?" says Angus. "He has earned the right if anyone ever has."

"That may be," says his brother, "but what about his mother? Soon she'll be calling for him to go to his bed."

"She will not," says the boy.

"You know she will," says his brother.

"I don't care if she will," says the boy.

"You may care to a tune out of the other side of your mouth," says his brother, "when she finds out."

"I will not! I don't care!"

With the solemn air of tribal elders they draw out his agitation until they have him all but dancing with rage and defiance and the awful fear that they may not take him.

At length Angus sums up. "I'll put it like this. He's got to start sometime, and it might as well be now as later."

"Maybe there's something in that," his brother allows, and then he doubles over, laughing. The boy attacks him, and his brother appeals to Angus for help.

"With that strength in him," says Angus, "it's a wonder he didn't hold the salmon itself by the tail."

But when in the darkness they are on the way, the companion-ship takes on another air, a wider air, like the air of the night. Into this companionship he has been initiated and is accepted. They tell him now that after his brother had left him he had gone to see Angus, that Angus had been speaking to the roadman whose job it is to keep the moor road in repair, and the roadman had been working far up beyond the pool and was finishing for the day when who should come along with his dogs but the gamekeeper, that the gamekeeper had been nearly as far as the Waterhead exercising his dogs and estimating the grouse prospects for the season, and that being so —

"He'll be snoring in his bed already," says his brother.

"He'll have earned his rest," Angus agrees.

All the same their tones are quiet, their eyes alert, and when his brother stops dead, the boy listens with all his being, for he, too, had heard something like a cough. The cough is repeated.

"One of Mairag's old ewes," whispers his brother, amused, and on they go.

They leave the Strath, for under the trees the darkness would be so deep in places that you would have to grope your way, and when you're groping like that you might grope into anyone or anything. The moor is different; it is open and wide, and if you lie down you can see a dark body against the sky. Besides, so long as you're on the moor you're not in the Strath, and there's no proof of anything so far.

The boy is learning fast, and when at a certain point they sit down to look and listen, to get the feel of the moor and all that lives and moves on it, they whisper and tell him things in between the listening, until his senses are held by something finer than a hair-trigger in the dimension of the night. The farthest the ear can listen is very far, through the near silence which is thick, to a finer silence, and then beyond that to a silence very far away.

"Safe as a church," says his brother. "Come on!"

His brother leads and Angus brings up the rear. He knows he has been put in the middle without a word so that they can look after him. The starlight is not good enough to see where a foot goes next on the dark floor of the moor, for if there is a track it can only be a sheeptrack, and how his brother can see it or how he knows where he is going, in this featureless dim-darkness, the boy does not know. But when he stumbles he picks himself up quickly, fearful he may fall behind his brother who is forging so confidently ahead. Then a "*Sst!*" from Angus and, as they stop, his harsh whisper to the leader: "What on earth are you racing for? I can hardly keep up."

"Right!" says his brother.

But the boy knows they have really been talking about him and their delicacy is not lost. The slackening of the pace helps him, too; the awful surge of fear that he might not last eases a little; for the long day is telling on him, and he knows it, though he will not know it.

His brother stops, then gets down flat. The boy and Angus lie down beside him.

"See it there against the sky, like the top of a peat-stack?"

"Yes," says the boy.

"That's the landmark. We go on a short way, then bear left to the road, cross the road, take a slant on the old burying ground, then down to the pool. No distance now. So let's take a rest. Isn't it a grand night! You're not tired, are you?"

"No, I'm fine."

"You had a heavy enough day as it was," says Angus. "And that brother of yours, you would think he was practising for the mile. He's always the same."

His brother laughs. "Boys, isn't this good!" He stretches himself. "The moon won't be up for a while yet."

"She's in her last half," says Angus.

"That's when I like her best," says his brother. "Not too much light to be seen, but enough to see. What a lot of stars! Do you know the North Star?"

"No," answers the boy.

"It's the only star he knows," says Angus.

"As long as you know that one you won't go far wrong. But first you find the Plough. Now look!" And so the boy found the North Star.

But when at last it came to finding the spot where he had hidden the salmon dismay descended on him deeper even than the darkness under the trees. For now everything is changed as though the trees had shifted position, not to mention unexpected humps, sudden drops, and the strange frightening feel of what comes up against a groping hand. Always, before, the hand had known what it was going to touch, or expected to touch. Now it doesn't know. Never before had fingers touched the air itself on the way to touching what they might touch next in a strange place that had shifted. And when they must be just about to touch, something hits the face. Then crawling out from under, he sees dimly a bush that shouldn't be there. He knows it is a bush, and yet. . . . He listens desperately for the others. He hears them, hears his brother's voice and goes to it on all fours.

"If it was here, it's gone. Are you there?"

"Yes," the boy answers.

"Come here. Feel this."

A hand drops on his back and he comes up against his brother's body. He feels the split sides of the rock, the cavity going underground. It seems altogether strange and yet — "Don't think so. No ferns." But he is not certain. "There was ferns."

"If it isn't the place, it can be anywhere." They might search all night and not find it. That's what his brother meant.

"Anyone taking the fish wouldn't take the ferns," says Angus.

"Who knows?" says his brother.

And the boy hears him listening. They all listen.

"If anyone took it, it was a dirty trick," whispers Angus. They listen harder than ever.

"How far would you say you walked back to the pool? Would it be as far as from the end of the house to the peat-stack at home?" asks his brother.

"Yes," answers the boy, "and a little farther."

"Can you remember anything special you passed, a rock or a jump, anything?"

"Yes, a wild rose, a high one, with pink roses."

"Was it nearer the pool or the fish? Think."

His walk to the pool comes back with the distinctness of a suddenly remembered dream and he says with confidence. "About half-way."

"Wait here for me." His brother vanishes.

Angus explains that this is nothing new. "You can search for hours round and round it. The great thing is to make at least two marks. For once you're not sure you'll begin to search on and on. I remember once. . . ."

The boy listens, but now the sinking tiredness is so invaded by anxiety that he feels queer and light-headed. As his distress grows he tries to choke it back. Oh, if only, if only he had made a mark! . . . Home . . . all the way home . . . with nothing. . . .

"So you're not the only one," concludes Angus.

But that he should be the one! It only makes it worse. His distress grows, so in desperation he tries to feel nothing, nothing, that he may endure. A thud, and his brother is beside him. "Farther down, I think. Come on!"

The boy is groping again on all fours, and now it doesn't matter what his hand lands on, not even supposing it's a face.

"Are you there?" It's his brother's voice, no longer husky.

The boy's heart stops. He cannot answer.

"God bless me," comes his brother's voice, clear and astonished, "it's not a salmon, it's a whale!"

Chapter 8

On the Way Back

The salmon in the bag, the companionship in the darkness, the feet that feel the earth is not so solid as usual, Angus's barn where they cut the fish and left behind the head half, and the last stretch home pale from the risen moon.

"Do you feel floating a bit?" asks his brother.

"A little."

"You're fine. You held up well. I'll say that."

"It was that time when I thought we wouldn't find him. That was the worst."

"I knew. But I wouldn't have given up, not supposing we had to wait till the daylight. Though you never know. Everything depends. I think Angus enjoyed it better than if it had been his own!"

"He's great, Angus."

"He's reliable. He would stick to you in a hole."

"I would think that."

"He's a grand man, Angus's father. The very best. Full of fun."

"He plays the pipes well, doesn't he?"

"He has the finger."

"I heard he said you had the finger, too."

"Where did you hear that?"

"I heard it from Sandy."

"Was that all!"

"Sandy said he heard Angus's father saying it to Dan Mackay. Angus's father said you could blow a grace note off his old chanter now and then better than many a piper."

"He's threatening me to try the full set next, not just the chanter. But don't mention that to anyone."

"No, I won't mention it to a soul."

"You must come up with me to Angus's some night."

"I would like that fine."

"Wait till he hears about you and the salmon! He's the old style, quiet and kind and full of fun, not holy and important. You know how Angus kept on tonight about salt on the tail. Well, I'll tell you the story behind that. It's when Angus was very little, and his father found him one winter's day stalking round the end of the barn where some wee birdies were eating the traces of the hens' food. Angus was throwing something at them, and when they flew off he would hide until they came back, then throw again. Do you know what he was trying to do? To throw some salt on the tail of a green singing lintie."

"No! Never! That's the funniest thing ever I heard."

"Yes. But now, look! there's the house. They'll be in their beds, but Mother will be awake."

"She'll be angry with me."

"Leave it to me. She'll say, 'What time of night is this to come home?' And I'll say we were up at Angus's. And she'll say something about you, but don't you say a word. It'll be all right. I said to her before going that we might be a little late. She has to use a stern voice at times."

"Has she any idea about the salmon?"

"Och, she may have her ideas, but what's that if we say nothing?"

"You won't say anything when we go in?"

"No, no. When she goes out to the milk-house in the morning she'll find the salmon on the floor."

"She'll know then!"

"She will. She'll ask how it came there. And I'll say, 'Maybe the gamekeeper sent you a present. I didn't know you were so well acquaint with him'!"

"She'll wonder!"

"Hsh!" cautions his brother. "We're here."

And so it all happened, the stern voice low but coming firmly through the dim dark around the screwed-down lamp, her face invisible. "You needn't tell me you were all the night at Angus's. They would never allow it."

His brother is silent now.

"And taking that young fellow with you! He may well be ashamed of himself standing there. But I'm not going to allow it. You have heard me. You can turn out the light."

Up in their bedroom, his brother sets down the candle on an old chest. "Was she awful wild?" whispers the boy.

His brother laughs silently. "She was a bit. She couldn't sleep. She gets anxious."

The boys laugh a little, too. But he becomes aware of his mother at the centre of the world.

"Would she be worse if she knew it was me?"

Laughter comes from his brother's nostrils. "She has a good idea already."

"How that?"

"She may have guessed something from the way you came home and that. But you'll find out tomorrow. Now into your bed and less talk."

With the strange feeling of being shy tomorrow, the boy gets into the off bed to find his younger brother fair in the middle of it. The middle!

"Don't waken him!" says his brother, for he knows the fighting that goes on sometimes. The boy heaves slowly with practised skill and is all but into "the warm place" when sleep, like a pair of shears, snips off that long day.

Chapter 9

Alone in the Dark

The companionship in the darkness: but there was the darkness when no one else was there. How young I was when this first occurred I cannot tell; somewhere around three or four, perhaps; for I can see myself darkly but clearly enough. I cannot see myself coming out of the house, though I must have just come out to perform on my own the quick natural act which troubles little boys often at unexpected times. Possibly, too, it was in the middle of that short but acute period when being able to tie a button is a matter of the first importance, when an interfering hand can touch off rage to the dancing point, and when, anyhow, secrecy helps towards independence. The position may have been more complicated by the fact that people had a habit of dropping into the house.

Anyway I was standing looking into the dark of the night, when a boy's fear of the dark came at me. I just managed to face it for the few necessary moments before I turned back in a blind run.

I should like to describe this little incident with some care because I am not sure even now how much if affects my subsequent thought; to what extent, for example, it influences or initiates a running commentary or criticism when I am reading a book like, say, Freud's *Totem and Taboo*.

For me, then, the important element in the incident is this: what I feared had neither shape nor form, neither containing line nor embodiment. It was there, not on the ground but in the air, in front of me, but not a distinguishable darkness in the darkness of the night. It was an invisible power, animated within itself. Yet even then, for a few moments, I took, as it were, a chance with it, before I turned and made for the door.

I don't remember going into the house, just as I don't remember coming out, but I'm quite certain that once I got inside I said nothing.

This incident is about as vivid and clear now as it was when I experienced it, and I find it remains so, however rigorously I test it. For example, when I subsequently saw in some child's book a picture of a demon or witch flying down out of the air with outstretched hand ready to grab, I knew at once what was meant. If my experience had taken shape, *this* is the shape it might have taken. And if I had told my experience at the time to an elder and he had asked, "Didn't you feel *as if* a hand was thrusting down for you?" I might, the picture being thus made for me, have answered, "Yes". Yet I would have known that in the moments of actual experience, there was no picture, no hand.

In short, the picture, the *as if*, are subsequent constructs. And by the time the demon has horns and a tail, not to mention red tights and an operatic background, the construct has been given very definite shape indeed. That is not to question the value or significance of the shape in its new context; though it may indicate how a primal experience can be elaborated.

To say it is "primal" may seem like begging a lot of questions and taking a jump, but I am using the word in the sense some anthropologists use it, or as Freud does when he is searching back for that out of which man created God. And created, too, spirits and demons and all unholy things that have haunted him at the core, too often blasting delight and making life a terror. Accordingly to follow up the boy's notion of how a primal experience can be elaborated might be very much in the hunt, though this time the terrain is within a very weird country indeed.

This country is the country of the mind and the hunt for some of the queer fish that come to inhabit it can be as engrossing and fearful as the boy's hunt for the salmon in the pool. We know as much from a book like *Totem and Taboo*, where the hunt is for spirits and demons and gods and, finally, God. This hunt takes place in the boy's mind, too, whether he likes it or not. It happens; but the way it happens will be conditioned by his own experiences, and that, for him, is the important, the guiding, and often the decisive thing.

So perhaps a tentative description of the nature of the historic hunt in this new country may be borne. Briefly, then, it ran through three phases. The first or earliest phase has got the name of *animism* because things in nature were then reckoned to be animated by spirits and demonic powers; the next phase has its religions and its gods; in the third or scientific phase the demons and the gods vanish, leaving only traces of an "omnipotence of thought" with some of the early "magic" still latent in it.

Actually, in the living of life today all three phases get mixed up in an extraordinary manner. Of the three, the earliest, the animistic, was most exhaustive and complete. As a way of life, a system of beliefs, it covered everything. This gave it its enormous penetrative power. In fact it is in this phase, says Freud, that myths have their sure foundation. And what the myth now means in our art and poetry, in the actual products — not forgetting the groggy novel — continues to astonish many, who see them as throw-backs to the primitive. They can even go further and, taking their stand on those sexual origins which Freud so rarely missed, assert that some of our more profound poems and pictures are but by-blows from a neurotic dalliance with the primitive (however "unconscious", of course, the dalliance may be).

But without going into this early phase too closely we may simply accept the notion of things in nature from trees to rivers being endowed with a living power or force that could come forth and affect the savage, usually not for his good, if he weren't careful. In due course he found ways and means, in the guise of sorcery and magic, of dealing with the power so that his good was maintained or even increased.

Now authorities have disputed as to whether in the beginning the savage did in fact endow all things with this power, or only certain things, or some things only at a particular time. The dispute is nicely complicated because many of the authorities did not themselves go and study the savage in parts of the earth which he still inhabits but collated the findings of those who did and by a wonderful exercise of acumen arrived at conclusions. But manifestly the exercise had to be performed within the individual and the process consisted in trying to make himself feel as "simple" as possible, on the principle that the simpler he became the nearer to a savage he grew. But the tool he used was his intellect, and when an intellectual achieves simplicity it may differ markedly from the simplicity of a non-intellectual. With all his Euclidean method of reasoning fresh upon him the boy approached the tail of the salmon with infinite caution. But the tail happened to be not a mental construct of all tails but a real tail, and, when he grabbed it, it behaved in a way markedly different from what he had anticipated.

So let us get back to the boy hunting in the dark for the salmon that couldn't be found, for here odd glimpses of animism in action may be caught. I find I have implied at one point that the boy was afraid his groping hand would land on a face. But this need not mean anything much in an animistic way because always there was the latent fear of the gamekeeper, who *might* have discovered the salmon in its cache and then come back in the darkness to lie in wait, or, if not the gamekeeper, then some other *real* man. For at the age of nine or ten, the boy was already more than half-way between the savage and modern man. Yet it was not always a face, a human body, that he feared, but something much less definable than that, as if the primitive world he was emerging from was still before and around him, and when he put out a hand it might land on something that would *move*. A black lump in the darkness had the air of *waiting*. And a bush seen in the starlight, a bush that *hadn't been there before*, was now standing watching on the outer fringe of the trees.

So the animistic phase was not for the boy a "psychological theory", but beatings of the heart in moments of vivid life as complicated possibly as the workings of an analyst's intellect. For him not all things are endowed with this animistic power, and he feels that it was the same with his remote forebears in the Strath for whom spirits, being alive, could instantaneously be here or be there, though they would have their special haunts.

It is when we leave this wonderful wonderland and come on the theorist trying to reconstruct the emergence of a god, and so of God, that uncertainty clouds the scene. To attempt to condense into a few sentences the intricately reasoned argument of a potent book like *Totem and Taboo* is to be left with that "sense of guilt" which it is part of the book's purpose to isolate. Even if the book may not be so solidly based in fact as was a totem in the actual life of my ancestors still it is a remarkable creation. That said, let me pick my way as quickly as I can through it, for its primitive background is not unlike the boy's, and it is within this background that Freud the hunter flushed God the Father out of a dark human thicket for the first time. If some speculative remarks are added their intention is to give a slant on the mind of the boy who will presently be seen in plain action doing his best not to find but to dodge God. Hunting Freud hunting God becomes one of those complications which inevitably attend the pursuit of any living quarry, not to mention a growing boy.

Darwin's conjecture that in the beginning man, little removed from the apes, lived in an unreflecting "primal horde" had clearly a strong fascination for Freud though he admits that "this primal state of society has nowhere been observed".

Freud proceeds, none the less, to draw his picture of the primal horde, with the old man, who ruled it, fully aware of the attitude of his sons towards his absolute authority, particularly where the females were concerned. Then he continues: "One day the expelled brothers joined forces, slew and ate the father, and thus put an end to the father horde. Together they dared and accomplished what would have remained impossible for them singly. Perhaps some advance in culture, like the use of a new weapon, had given them the feeling of superiority. Of course these cannabilistic savages ate their victim. This violent primal father had surely been the envied and feared model for each of the brothers. Now they accomplished their identification with him by devouring him and each acquired a part of his strength. The totem feast, which is perhaps mankind's first celebration, would be the repetition and commemoration of this memorable, criminal act with which so many things began, social organization, moral restrictions and religion."

Surely never have the bare bones of a plot contained so much. And one can see it developing. When the brothers had killed the father they found themselves in such a hot welter of rivalries and difficulties that they began to wonder if life under the old tyrant hadn't been so bad after all. Brotherhood wasn't working out, with each receiving according to his needs, much less his desires. They began to remember good points about the old man. If they had feared and hated him they had also admired him. Hatred may have suppressed the admiration, but now it is released in tender feelings, quickened by the sense of guilt. All the time in their attitude to their father there had been this double emotion, this ambivalence. Hatred, with love concealed; love, with hatred now buried out of sight. Their guilt haunts them and they propitiate the dead father; the feast becomes a sacrificial commemoration, and as the father recedes in time he becomes the original father, the all-father, the god or, in the Christian religion, God.

Not that even all the bare bones of the plot are here, but enough of them perhaps to permit Freud to insert with marvellous skill one or two bones of his own by way of a sub-plot, which is yet for him all-revealing.

Exactly how a tribe or clan came to have a totem animal we do not know, but the kinship between the totem animal and the clan was in the nature of a blood kinship, the totem being called the ancestor and primal father. "If the totem animal is the father, then the two main commandments of totemism, the two taboo rules which constitute its nucleus — not to kill the totem animal and not use a woman belonging to the same totem for sexual purposes — agree in content with the two crimes of Oedipus, who slew his father and took his mother for wife." And so we find ourselves at the core of Freud's psychoanalytic findings and theories — the Oedipus complex, the relation of the child to its parents. "I want to state the conclusion that the beginning of religion, ethics, society, and art meet in the Oedipus complex."

To revert now to the primal horde and the tragic drama of the sons killing the father. When I begin to probe into it an astonishing change takes place. It is as if its backcloth were removed to disclose a still earlier drama where the central figure is not the old man of the horde but the old woman. In a word, matriarchy preceded patriarchy and the first gods were female. This is now generally accepted. Freud, need I say, was perfectly aware of it, and admits "I am at a loss to indicate the place of the great maternal deities who perhaps everywhere preceded the paternal deities". Leaving it at that, he then proceeds with his own argument about the father horde.

So where are we now in the hunt for the first god? Assuming there had not been a change from matriarchy to patriarchy, what kind of story would our learned old women now be telling us about the creation of deity in the earliest of all organised hordes, the matriarchal?

A working man, in truth, may still refer to his busy wife as "the old woman" and even, with a touch of swagger, as "the old girl", but the poet, penetrating into further dimensions, can find the fatal woman, *la belle dame sans merci*, the goddess. Indeed in his book *The White Goddess*, Robert Graves opens up the earlier drama in a way as exciting and tumultuous as the interactions of Freud's all-male cast are dark and dour and deadly.

Yet to us as boys, for whom the Old Testament was required reading, the word patriarchs meant the old men of the Jewish clans. I was a member of a Highland clan. If the Jews were "a persecuted people" it was in a religious sense, and accordingly any thought of our persecuting them was high taboo. Scotland has never persecuted the Jews.

So I may be permitted, perhaps, to fancy I detect in Freud if not a motivating at least a directing influence out of a long patriarchal past. The drama of the father horde is a man-made drama for men, and all that follows from it may be expected to be bloody in a terrible and terribly dull way. On the other hand the female deity, the White Goddess, also did some human eating, but with what a difference! for she had apparently an eye for dynamic poets; indeed if the poet today is not consumed by her, we are told, he is no true poet; from which it may be gathered that at least her diet at its best was sauced with immortal song, toasted in blood-red wine and concluded in a resort to arms at once ecstatic and unambiguous.

So it seems, after all, that we can choose our drama. There appears to be no certainty of how the god, male or female, or God, was first "created" by those remote savages, our ancestors.

A little more patience is needed before I can get round to the little boy of three or four performing his small act beyond the gable-end of his home in the face of the darkness. For I am finally concerned to find just how much there was in that encounter with the night, in how far it may have been the primal atom that was subsequently built up into so many peculiar psychological structures.

Some of us are inclined to call primitive man a savage in the sense that he was brutal and his psychic responses blurred and dull. This, as field research has shown, is a great mistake. His responses were, on the contrary, vivid and rich. His emotional ambivalence was more intense than ours. And as it was with him so it is still with the child, as Freud knew so well: "I think that we may easily make the same mistake with the psychology of these races who have remained at the animistic stage that we made with the psychic life of the child, which we adults understood no better and whose richness and fineness of feeling we have therefore so greatly undervalued."

So much, then, for as far back as we can go into the "animistic stage". But what about the stage before that? Says Freud: "We have practically no further knowledge of pre-animism as no race has yet been found without conceptions of spirits."

In short there never seems to have been a time when man did not believe in the existence outside himself of what we may call a psychic something, an active independent psychic power (*mana* is the Oceanic word for it). And I am inclined to credit it because of the experience the small boy had in the dark beyond the gable-end. It was spontaneous in the sense that the capacity for the experience was as it were latent in his psychic stuff. And in that sense, if there is any parallel at all between the earliest experience of a boy and the experience of earliest man, we are very close, if the comparison may be used, to that which is inalienably inherent, like the *given* in mathematics. And upon the *given* in mathematics vast superstructures, resulting in wonders and terrors, have been reared as we know so well.

Let me add at once that of course I am aware of the theory that (to quote Freud again) "spirits and demons were nothing but the projection of primitive man's emotional impulses; he personified the things he endowed with effects, populated the world with them and then rediscovered his inner psychic processes outside himself". But when I want to know why he should have gone to all this involved trouble, I cannot find any answer beyond Freud's, "we want to avoid the problem as to the origin of the tendency to project psychic processes into the outer world". But that is precisely the problem which I do not want to avoid. However, if "tendency" may be taken as innate, then it is merely another way of saying it is *given*, and my point comes sufficiently clear.

The nature of the reality or otherwise of all the spirits, demons and gods man has evoked in his own or other more dubious image is not, of course, my concern here though it has been, as I have tried to indicate, the concern of a host of learned investigators in a way that rouses my admiration. My concern is with the experience of the small boy, for this I know, and in isolating it I am doing no more at the moment than suggesting that this whole trafficking with spirits and gods derives from an innate tendency, in short that it is functional in the psychic stuff.

Chapter 10

Speculation

Although pure speculation is beyond my purpose here, I confess to an urge to do a little elementary speculation about this psychic stuff, as though something further were needed at this point to tidy it up.

We have gathered that the psychic exists only inside man, and if he finds it outside, whether in an actual tree or an imaginary god, he finds no more than what he has projected or placed there. That he may not do this consciously merely means that his unconscious has done it for him.

But when it really comes to the question: does psychic stuff exist anywhere else in the universe? then we enter the realm of pure speculation; at least my purpose for the moment becomes a purely speculative one.

First, then, simply as a matter of probability, it seems to me unlikely that in the countless galaxies throughout space our relative speck of a planet is the only place where this psychic stuff is to be found, particularly as we have good reason to believe that the matter of our planet is found throughout space. When it comes to assessing the value of this psychic stuff, with its known capacities and apparently inexhaustible potentialities, still more does man's claim for its uniqueness in himself become difficult to entertain, short of, it seems to me, a colossal vanity. We learn about probabilities from experience. We are satisfied that our "fundamental laws of matter" operate universally. About the nature of mind and how it operates we know as yet comparatively little. It is reasonably probable that we may learn a lot more and that the sphere of the inquiry may extend.

Here, anyhow, scepticism is not enough, because we know how sceptically our ancestors reacted to the notion, when first propounded, that the earth went round the sun, for with their own eyes they could see the sun going round the earth daily. And as for the notion that the earth was not flat but a round ball, then literally how on earth could people walk and sail round it and yet keep right side up? Strangeness in any notion is not enough.

To leave ordinary probability and take a slightly more difficult step towards the materialistic conception that mind is a function of matter, I find from experience that this is, in our childhood's phrase, "very like the thing". But, again, there is such an enormous amount of matter throughout space that it seems less probable than ever that this planet should be the only spot where matter functions in this particular fashion. The more materialistic or mechanistic one conceives the functioning process to be the more likely is it to manifest itself as a normal process throughout the range of a mechanically operated universe, and certainly in the sense that it would tend to dismiss a "special creation" for this earth.

But just here an extra difficulty arises because if matter and mind "gang thegither", as Burns said of whisky and freedom, then just where does the partnership begin or lapse? To our senses the presence of life is the criterion, the activating principle that demonstrates the partnership. Where there is no life matter is "dead". But the range of our senses is very limited. There are sounds that we cannot hear; atoms that we cannot see. In brief, if life-mind is a function of matter then it would seem that the capacity of matter to function in this way must be latent within it. Either that or it is endowed with the capacity by some outside power at some particular point; in short, something in the nature of a special creation takes place, and that is pure mystery and not in accordance with the unvarying way in which the laws of nature are observed to work. Even granting that man projects these "laws" into nature, as the savage projects his psychic impulses into tree or river, still we can depend, on the whole, more absolutely on our laws than the savage could on his spirits. For that Freudian "tendency" to project our psychic processes into the outer world has increasingly taken the conscious form of desiring to eliminate mystery, or at least of trying to find out how "mystery" works, and this, to me, is a fascinating development.

Now if all matter is potentially psychic, if the psychic is latent in it in however infinitely tenuous a manner, then the need for anything in the nature of a "special creation" is at least lessened. Granted the "tendency", we can go ahead with "development" under our own steam.

But where are we now? Certainly a fair distance from the "projection" by the savage (or by any of us) of the only psychic stuff that existed or exists. If, to take the simple example, and bring the matter to a focal point, there are beings, so to call them, on other planets that differ in many respects from ours, then the stage of their "development" is probably different from ours. From that, it is a reasonable step to postulate a development beyond ours. But once we start out on that road (always remembering that in our earthly experience the psychic stuff has an innate urge to find out how "mystery" works) where do we end? At an absolute knowledge, somewhere, of the whole mystery? But the experience of the small boy by the gable-end has possibly taken me far enough for the moment.

Chapter 11

In Woods and Wild Places

So far, then, the boy of the Strath seems to have caught what I may call two atomic glimpses. The first was when, sitting on a stone in his river cracking nuts, he experienced an extraordinary state of well-being; the second, when he had his encounter in the dark by the gable-end. Having dealt with the second at some length, let me return to the first.

The only way I know of testing whether an intimate memorable experience can be communicated to others is by finding out whether others have had an experience of a sufficiently comparable kind. If they haven't, then no effort of mine will rouse a response. There can be no question here, at least, of projecting a state of mind into another mind and then finding it there *unless* the other mind has a capacity however latent for entertaining it. All literature, it seems to me, consists precisely in a communication that touches off an innate capacity for its acceptance and so induces an immediate response. Thus a reader may exclaim, "How wonderful! I never thought of that, but it's true!" There a latent capacity has clearly been roused. But the response may be, "I thought no one had ever experienced that but myself!" Here the communication has been of a unique kind. Great literature brings into consciousness the wonderful and unique, and leaves behind by way of extra marvel the reflection that the wonderful and unique are true. After that and according to our capacity, we mark our passages.

But sometimes the person at the receiving end, the listener or reader, may think or feel that the communication is inadequate, that a deeper understanding exists of what is being conveyed. At that point true criticism begins.

Let me try accordingly to place the boy's early experience of well-being in his particular strath against comparable experiences by three great writers in different countries in order to see how communication and responses work.

In *Letters by W. B. Yeats* (edited by Allan Wade) I come across this comment by the poet on one of his poems: "The poem means that those who in youth and childhood wander alone in woods and wild places, ever after carry in their hearts a secret well of quietness and that they always long for rest and to get away from the noise and rumour of the world."

That arrests and sends me wandering in a few old woods. Here is communication that touches off more than a few responses, with overtones dying away into a sort of transcendence that may be vague but is none the less apt for that. He knew about it! Bless him, too, for the "alone" that is no longer alone now, yet will ever be alone more richly.

But the small nut-cracking boy of the woods is not dead, I find. He stirs. For his forays, he had one or two special companions. Wandering alone occurred, but it was not normally an aim in itself. There were other aims, vivid actual doings, handlings or pokings into, sudden "queer" things in a place just beyond the known place, "something" in the shape of a rocky outcrop or gnarled tree roots that called for a wary approach, circuitous rather than direct, the crack of the branch that was not strong enough, the crashing leaf-bashing fall, a pain, inside, blood on the hand, on the knee, a pain! gripping inside, I've got a pain! the slow squirm, the relaxing grip, ah-h it's going! I shouldn't have chanced it, but I chanced it, I am fine, I am all right, if I wash the blood away no one will know, no one will be able to laugh, and at home no one will threaten if I can hide the cut. "Where did you get that cut?" "What cut?" "That cut." "Och, that!" As if a boy could remember everything! Behind it all, the freedom of the woods in the Strath, the delight, the certainty of "next time".

Some essence of all this comes from memory's well and in a circuitous swirl has, as it were, a look at the poet's well of quietness. It's a beautiful well. It's safe, too, perhaps. All the same there's a something missing, a contact of hand to tree, blue eggs in a thrush's nest, warm to the touch, the mysterious warmth of life in *that* world, magic with its smile on his face as the hand slides away, as the boy backs away, hoping the bird won't know the hand had been there lest she deserts the nest. . . .

The poet's longing for rest, to get away from the world — but into what? resignation?

The swirl has a look at this resignation. . . . The poem issues from woods. Resignation in woods? In woods!

There is something wonderful in and between the quoted words all the same — if resignation does not mean a negation. The boy cracking nuts on the stone did not fall into a resigned state. Anything but. Mindless, possibly, but in the sense that the essence of his woods had taken possession of his mind, and the rare feeling of timeless delight, like himself, simply was.

The trouble about having a close look at a chance passage is that it may seem to imply a criticism of a writer's whole work. No such implication will be found here where the chance moment is all. Indeed years later Yeats wrote to George Russell (Æ), "In some of my early lyric verse there is an exaggeration of sentimental beauty which I have come to think unmanly . . . a womanish introspection. . . . Let us have no emotions, however abstract, in which there is not an athletic joy." Some twenty-seven years later still, he wrote to Olivia Shakespear, "I went for a walk after dark and there among some great trees became absorbed in the most lofty philosophical conception I have found while writing *A Vision*. I suddenly seemed to understand at last and then I smelt roses. I now realize the nature of the timeless spirit."

If the nut-cracking young savage on his river stone may think that athleticism came a trifle late in the order of the poet's years, he also finds — abstract emotions and philosophical conceptions apart — a relationship between the first quotation and the third, as near, say, as the blue egg to the hatched bird.

When I had to hunt for something which one of my brothers had hidden he would encourage me by saying, "You're getting warm". With a vague feeling of this warmth about, let me have a look next at that wonderful evocation of boyhood: Marcel Proust's *Remembrance of Things Past*.

No boyhood could have been more different from the nut-cracking savage's than that of the little fellow who, carrying his umbrella and wrapped in his Highland plaid, set out with his parents for a walk on either of two ways — the "Méséglise way" or the "Guermantes way". Never the two on the same day; never

a wild foray from one to the other; everything arranged or understood beforehand, today on this "way", tomorrow on the other,
passing the same objects, those apple trees, that lilac bush, like
figures in the order of a ritual; and even on the days when he goes
alone he goes the same, the proper way; until in advanced
maturity as Proust looks back on that beloved countryside of
Combray, with the small French boy, Marcel, pursuing the
"ways" in an order that almost has the mathematical nature of
being *given*, that order itself seems to secrete an entrancement in
which the familiar objects are perceived with the heightened
intensity that gives them so remarkable, so unforgettable a
precision; until, finally, they remain, together with the
containing, the unvarying outlines of the "ways", permanent
within a time that never changes. And that, of course, is not all, or
even the more remarkable part of the total experience, for
accompanying the acts of perception are feelings and thoughts,
the light and shadow of moods, their most subtle evanescent
colourings, and these, too, are caught, as Proust looks back, with
the same precision, if not now indeed with an extra exquisite
capacity that arrests in the moment of its vanishing what was
hardly felt at the time as even a fleeting sensation; until the
Combray boy, too, achieves his permanence within changeless
time.

Clearly he was not a boy among other boys for whom the order
of any "way" means the hope, the expectation, that it may be
excitingly broken. He was a solitary among grown-ups. He never
raced *out* of himself — I'm off! I'm away! — he always walked
with himself. And when the walk was over and in due time he
went to bed, he lay awake hoping his mother would come and kiss
him goodnight. If there were guests and she might not come he
was tortured by hope and doubt. That he may have been kissed
goodnight already made no difference. He wanted this special
visit and longed for it with an aching intensity.

So for Proust, as he looks back, that place and that time affect
him not simply in what may be called a nostalgic way, but with a
sense of reality which he never encountered again. "The
'Méséglise way' with its lilacs, its cornflowers, its poppies, its
apple trees, the 'Guermantes way' with its river full of tadpoles,
its water-lillies, and its buttercups have constituted for me for all

time the picture of the land in which I fain would pass my life. . . ." No other land, even with finer flowers of the same kind, would do, any more than it would be enough, "for any strange mother to come in and say goodnight to me, though she were far more beautiful and more intelligent than my own. No: just as the one thing necessary to send me to sleep contented (in that untroubled peace which no mistress, in later years, has ever been able to give me . . .) was that my mother should come. . . ."

Here the French boy is father of the man in a way that is strangely *fixed* to the boy of the Strath running wild in a fluidity that never got fixed. Here delight has been; its land is a memory, is contained within the mind; it can never again be actively achieved, never athletically in the sense that Yeats went on in his old age to find "among great trees" his most lofty philosophical conception, to "realize the nature of the timeless spirit". What exactly "the timeless spirit" meant for Yeats we may not know; what it meant for Proust we know precisely. The perfection of his creation of "things past" could not, being perfect, excel itself, and if I use the word creation instead of some other like evocation, it is because I cannot at the end be quite sure in how far the writer, the artist, was important into his memories some of that imponderable stuff which inhabits and directs the creative act.

Let us leave these brief considerations and pass to one other great writer who had notable dealings with nature and recorded them occasionally in an imperishable way. But now, for a change, let us have something quite definite, as definite for the boy of the Strath, anyhow, as the feeling he had, when hunting for the salmon in the dark, that the inanimate would *move* under his hand. Wordsworth may have his "clouds of glory" around childhood, his alleged exaggeration of sentiment at times, his nostalgic backward look, but the athlete in him was once caught by that animism, which we have considered, so directly on the quick of the heart that I am happily left without any kind of qualification whatsoever. Here is what happened:

> *I dipp'd my oars into the silent Lake,*
> *And, as I rose upon the stroke, my Boat*
> *Went heaving through the water, like a Swan;*
> *When from behind that craggy Steep, till then*

The bound of the horizon, a huge Cliff,
As if with voluntary power instinct,
Uprear'd its head. I struck, and struck again,
And growing still in stature, the huge Cliff
Rose up between me and the stars, and still,
With measur'd motion, like a living thing,
Strode after me. With trembling hands I turn'd,
And through the silent waters stole my way
Back to the Cavern of the Willow tree.
There, in her mooring-place, I left my Bark,
And, through the meadows homeward went, with grave
And serious thoughts; and after I had seen
That spectacle, for many days, my brain
Work'd with a dim and undermin'd sense
Of unknown modes of being. . . .

Chapter 12

Trees in Church

As I think over it again, that picture of the small boy on the "ways" of Combray, while wonderfully precise, may have something added from the mature Proust in the nature of a sentiment with an illusory life of its own, like a sheath about the boy, or like his sentient double, his doppelgänger. That the boy himself experienced something of the kind in moments of reverie, which were many, is no doubt true, but there would also have been moments of an actuality that escaped from the sheath, that was unaware as it were of the confining, defining rhythm of the artist's prose. But when all allowances of the kind have been made the picture remains essentially clear of a boy wrapped in himself as in his Highland plaid, if never quite enwrapped like an umbrella.

The contrast here with the boy of the Strath, whose delight was to be off and away, who never even in his after life became the possessor of an umbrella, is so marked that some effort must be made to understand such apparent "opposites" or I shall never get into that climate of delight, that actual "land" where Proust would "fain" be. As genius needs a given culture to emerge from, so there must be a land of delight before the achieved, the timeless moment, may emerge, even if its emergence remains, like that of genius, a matter of chance, something that occurs "by the way". The atomizing of the moment can only be attempted later.

The young savage of the Strath, then, was off and away from precisely everything that confined the culturally conditioned young boy of Combray. He burst loose and raced so fast that in a real sense he had raced beyond himself, he left himself behind. And the self he left behind was the self that knew grown-ups, restrictions, home lessons and other home tasks. It was as if he had two selves and found the second self after going through the

speed barrier. Here we have, I feel, the clear separation of the
"opposites" in a way that was never vividly experienced, not
anyway from the urge of a sufficiently strong primal need, by the
Combray boy. A boy may either stay among grown-ups (with
whatever wayward thoughts and fancies, with whatever enrich-
ments) or he may deliberately break loose, like a man from a
prison, into a known land of freedom; but if he breaks loose in
this way then his attitude to the grown-ups is conditioned accordingly and particularly to the two important ones, the father and
mother. The boy of the Strath, for example, has no memory of
having been kissed by his mother either in bed or out of it, nor of
any shred of desire so to be dealt with. Fathers didn't kiss
anyway, of course. I can imagine the boy's round eyes at the mere
rumour of such a proceeding! However, leaving theory alone, in
actual practice the boy did not encounter this parental trait or rite,
and he certainly can remember fighting successfully against all
efforts by visiting females, particularly those with the scents and
manners of the south, to entrap him into a performance of the said
rite. Indeed it is highly probable that when he himself went south
he may, out of an inadequate knowledge of polite usage in this
matter, have kissed a woman at the wrong time.

That there was no inclination of the boy towards the mother in
any over-affectionate way, however far back I try to go in
analysis, may seem like a comment on the Oedipus complex, but
nothing so profound is intended. I am describing only what was
normal then and seemed so absolutely natural. And I am trying in
particular not to endow the parents with qualities which the boy
did not consciously perceive at the time, however he may have
perceived them subsequently. In his bones he simply knew that as
parents they were "good", so good that once he had got beyond
their reach — beyond the errands and tasks of a busy household
— he could forget them. If there was an errand which he managed
to jink — and often a sixth sense told him that if he stayed at home
another minute he would be caught — then the sense of guilt, if
any, did not last long, and if it recurred it was only when he came
in sight of home again and he wondered just how much he was in
for, particularly if he had skipped a meal and left the whole household to do its best without him.

That his mother had a sixth sense, too, he knew, though he tried

to defeat it. "Where have you been all this long day?"
"Nowhere." "Where's nowhere I should like to know?" As he
could hardly say "Nowhere" again he remained vaguely or
moodily silent, not with too great an air of being wronged but
still. . . . "Were you wanting me for anything?" he might ask,
though still not sufficiently implicated to meet her eyes. The
answer to that question would begin to relieve pressure and soon
he would find himself round the corner once more. There were
variations in the small drama, where the acting revealed more than
the words, and on the whole the parts were skilfully taken. To
withdraw intact was the great thing. And this must generally have
happened because he has no clear memory of having been
thrashed by either parent. A cuff or a slap in the by-going from
older members of the family was in the run of play and would
leave no impression. If he got it he knew he had asked for it. To
have an instant way of retreat open and to "ask for it" from an
elder brother was sometimes irresistible. Invariably the cry
followed him, "You'll pay for that!" and invariably he did. But if
to the payment "interest" were added, then at once a sense of
outrage was engendered and the transaction was continued until
a reasonable balance was struck in some moment of mutual need
or conspiracy when they seemed to come closer to each other
than ever before. Blows did not matter; it was not primarily the
body that got hurt. That was why a deliberate thrashing from a
parent would have been something in the nature of a disaster. It
would have been an onslaught on the second self, the one he
found when he went through the speed barrier.

That, and yet more, for here there is implied a field of subtle
family relationship as native to the boy as his blood.

In some way that I find even extremely difficult to define now
the boy himself by invoking and receiving the thrashing would
have broken some taboo that had to do with the wholeness, the
balance of the family as a living active concern, as though it, too,
had a second self. And it is always the second self that holds
within itself what is inviolable. When the brothers in the story of
the human horde killed the father and were pursued by a sense of
guilt, that sense of guilt would have covered *more* than the killing
of the father.

When I try to test this I find at once that a thrashing by the headmaster, or any other master, was a matter of no real concern, beyond, of course, being able "to take it" within the recognized standard of stoicism. If one were jeered at by a classmate for not having maintained the standard, a fight followed. Certain responses were automatic. They had to do with what I have called the first self, the self that interacts with grown-ups and their rules and orders, with the pressures and accidents of life in the mass. The boy had many fights. Not that he ever sought them; they just happened. And the more fights any boy won the more he was let in for. Sometimes the preamble to a contest was very formal. One or two of the older boys (two years made a vast difference then) after school hours would bring along a boy of one's own age or size with whom, up to that moment, there had been the most friendly relations, and he (having already been put through the ordeal of *daring* to challenge) would hold out his arm and say, "Spit over that". Not to spit would be unthinkable disgrace. So one gathered a good spittle and shot it fair and square over the arm. The fight was on. Somehow, anything in the nature of a boxing technique was never learned. The contestants stood up to each other and slammed away with all their might. The nose was the important objective, for when a nose began to pump the contest was stopped, with honours resting upon the intact nose. My memory of them is actually rather hazy, for cuts and bruises of one kind or another were not uncommon. And if I remember one with distinctness it is because of a particular feature in it that vastly astonished me at the time. Possibly I had been having a run of luck for somehow I got matched against a much older, heavier, and stronger boy who had what was doubtless a compensating disadvantage in being mentally weak. I had never before been physically staggered by a single blow, and possibly then for the first time I got a glimmering of the technique of avoidance and of dancing around until I could land a welt of my own. However, the time came when his face was there wide open and all I could do, being all in, was lift an exhausted numbed arm and sort of push the face away; and all he could do in return was the same. That I couldn't hit that nose a bash really did astonish me for the spirit was still very willing. As no contest was ever settled on points, the result was declared a draw, both noses, so far as blood went, remaining intact. I have said that I never sought these fights, indeed in prospect I disliked them, but while they were on they were remarkably exhilarating. The something that won't give in has more than the life of an eel, and a stunner is more of an outrage than a physical pain.

But in all these natural accidents and happenings, which are so often vastly exaggerated in importance as indeed in number, there was one element that just seemed to be about as basic as life itself, and that was, whether the occasion were a thrashing at school or the imputation of a motive, a sense of justice. A child's experience of this sense is extraordinarily acute. Where a mature man may "make allowances", the child can't and won't. The child has to be taught to "make allowances".

But when we come to the second self even the sense of justice is left behind. I have tried hard to think of ways of describing it but cannot get beyond the mere assertion that it simply *is*. It has won free and now it *is*. If I remember my school Euclid correctly the four or five basic axioms *were* in much the same way, yet with the difference that in being taken for granted they are assumed to exist, they remain assumptions, even though they "work" with unvarying success. The second self is not an assumption. It is the fount from which assumptions proceed. In the beginning it is. I am itself, trying to describe it.

I feel an urge to make this clear, as I did when the boy had his experience of the darkness beyond the gable-end and again when, a few years older, he was nut-cracking on the stone in the river, as though here in the second self we have what was central in both experiences. If there has been talk of an atom, here is the nucleus. That I may also feel like a coral "insect", grown vaguely conscious of itself, is not so much an indication of self-consciousness, perhaps, as a dim view of the kind of humour that inhabits the second self when it gets off on its own. I'm off! I'm away! and sheer into the freedom of the Strath the boy flew. It was delightful; it was positively laughable. And if he had escaped by a hair's breadth it was more laughable still. Here he was with himself, intact. It was wonderful.

If all experience that is blissful comes from this second self, then very naturally it is going to take care of itself, to protect itself against any kind of interference from outside. And in the boy's case this happened to the extent, if a pictorial representation may be attempted, of putting a circle round itself, not unlike the magical circle of the primitive, always remembering that magic is our learned word, a concept, whereas to the primitive magic was in a powerful sense more real than the nose on a face.

Now within this circle the boy was protected not only from the good intentions of his elders but also from whatever adult evil was let loose among them. In a very literal sense of the simple saying, he bore a charmed life. He had the power not to let either the good intention or the evil actually *touch* him. He could become aware, for example, of the evil to an extent his elders never dreamed of, he could even in a quietened, wondering way be arrested by it though never fascinated to the extent of being spellbound for always he "kept his distance" so that it could not come and touch him. *Touching*, of course, can be a vivid affair in primitive taboo. There was the object that must not be touched. To touch it was to let loose its mysterious power upon himself, if not indeed upon the whole clan. But I suspect that in a clan where a certain way of life had been established for a long time, the taboo would work more normally in reverse, for the then latent or active fear would be not so much of touching, which could be avoided, as of being, somehow, touched. When the boy searching for the salmon in the starlit darkness saw the bush that "shouldn't be there" his whole being experienced the fear — the one-way fear — that something in it might come and touch him. Here the Freudian "emotional ambivalence", I submit, did not exist. Not even in the boy's deepest unconscious did there exist *at that moment* any kind of counter impulse to go and touch that bush. In the neurotic it has been found that love of another may become excessive or obsessive because buried in his unconscious is the desire to kill that other. Tribal ceremonies conceal the same ambivalence. Where there is love there is concealed hate and vice versa. When any emotion is analysed in depth there appears this two-way traffic. No man is "normal". Until back in our beginnings the child of the Oedipus complex emerges from his sexual ordeal in the guise of what is sometimes considered by the uninformed a shocking little monster of unconscionable iniquity.

I am not disputing this analysis in any way, not so far as it has gone. I have neither the experience nor the knowledge to do so, nor any particular desire, and indeed accept it with, I hope, some elementary understanding. But I am submitting that it is not the whole, the invariable picture. An experience like that of the boy with the bush — and many others that I could readily adduce in the realm of the young boy's emotions — suggests to me that a state of profound emotion can be experienced in its purity without any ambivalent admixture. Now Freud does admit that for man in some pre-animistic stage this emotional ambivalence may not have existed. Precisely what kind of glimpse he had of such a man, and precisely from what within himself he was capable of having the glimpse, I should not care to offer an opinion, even if hereabouts I feel we are getting "warm".

It links up, anyhow, with the notion that a child or young boy may re-experience the mental states of earliest man and that even an adult may have a glimpse now and then of a "pure" state.

That the boy raced away from the social complex that normally had him in its toils, from the breeding ground of emotional ambivalence, into a freedom where with his second wind he got his second self and a powerful feeling of delight there is no doubt. This second self was his own, his very self, and he knew it, and when he stopped skipping or dancing or otherwise expressing his joy, ceased being the joy itself in its pure moment, and glanced around with a quick wary eye, he was simply making sure that nothing was going to *touch* him now.

From the adult viewpoint, this boy in his purity of joy is actually a selfish young rascal, cunning in avoiding a task, not only not shameful but gleeful over having manoeuvred his younger brother into being "caught" by the task, doing unto him as he himself had so often been done by from above in the brotherly sequence with interest added if possible, an expert in bloody noses and every kind of game from the wildest form of shinty to swinging from one treetop to another in a way that often enough might have cost his parents the price of a coffin. He didn't even have haunting nightmares over groping for a crack in a rock face. If he was pure in any way it was as the savage whom realist novelists make no bones about.

The boy knew this quite well and what he didn't know was on occasion told to him, with gloomy pictures of his future added by way of compound interest. But that made little difference to the boy at the best of times and none at all when — "Oh, boys! isn't it good to be off!" He came out within his circle then and in his joy felt as pure as the lily, except, of course, that he never felt in any such verbal way. To have mentioned the purity of the lily to him at that moment, with its associations of church and school and adult solemnity, would have made him wary indeed, something to be dodged with extra cunning. His joy in its moment of experience was so unique in itself that even a simile or analogy held the threat of a *touch*. The suggestion, for example, that there were "clouds of glory" still trailing about him would instinctively have set his hands brushing them off, as if they were dubious spiders' webs caught in a cave he hadn't been too sure of.

In his "Ode on the Intimations of Immortality", Wordsworth drew a picture of the child at which distinguished critics, like Coleridge, have scoffed. To say that a child can read the eternal deep, be a mighty prophet, a blessed seer, is no doubt absurd, but so absurd that surely something less absurd was intended by so great a poet. I have tried to isolate a child's moment of joy in its purity, and I suggest it can be so pure that literally it is ineffable. One can only say it *is*. Being of this unalloyed nature it is innocent, it seems to me, that the poet — and others of the pre-Freudian age — were concerned when they spoke of "the innocence of childhood". It may be "a primal innocence", and, so phrased, give an "intimation" of why man has in his time been haunted by, and hankered back towards, a Golden Age. But it is in the nature of man's psychic stuff, as has earlier been suggested, to hanker forward as well as back, and when he hankers forward in terms of innocence and pure joy he is given the name of prophet or seer and finds his Golden Age in an immortal realm or, if his seerdom is very advanced, in an eternal Now. The child's actual experience of his nut-cracking timeless moment of happiness becomes an "intimation" to the poet or seer of the blessedness of the state towards which he aspires, and the child himself by inhabiting the blessed state becomes, for poetic purposes at least, a seer in the eternal deep.

If there remains something dubious, or taken for granted, about my use of the word timeless, all I can say is that time was often forgotten or lost so completely that the boy of the Strath awakened to it with a peculiarly startled feeling, but once he was sure it was "real" he started off for home, stung by guilt and similar attributes of his first self, making up as he ran the excuses that might fend off a disastrous conclusion. If nothing else, at least he achieved an "intimation" of the timeless. He did indeed, and was prepared to pay for it, too.

Wordsworth also talks of a Superior Being by whom the child is "forever haunted". This is much more difficult for the boy of the Strath to get a grip of. That God did a lot of haunting at times there is no doubt, but when this happened, say in church, the boy drew his circle so closely around him that he could feel it. God wasn't going to get past that circle if he could help it. No fear! And usually there was no fear, for as the great sentences poured forth from the white-bearded, tall, erect, square-shouldered figure in the pulpit — archetype surely of all patriarchs — and the congregation settled down for an hour-and-a-half's sermon or thereby, the boy could let his circle relax and even discreetly shift from one hip to the other on the hard seat, observe the grain in the pitchpine, or become absorbed in the way the outermost twigs of an ash tree swung idly beyond the window. That the branch could swing like that in the wind, as if there was no sermon, just showed you what a tree could do, out there, as if it wasn't even Sunday. A tree was like that. Once all the twigs gathered together and in a wild swing thrust their fingers towards the window but couldn't reach, though they did their best, then back they went, nodding as horses do, gradually settling down, but not really settling because they were waiting (they knew fine) for next time — waiting — and there — yes! — look! — they were beginning — up and down — they were feeling it coming — it was coming! — here it was! up they went, tossing high, curling over, but held, reined in —

A nip in the thigh brought him back like a nip from an adder. He met his elder brother's eyes slanting down at him from their corners. He kept his own head as still as he could and turned his eyes right, but his parents had seen nothing. The awful surge of internal heat began to ebb; he hadn't been caught; from under his brows he looked up at the pulpit, and the minister's eyes seemed to be on him, but in an instant they were off, sweeping the church, and his hand, which was aloft, an almighty hand, banged down on the Word of God, over which he now leaned dramatically, and, with the unexpected intimacy of a conversational voice, said of the biblical character whose delinquencies he had been expounding, "Of course the man was a fool — he was a *great* fool — he was a *very* great fool." And the boy knew he was safe once more.

But not altogether, for the temptation, now that he was safe, to twist his eyes round for a glance at his brother, was very strong. He had the awful feeling, too, that his brother was waiting for it. For these words which the minister had used were not new. He had used them before, often. They were known, and were used among the boys themselves on secular but apt occasions with convulsive effects, tumbling them around in laughter. To keep himself from looking at his brother, he looked at his younger brother on his other side who was restless but so young that he could afford to be restless now and then. His younger brother looked at him frankly, with what seemed a touch of distress, as though the sermon was awful long and he was needing to get out; so he frowned at his younger brother, but with helpful understanding, imparting the knowledge that this is what happened in church so it was no good pretending he needed to get out, he must just contain himself; and at that moment he was not nipped but nudged by his elder brother, and he looked down at his brother's hand, and in the hand was a round hard sweet called a pandrop, and as he took it he glanced along the pew and met his mother's calm face, smooth as a calm in all the storms, and gave his younger brother the pandrop. His younger brother, aware now of what had happened, grew shy and looked at the pandrop, and looked up at his brother slowly, with a little smile, and then more slowly from under his brows at the minister, whose hand was aloft dealing with the Amalekites, or it may have been Nebuchadnezzar, if not Daniel in the den of lions, or Shadrach, Mesach and Abed-nego in the fiery furnace, and he popped the pandrop into his mouth and forgot about the need for getting out. All the same this shouldn't happen, not in their family, for disgrace on the family was a hundred times worse than on himself or his little brother. Perhaps he could take a glance at his elder brother now, if only because everything was all right. So his eyes moved sideways and slightly up and met his brother's eyes in a face almost as calm as his mother's, except for a small crinkling of the skin around the near eye, an infinitesimal lowering of the eyelid in an objective solemnity, before the eyeballs swung away and came to rest on old Geordie in a pew in front, across the aisle. Geordie had a grey beard, not long like a minister's but short and bushy like a bird's nest, for he was so hard-working a man that a long beard would get in his way. As the boy, following his brother's eyes, saw Geordie he realized that he was in the throes of a power stronger than the minister and the king Nebuchadnezzar, not to mention the lions. Geordie was nodding, but with little upward jerks of his head that showed what a desperate fight he was putting up, gallant even while he was surely sinking. The boy, having ears that could hear the squeak of a bat, heard a crinkling of paper issuing from the lap of Geordie's wife, a kindly stout woman, black in her Sunday best, with eyes reverently on the minister. Geordie's head suddenly gave a decided jerk, not like the jerk a horse's head gives when its body is unexpectedly poked, but not unlike it either. After finding his bearings Geordie glanced down at his own lap and his arm perceptibly moved. But his eye soon found the minister and his ears were assailed by the eternal tidings, and solemn was Geordie and earnest. Up came his hand as a man's hand will and thoughtfully encountered moustache and whiskers and the boy knew that another pandrop had found its way home.

Terrible is the bodily swelling that must not be allowed to burst in a solemn place, the internal pressure that a boy must contain against the odds. Never would he dare look at his brother now. It was his brother who made it far worse. But he couldn't stop his eyes turning, not far but just a little, so that he needn't see his brother's face quite, but just only so that . . . and then he saw it, and it was not looking at him, but it held a stern warning. At that moment the minister cried "Fourthly", and that was a help, for it meant the minister was well into the second half of the sermon, because he didn't always go to "Sixthly".

Not that God, and Sin, and the Devil that went about like a roaring lion, could be kept outside his circle as easily as that. They knew their own minister, he could be relied on, and if he didn't stand for any backslidings it was because he was like the Rock of Gibraltar — not the Rock of Ages, for no human being could be like *that* Rock. A man who had been doing wrong things would certainly founder on the minister's rock. He was, as was said, highly respected and ruled in a way befitting his station.

But there were visiting ministers at the time of The Communion. And one Sunday evening a visiting minister preached to a church packed because his "gift" was famous. His sermon must have had to do with damnation, which the boy knew as a word his own minister could use in church (but, normally, no one outside) so it was quite safe, for among themselves boys never swore. But their own minister just used the word damnation; he never went "into it". This far-famed minister went "into it". It was the picture of hell that stuck in the boy's mind. It was spread before him as a vast unending lake of brimstone, lurid with flame upon boiling movements big as currents in a tumultuous sea. Even *that* the boy might have kept at its distance: it was the depth that got him, for the minister described how if you were cast into it, and sank down — and down — and down, you would never reach the bottom.

This depth got him because at once his mind saw the clifftops from which he had thrown stones into the sea, for the astonishing thing about that precarious game was the length of time it took a stone to reach the blue-green surface. Often the stone disappeared in what was called "a dead man's dive", that is, it threw up not a drop of water. The ear caught the sharp *hst!* of the impact and the stone was gone into that element of which the local fishermen sometimes remarked, "We couldn't find bottom". And this was made the more fearsome for the boy because he had a poor head for great heights — his one and awful secret weakness, driving him to a courage of foolhardiness which it still makes him a little sick to think of.

So there wasn't much in the conception of depth which the boy had to learn; nor did it help that the dead man was immortally alive as he forever failed to plumb the fiery brimstone lake. The picture haunted him, and it is possible that "the other world" came pretty near his circle often enough. Not, let it be clear, that he ever for a moment doubted the existence of the other world. It was taken for granted, like the church and the school, or, more precisely, like the sky. One Sunday evening about this time he and his elder brother heard a man in the deep twilight coming down the brae on the off side of the Strath, whistling a bagpipe tune. To whistle on a Sunday as this man was whistling was sure damnation. Yet he did it; and he did it well. It was not boastful whistling. The notes were liquid and clear, and the man threw off the "turns" or grace notes with a lovely precision which his brother obviously admired; it was like a whistling in some fatal and enchanted region — before the blow, the lightning, strikes. Oh *why* did the man do it? Why take that terrible risk for nothing? If ever a man was a fool, a *great* fool, a *very* great fool, this was the man and the moment; yet the boy did not think in such terms. To mock the minister's lightest words could not occur to him now. The folly of the man was beyond words, in that region where the lightning at any instant may strike and blast. The whistling stopped. The calm of the deep dusk grew calmer, more still. Without a word, they turned back towards the house. Presently his brother said, "Boy, he could whistle well!" "He must be a stranger, mustn't he?" "If he wasn't a stranger I would know him by his whistling."

It is possible that the boy became comparatively "good", that he may even have asked what errands had to be run before he absented himself. It is almost certain that he did not observe "It's queer it's always *me* that has to go", a remark to which he was partial when "caught" in the normal way. Yet no very definite memory of this period remains, no memorable moment, that, is, when God or the other world got within his circle, now drawn surely as tight as the shell round a nut, no "conversion" which breaks the circle open; even the brimstone lake didn't quite drown the outworks.

This sheer tenacity of the inner core of himself, the second self as I have called it, is remarkably strong in a boy, if not indeed imperishable. And it operates equally, as I have said already, against good and evil, heaven and damnation, as our adult or tribal conceptions of such states attempt to impinge upon it. Otherwise I should fail to understand or credit those stories by travellers who found in certain areas of Europe children who took bombs and devastation as natural manifestations and contrived their fun and games amid a rich welter of shell holes and ruins as inevitably as the sun rose or set. This might well be the profoundest of all surprises to any traveller. And if one were to indulge the now popular phantasy of a world rained upon by the new bombs and of mankind being blotted out, so long as the blotting wasn't complete, so long as a few were left here and there intact, then, in the search for food, the boy would once more hunt his salmon in the pool, once more crack his nuts on the stone in the river and get lost in his timeless moment. If there may not be much comfort in such a thought, at least, in the realism of a boy's terminology, we "asked for it".

That this may be a particular kind of adult reconstruction of one boy's mind is no doubt true and accordingly it may hardly be permissible to generalize from it. Doubtless there may have been a boy here or there whose circle did get broken open, who, as a result of the assault, did "walk with God". The mind can be brought "to see the light", whether of a religion then or an ideology now, as we know. But in this seeing of the "light", this breaking down of the circle to let the "light" in, what exactly happens?

In the boy's case an answer may be attempted in two parts.

If fear has been the total or principal element in the successful assault, then the boy's second self will remain within the ambience of the "light", he will see that the "light", as explained to him, is "right", that a boy must be guided by it for his own good, and for the good of everyone else, including his parents, for if he isn't so guided then something terrible will happen because he will call down the wrath of the terrible "enemy". The particular form the "enemy" may take hardly matters, because he already has had an experience of a terrible invisible "something" (as at the gable-end), and if his teacher is psychologically clever enough to metamorphose that "something", with its power or mana, into the "enemy", then the realist situation, which a boy so acutely perceives, is given shape, and conversion to the "light" is achieved. But though the circle round his second self has now been broken down, the second self does not expand because the "light" proceeds from fear, and fear has not an expansive but a contracting effect; it does not open the hand, it contracts it; the second self becomes tight as a fist. The boy may appear to become expansive, even to grow braggart; but the more he behaves in this way the tighter his fist behind the appearance.

If, however, the opposite emotion to fear has been the principal element in the successful assault, then the boy accepts the "light" after the fashion in which he accepts anything that is "good", like the taste of a nut or a special kindness shown him by someone he secretly admires. Here complete confidence in what he knows is good may break the circle, as in the first case, but the effect on the second self is expansive; it glows. The "light" hasn't to be explained as something that is "right", it has merely to be appreciated as something that is good; it isn't an argument, it just is. And the wonder of it makes him glow. He was ready for it as it were without knowing, like the boy nut-cracking on the stone.

In either case the "light" may prove illusory as the boy grows in years and experience of life, for now the element in him which has been called his sense of justice comes into play over widening fields. Gradually he becomes aware of the machinery which produced the "light" — the religion, the ideology or whatever it may have been. It is examined by his sense of justice and the quality of the "light" assessed accordingly.

If, in the first case, the examination results in the repudiation of the "light", then the grown boy or adult turns against the machinery that produced it, and as fear was the operative or dynamic element the self becomes, if necessary, an active fist. The process may be drawn out and bitter and full of despair, but in the end the "light" is blotted out by the dark anger of the fist.

If, in the second case, examination results in repudiation, the repudiation is more of the machinery than of the "light", because here, however he may think he has been tricked by the machinery, the "light" contained the expansive feeling of joy, of delight, which he has tasted and already knows in himself, which he raced into, and which, if he can help it, is never going to be *touched* by any machinery. His sense of justice is not against it but all for it. Here the "light", the forever desirable, can undergo metamorphosis in two absolute directions: into that nihilism which after experiencing the soul's dark night knows itself in passivity as an utter absence of the "light", or into that ultimate apprehension of it as the Light. Between these two extremes there remains at however deep a level a memory of it; and though machinery may *touch*, or attempt or even seem to destroy it, it comes back, it suddenly in some unexpected moment *is*; for it is implicit and as imperishable as the second self.

Chapter 13

The Sea

As his existence had two parents, so it had the earth and the sea. If his mother was the earth, his father was the sea. In fact he could hardly think of his father without thinking of the sea. Out of the sea came the livelihood of the household. They depended on the sea, and of all the elements in nature it was the least dependable. You could never be sure of it as you could be sure of the earth. When a storm blew up on land, you could get inside and shut the doors; in bed you could curl up and listen to it; you were safe and could wait; but at sea you had to fight it out, with only an inch of planking between you and what lay underneath. The sea reared and sprang, it hit and battered, it was remorseless; its blows staggered the boat, her planking shivered, and when she reared again, lifting her fighting head, again she was struck. Snatches of such fights the boy heard now and then when on a winter's night a half-circle of men hemmed in the kitchen fire, smoking their pipes, at ease, their weathered faces lit by their eyes and the oil lamp and the lazily flapping peat flames, telling stories of one kind of another. There was always some good fun going then, for if the man telling the story was himself the principal character, he could get his leg solemnly pulled. This he took "that same way", meaning in the spirit of the fun, but defending himself, too, perhaps by passing the real tribute on to the boat, "Ay, she had it in her. I'll say that." Often these stories were of earlier years, of memorable storms, of landfalls and ghostly adventures (that might explode in laughter), of skippers who were "no more" and had had the extra seamanship which connoisseurs will salute to the end. Time or age was needed to mature a story, to give it the tone of voice that went into the past. Recent happenings were conversational. The boy might overhear one man say to another, "Ay, it was dirty. One lump of sea hit us when we were rounding the Head and I thought she was away with it." A quiet seaman's comment on what was thankfully over. To boast about one's own skill at sea was unthinkable; the essence of taboo. The sea could always wait for "the next time".

But if humility was the sea's unended lesson, it was the humility that stood on its own feet, fighting it out, with the long steady look, and the look at "the next one" — the next lump of sea or wind, the steering hand gripping and the word of command ready for those who would leap to it.

Not, to be exact, that it was always possible either to stand on two feet or to issue the word. The boy was grown into manhood before he heard an illuminating story about his father from an old stooping man who had sailed with him. The deep-sea sailing boats then were little more than forty feet long and carried a great brown mainsail hoisted to a creaking of sheaves in the blocks that was rhythmic and pleasant to hear as they crossed the bar. According to the season of the year, they fished off their home coast on the Moray Firth, or went north-about and through the Pentland Firth, with its racing tides and whirling tumults, to the West Coast fishing; north to the Orkneys or Shetlands or round to Peterhead, or even south on the long haul to Lowestoft or Yarmouth, hunting the herring that had their seasons and migrations, with a portable marine compass on board but no chart.

This incident the old man remembered took place somewhere off the Outer Hebrides. The boat's name was *Isabella* but she was called the *Bella* for short. Apparently she had been dismasted once in a storm. Said the old man, "It got so bad that in the end we had to lash your father with a rope to the tillie (tiller) and leave him sitting there. She was taking it clean in over. We had everything battened down, and we got down into the den ourselves and drew the hatch and left himself and her to it. We were in his hands now. They were good hands. Never better. It was some time after that that a great lump struck us. We all thought she was away with it. I sprang up and pushed the hatch back, and looked out. It was breaking over her in white smoke, but there the skipper was, boy! with his head up, his eye on the mast and the peak of sail that was holding her to it, and as sure as I am alive and will go to my judgment, I heard his voice cry above the storm: 'You have cast one mast before, Bella my lassie; you can cast a second — and welcome!'" The old man, who was tall and lean, unfolded as his head tilted and laughed a soft husky laugh of triumph and pleasure, exposing the gums which had only the eye teeth left and they were yellow. "He had great spirit in him had your father!"

And once at least, to the boy's own memory, even the skipper was battened down with the rest, leaving everything to the boat; for the storm caught them in the western ocean, west of Barra, with no hope of fetching shelter. So the skipper shot his fleet of nets for a sea anchor, hitched on to them, and rode the storm out through three days and three nights.

After that, there is quiet, an easy manner with the upsets that meet a man on land, a balance between great and small; herring baskets are filled to overflowing; a generous hand gives without seeming to give; a niggling meanness would neither last long against the sea nor gather its harvests. Then the way home once more.

Once the boy met his father in his long leather seaboots as he was coming up a flight of stone steps near his home. The boy must have been very young, for being able to go down and up the steps on his own was a new accomplishment. He stopped going down to meet his father as his father ascended. For here was his own father, coming. "Is it yourself?" said his father, a smile on his face and a kindness in his eyes as if he had come from a far place, like a stranger, back to his own. "Your hands are cold," said his father; but probably his own hands on that cold day were not much warmer for now he got to his knees on a lower step and brought the small hands in among the thick hair on his head and warmed them there in a way that was new and strange, like the shy wonder of the meeting.

The "big boats" were hauled up the shingly beach on the off side of the harbour, and the "small boats" (*Rose of Sharon* was the small boat's name) prepared for the local winter fishing of white fish. Then as the year came on again the big boats were tarred and painted for the new herring seasons. That was a busy time, bright and tarry smells, hammering, sawing and voices. The small boy conceived the great idea that he himself would like to renew the name *Isabella* in white paint. Someone had to do it so why couldn't he be the one? Why couldn't he? Won't you let me? Not that he would express his consuming idea to his mother. She wouldn't understand. She thought that the less boys had to do with the sea the better. But his father was quite different about the sea, and he let him. When his elder brother heard about this the amount of amused scoffing that went on was the worst yet. But he didn't mind. When driven to the dancing stage he could always pick up a stone and threaten to let fly. That only increased the amusement, the scoffing. Life was often complicated and difficult, but nevertheless if you stuck to yourself you would find a way; as the small boy found his way to the small pot of white paint which his father stirred and mixed with oil until it dripped off the stick in a satisfactory manner. Then his father showed him how to use the small brush so that there wouldn't be too much paint on it at any one time. It was easy, and wonderful, and he was going to paint the name.

When he had climbed the ladder on to the deck it looked a long way to the ground, but, as far as he can remember, his father did not lash him to the gunnel. In truth much of the active detail is forgotten, but not the actual painting, for now he found to his astonishment that it was not easy at all but very difficult. The old white paint was there clearly enough but oh! how difficult it was to keep the brush from going over the edge of the lettering, and yet the brush had to work out to the very edge. And the letters were all curves. The *I* itself, the first letter, had no end to its curves. Try as he would, and shift his position as he liked, the edge would have a small waver at times. "You're doing fine," said his father, directly below him, swishing away with the long-handled tar brush. But he felt he would never be able to do it. There was no fun in it now, and if it hadn't meant giving in he would have been glad to stop. Doubtless his father realized what was going on and came to his help so unobtrusively that the help is forgotten. The name was painted and, seen from below, it stood out white and gleaming, *Isabella* without a sign of any wavering. It was his mother's name.

On a fine summer morning the sea had a wonderful swing. Great wheels of light whirled one into another out and away. The light fell on the face, on the eyes, on the hands. It was warm and bright. It was like something newfound, and so clear that a small object here or there glittered unexpectedly like a bit of treasure.

. . . Off flew the feet and, would you believe it? it was only a small stone. But look at it — queer, isn't it? See that vein. Like silver. It couldn't be silver, could it? Silver is found in stones, and gold, too. . . . Silver! Ho! ho! . . . I didn't say it was silver, I said it was *like* silver. . . . As the stone turned it glittered into the eye. I'll make it shine in your eye. It flashed like a sixpence of sunlight. With cries they scattered and swooped, like the gulls, waiting for the boats to come in on the flowing tide. A wooden station for the herring, big as a dance floor, with upright sides that could be straddled or leapt over, became the stance for a four-corner game. One in each corner and odd man out in the middle. *Feelie-feelie-four-corner!* From one corner to the next each charged, keeping the odd man from gaining a corner. For if he got "in" first the other was "out". The floor boards clattered and resounded. The women gutters, in coveys here and there, in stiff rustling oilskins, cried their shrill laughter as a joke was cracked or some man got more than he asked for. It was such a lovely morning, bright and young, it affected even the harbourmaster, who had to keep order without keeping order. Now, now, boys, you'll go through the bottom of her if you jump like that! . . . As if they would go through her bottom! What a joke! *Feelie-feelie-four-corner!*

Then they were coming, the boats were coming, far off. The gamble now, the gamble of the sea; who was well-fished, who had the biggest shot? This came near home, this touched the marrow. For the best skippers, the luckiest boats, had bad spells. Down at the quay-point, the incoming tide brimmed among the boulders, lifted the seaweed and with a seething and rustling let it fall until it plastered the boulders like wet hair. The sea was so full that it sighed. On the other side of the harbour entrance the small wave ran along the wooden piles of the breakwater, lipping them; and beyond, on the shingly beach, it broke in a small edging of white lace that shone before the bubbles died.

The wheels of light whisked out and away, for all the world, to the boy, like magical girds (the slim hoops of iron which they trundled, full speed, on the roads). Sometimes they made spangles in the eyes, coloured, and then the eyes had to blink as they looked for the boats. The "air of wind" was off the land and affected the sea's surface only far out. Every inch of brown canvas was spread, and soon the oars would be out, the great long sweeps

that lifted and fell like slow-going legs, to the side, crab-like. Soon
it was this boat or that, known by the sail, by "the cut of her".
Keith has got some gulls about him! There was going to be a
fishing. Ay, and Hamish is well down, too. He's got a fair shot.
You can bundle up your knitting, women!

His father's boat, coming at last with her consort of gulls,
weighted well down — oh, the joy of that, the relief, the wonder
that it should be so! The feet raced themselves nowhere and back.
A staring boy's cap was sent spinning with a flick of the hand.
Things got busy now.

Then she came, his father standing aft with the tiller against his
knee, his Gaelic-speaking crew from the Hebrides taking her in,
silver scales on his leather thigh-boots, on the decks, and, when he
spoke to the harbourmaster, speaking with the quiet voice of the
sea.

Chapter 14

The Cow

Anything could happen to the boy in the way of a task if he wasn't careful, though sometimes it made no difference how careful he was, with what skill he read the prognostications. He might be doing his best not to appear to be bolting his food when his mother would begin, "I want you to run a message. . . ." And the other boys waiting for him, the kick-off in ten minutes . . . the long jump, the high jump, the playing field . . . the Strath! It was terrible! His spoon would fall in his plate and scatter sparks of milk or soup. The voice of warning rose. My boy you are running on it! The surge boiled up inside, the surge that could hardly contain the wet spindrift of rage. It was queer it should always be him! . . . It wasn't. His elder brother was at that moment. . . . What about his younger brother? . . . He was too young, he didn't like to go and. . . . Didn't like! Didn't like!! . . . It was argued out, so long as he didn't splash his milk, and in the end off he went like an angry arrow. He could just see the justice in it, but if so, my word! he would make his younger brother see it too! Just wait!

However, these were merely the chance errands, even if they were as permanent as the merchant's shop or the post office. Occasionally there was a special message, like a gift of fresh fish to some poor old widow woman who lived a mile off. That was too much! It really was! Her! Couldn't it wait? And sometimes it was agreed that it could wait if a promise was given that it would be undertaken when the game or match was over. Behind the relief of the accepted promise was something final, and the promise was never broken.

But apart from these odd and irritating interferences with the main purposes of life, there was one permanent task — the cow. That cow! Not one day but every day! For they kept a cow for their own use. The family cow. He knew her from the look in the

corner of her eye to the last strands in her tail that could hit the
face like a whip. Not that she meant to hit you, but all the same if
she did she was not let off with it. It was her tail.

The sea being the harvest ground, they owned no land, so the
cow had to be driven to the park or large field of permanent
pasture where the cattle of the Home Farm grazed, a rent being
paid for the privilege. The distance from the byre to the park was
well over half a mile, and for a boy of seven or eight that was a
long way, a twisting way, with a stretch of public highway
thrown in, not to mention the vagaries of a cow with decided
notions of her own at certain times. This had to be done before
school in the morning and again in the evening when games
would normally be in full swing. Somehow in the ordering of the
family, in the long brotherly sequence, a boy fell heir to the task
for a spell. There were all kinds of let-offs and chance aids, but on
the whole it was his job. He could do it. Off you go!

Not, in truth, that it was always an unpleasant task. In the long
summer holidays there were mornings when the boy could
dawdle like the cow, for if there was a good bite in passing she
never missed it. And there was something, too, about driving a
cow, as if you were grown-up. From the way she swung her head
round as you first entered the byre, the glance in her large brown
eyes, you could see she had been waiting. Up went the small hand
and clapped her authoritatively. Stand over! No need to get
excited, you great fool! Firm but friendly. Then you reached for
the chain round her neck, slipped the catch, and nimbly got into
the calf's stall as her great bulk came about and she headed for the
door, her massive sides giving the jambs a crush in passing. If in
her desire to be off she began dropping pancakes before she was
quite clear of the byre, you yelled at her in explicit terms. She
might have kept that, the old fool, until she was beyond the area
that had to be cleaned. But no! Would she!

Sometimes when the boy met another boy a long conversation
would ensue about very interesting things and when he remembered the cow she was nowhere to be seen. Off he would pelt,
looking this way and that, round the corners and on, until he
would happily find her waiting for him down at the iron gate of the
park. She was wise. Everyone knew she was a wise cow. He let her
in, and then, pushing off with one foot, had a swing back on the gate.

Like the other members of the family she had a name: Nanz.
She was a big Ayrshire cow, sleek, with sides bulging like a great
cask and with a wonderful nose for a tasty bite. She was
condemned with affection as the best scrounger in the district.
And one evening in particular she gave him a fright. For some
reason he had been late and when he reached the park he found
that all the cattle had been driven home. The park was empty. He
went beyond it to unfenced braes near the sea, but she was not
there. From gleaned information, he went beyond the braes to the
cliff-heads. It was a long way and fear was in him now. It was so
easy to fall over the cliffs that neither cattle nor sheep were
allowed there.

He climbed up over the Head, keeping well back against the
dry-stone dyke that separated the top fields from the cliffs. At
first the distance between the dyke and the cliff-edge was fairly
broad but soon it narrowed to a mere passageway and then he saw
her in front, the dyke on her left side and the sheer drop on the
other, revelling in a growth of rare succulence.

At once the boy stepped back lest she see him, for he
instinctively realized that he mustn't frighten her now. She knew
she was doing wrong. She knew she would be for it. A wild swing
round or a barging on, and she might finish at the foot of the cliff.
Out of her sight, he climbed over the dyke and noiselessly went
forward in its shelter until he had got well beyond her. His heart
was beating strongly and he was feeling a bit sick, for the height
of the cliff could get inside him. Then carefully he climbed and
put his head over the dyke. She saw him and her head swung up.
She looked at him steadily, a thing she rarely did. She stopped
munching, with the grass sticking out of her mouth. They might
have been strangers meeting in very remarkable circumstances.

"Go on now," he said.

"Moo," she said.

"Home," he said, keeping the conversation up as best he could.
She had another tear at the grass and lifted her head.

"That's enough," he said. "Go on now." His voice firmed.

She began to go about, backing her haunches towards the dyke,
her head over the brink; then she was round and walking away. A
weakness of relief went over him. He kept inside the wall,
following and exhorting her, until the passage broadened and she

was clear. Then he climbed the wall and came in behind her. He had her now! The time for payment was not yet. Over the root of the Head, and now the descent of the steep brae. He hung back, giving her time. Once a hind leg slid and she sat down, but she never lost her balance, heavy as she was. There was no denying she was wise. He even told her to take her time. Take your time, you fool! In his anxiety, he encouraged her strongly until she was down on the level and then he told her that she was in for the greatest hiding of her life. He even stole forward to give her as foretaste one wallop with the small stick he had picked up. But she knew him and got out of reach, and then he saw something that stopped him for as her udder swung from side to side milk streams came from the teats.

She was so full, she couldn't hold any more. Wasn't it like her! But the milk remained in his mind.

At long last the byre, the chain fixed round her neck, and she was at his mercy. He picked up the hoe, prepared to belabour her with its handle. His whole evening had been ruined, she might have killed herself.

"Ah, you!" he said and gave her a wallop on the haunch. She stepped about the cobbles and swung her tail.

"That will learn you," he said, "not to go to the cliff heads!" And he gave her a second wallop.

She swung her head, looked at him and gave a double switch with her tail as if there were a lot of flies about.

"Ah, you!" he said and half-raised the hoe, leaving her to understand that she was very lucky not to be given a third blow.

"Maybe you'll remember that!" he added powerfully, putting the hoe away.

"Hooo," she said, still trying to whip flies.

He was surprised to find afterwards that though there were head-shakings about that encounter on the cliff, still he had done something that might not have been expected of his years, something even remarkable. He could read the look in an eye, the suppressed smile, and even his mother's grave face had something behind that he wasn't supposed to see but that he saw. If anything can be subtler than a boy's insight into elderly attitudes it is his vanity. But alas, the rare, comforting, swelling feeling of vanity wasn't given a long life in that milieu, not even supposing you tried to hang on to it and at the same time blow it still larger, like a soap bubble at the end of a clay pipe, by discounting the importance of the incident. Och it was nothing! His elder brother got the whole story out of him, including what he had hitherto suppressed, the almighty thrashing he gave to the cow in the byre. This was the final, grown-up touch.

"Boy, I fairly gave it to her!" he said, feeling very big.

"What did you do that for?"

"Why not? She needed it, didn't she?"

"But she would have forgotten by that time what it was for."

There was a pause then. "She would not! She knew fine!"

His elder brother laughed. "She would. Nanz is just a cow. She would have forgotten."

"She isn't! She would not!"

"She would so."

"She would not!"

His brother laughed.

A burst soap bubble is cold even on the hand. For he saw that Nanz may not have understood. It spoiled everything.

"Will you come with me?" asked his mother when the nights were long. "It's dark and I don't care going alone."

"Yes. Will I light the lantern?"

"Do."

He lit the little lamp inside the square lantern and shut its glass door. There couldn't have been others about, for between his mother and himself there was all in a moment a rare confidence, quiet and grown-up. "Are you ready?" he asked.

"Yes." She took the shining tin milk pail off its hook and they set out for the byre, up a short flight of steps, which he mounted sideways, in front, so that she got the full light, past the peat stack and the hen-houses, and so into the tall plantation of trees. Every foot of the path he knew. "Watch the roots there!" he cautioned her, shedding the light on the grey ridges that crossed the path like snakes. "I'm seeing fine," she said. "They're that slippery often," he explained. The shadows of the trees swung with the lantern and they were there in the night and he was all eagerness to make sure that his mother didn't slip. It was a rare feeling, looking after his mother; just the two of them. Then they came to the stone dyke. Here was a difficulty now! Two or three stones stuck out from the wall as steps on either side. He has a confused memory of being if not on both sides of the dyke at once at least so positioned that the light shone fair on one step after another as his mother mounted, got over, and descended. "That was a great help," she said. "It's not so easy in the dark," he said. "It is not," she agreed. "Mind your feet now," he warned as they approached the byre door. Then he lifted the latch and swung the door open.

"Moo," said Nanz.

"You're there, are you?" said his mother to Nanz, and Nanz shifted about, and gave another strong "Moo" as the new calf danced in its stall.

"I'm hearing you," said his mother.

Where she was everything else was about her, naturally, each in its own right and pleased to be there. The byre was warm and full of its own smells, rich and comforting, a little world of its own, and they were inside it, and the door shut to keep out the cold. Nanz tossed her head as usual and some strands of the hay she had been given got about her horns. He found the little stool and his mother sat down to the milking. The calf was excited and danced and butted. But his mother never got excited; she was calm and wise, and she liked his company because it was dark. So if he could see beforehand what she needed, he was quick then. Not that he could do anything to Nanz when she switched her tail and hit his mother, beyond saying powerfully, "Stop it!" But Nanz, hearing her calf, forgot to stop it, and his mother at last took hold of the end of the tail, divided the long hairs, and tied them round Nanz's rear leg. That sorted Nanz! When she tried to switch her tail now it wouldn't switch. His mother wasn't angry with Nanz. So Nanz ate her hay and the milk went into the pail, *switch! switch!* and the froth began to mount. Sometimes he cried out when his hand got tickled by the ridges inside the calf's mouth. So he asked his mother when the calf would get her teeth and they had a conversation about such things; not about lessons and school and all that, which people who weren't wise asked about. The whisks of milk got shorter and soon there was none left in the udder. The pail was nearly full. "She's a good milker, isn't she?" he said. "Yes," answered his mother, "she does well." She was a good cow. Of all cows, she was the best. He gave her a clap, and when the tail was released Nanz gave it some powerful switches to make sure it was working. At the same time round swung her head for now her precious calf was about to be fed. "Moo!" said Nanz. It was one thing pouring the milk into the calf's basin, but another holding the basin when the calf butted it. It was a job, and once he was nearly beaten but he held on. A little of the milk was spilt, but his mother said, "It's nothing". He helped to bed Nanz down, and soon they were outside once more. "What a night of stars!" said his mother. "Mind your feet," he said. It was worse going over the wall this time than before because there was milk in the pail, but he told her how to go, and lit up each step, for, as he explained, "You never know with a shadow." "How true!" she agreed. So they both knew exactly, and it was easy — the roots, and the small tree-stump to one side, and the step down, and the loose stone.

At last here they were at the back door; everything had gone right and it was fine. But who was this in the kitchen? Whenever he heard her voice he knew her. What was *she* coming here for? But his mother was welcoming her, as she was always welcoming wifies and people. And the woman, a skipper's wife, dressed and bright, explained that, "they were out and I just thought to myself I would take a run up to see you". And then in her laughing voice she turned to the boy. "Has he been lighting the way for you? Your chevalier!" He tried to smile politely but it was difficult, and when he slid out at the front door his mother didn't call him back. He couldn't even mimic the woman's voice he was so angry. Then he mimicked it, but didn't feel any better. Coming to the house like that at this time! It was too much.

Chapter 15

The Community

Scents, smells, beasts, birds, eggs, trees, the wild rose, the loose stone, the feel, the touch, the precarious hold . . . stringing the words is like plotting a course. What happened was outside the body rather than in; tears were for rage rather than sorrow. The social structure was so simple that it didn't consciously exist. Even much later, long after the boy had left his Strath, he found difficulty with those fine English distinctions between classes. He had to puzzle out an expression like "upper lower middle class" — and even now, as he writes the words, he feels he has probably got them wrong. But an expression like "the classless state" presented little difficulty, though it may have needed some reflection, the kind of reflection required when a stranger referred to "the fresh air" in the Strath. But once the surprising expression was understood it was so obvious that it was almost laughable. That one should come to the Strath for "fresh air"! Whereupon out sallied among the boys themselves an old saw like "Wonders will never cease" or "It takes all kinds to make a world". The "fresh air" was full of fun.

For that northern world was still in large measure self-sufficient, with the mail coach and its horses bringing letters and an occasional visitor from a remote railway station. Not that the outside world was unknown; indeed round the fire on a winter's night the talk could dwell on countries "beyond the seas", for already local men were in Canada, Australia, New Zealand, the States, and at least one old man, who had been in the merchant service and in most of the great ports of the world, could tell of "customs among the natives" that were strange and astonishing. Then, too, Highland soldiers had fought in most parts of the world, and the Relief of Lucknow with the bagpipes playing was more intimately Highland in a boy's ear than the Massacre of

Glencoe. When a voice sang "My bonnie is over the ocean, my bonnie is over the sea", to a boy's ear, at least, the sense of distance was real enough. The world was wide.

Perhaps this "classless" feeling came out of the old Gaelic clan system, wherein the chief was not a landlord but a leader, the head of the tribe, the father of the clan or *clann*, the children. In the Latin tag, he was *primus inter pares*, the first among equals. And if he wasn't going to be fit for leadership he could be passed over. The principal men of the clan, and even the reigning chief himself when it came to nominating his successor, saw to that. Primogeniture did not run as a law, and this the Lyon King of Scotland still recognizes. So usually the chief was fit for his task and the spirit of devotion between chief and clansmen was not only complete but vivid and bright, lifting the feet so often on a hopeless cause that it came to be said of the Gael, "He always went forth to the fight and he always fell". But he went. The boy wasn't conscious of being driven to the Strath. He went.

Still farther back, in the legendary days, the hero might be a man living in the next hut, the next dun. He came and went among his fellows, one of them. What distinguished him was some personal attribute, some remarkable skill or power. His name became legendary because of what he was in himself. Exaggeration did its best in the way of wonder.

This clan fellowship, with its devotion, mutual trust and social warmth, got broken down in historic processes that included the "hopeless cause" of Bonnie Prince Charlie, with the bloody aftermath of Culloden Moor and laws proscribing the wearing of their tartan by the clansmen under penalty of being banished beyond the seas to a penal settlement for seven years, and that included also, and finally, the bitter tragedy of the Evictions or Clearances when clansmen were driven from their immemorial homes in the glens to make room for sheep. So great was this betrayal by those who had now become mere landlords that men of the clans were bewildered and broken, more hopelessly broken than on "dark Culloden Moor", and this time they were driven out, their homes in flames behind them.

In his own place, the boy had no chief, though it was in the region of the old clan territory. There was a landlord or laird, but he was an absentee. However, you cannot rub out the whole way of life of a people by manipulating the powers in a charter, not unless you rub out the people themselves. And even if you add a new rent and protect the salmon, the old blood has its memories.

And the people got on very well without a chief. The old feeling of equality among themselves remained, of that independence which being independence on oneself was not directed against any other but, on the contrary, respected a similar independence in all others. A man could do what he liked with his own, whether croft or boat, and if he didn't do well he suffered. If bodily or other misfortune was the cause of suffering, then the others helped; as naturally as each, in his time of difficulty, would be helped; as naturally, in fact, as a storm spread havoc or things grew in their season. This may be difficult to understand now; and even seem to border on the sentimental or absurd when it is further suggested that often more amusement was derived from helping another than from helping oneself. But it was so. The boy, for example, might hear some of "the young fellows", an elder brother of his own among them, say, "Poor old Geordie is laid out with the rheumatics — oh cruel! he can't bed! What about giving him a hand?" And off they went, working into the darkness, scything hay or threshing oats in the hand mill, and afterwards, "making a night of it", with Geordie's wife not able to do enough for them, she was so pleased, though she could always be helped by a merry girl or two and a fiddle.

But this pleasure from mutual aid, from co-operation, was best seen at the time of peat-cutting, when friends combined to form "a squad". The boy can remember a real bout of tantrums, culminating in defiance and intercession by others until his mother said, "Well, he can go. But if he gets a thrashing at school tomorrow for being absent, he'll have himself to blame." A thrashing! A mere thrashing! The picnic baskets, the bottle of whisky — be careful with that! — up the Strath for a bit, then across the moor, past new places and little streams, on a whole holiday, in a wide world, with horizons far off, to the family peat-bank, for the first time. It was strange and wonderful, for everyone appeared to be on holiday, and the jokes that went flying were juicy enough sometimes, if never "beyond the thing".

This pleasure from co-operation was something added to work, as pleasure is added to the co-operation that makes a dance or a game. It was natural and spontaneous. Perhaps the spontaneity came from an absence of compulsion by one neighbour over another. This may have been the "free" element in the delight. However that may be, this pleasure was added to work. It happened.

Admittedly a boy is out for his own fun and, being selfish and full of vanity, does not want to be touched by the disagreeable, by misery, hard times, and the ills that afflict a community thankful when the fundamental needs of existence contrive to make ends meet. Looking back, too, he may let his own memories gild the dark times. But in the simple economic picture there were a few basic safeguards. The cow meant milk, butter and crowdie or cream cheese. The stack of peats provided fuel for a year as the potato-pit potatoes. When the new oats were ground at the mill, the meal chest or kist was packed. Flour was laid in and a barrel of cured herring. Fresh white fish, hens and eggs were always around. Rabbits were never far off. A crab or a roasted mussel might interest boys more than adults. Some kept a pig. Cabbages, leeks, rhubarb, garden berries. At least the normal basic picture gave rise to the joke: "We never died a winter yet!" People worked hard, for they liked to keep their heads up and preserve their independence. The boy can remember a load of peats being tipped off at the end of an old widow's house and his father getting clear before she could come out and thank him for the gift. That it was more difficult to receive than to give they all knew. Only once does the boy remember a dark shadow that overspread the whole community. He heard his parents talking quietly about it. An old woman who lived alone in some outlying small cottage could no longer look after herself and apparently she was going to be "taken away" to the Poor House. Never had the boy experienced this sense of tragedy before, with its dark shadow implicating everyone, as if in some mysterious way they were all to blame. But they could not help her any more. It had to be.

Chapter 16

School

Perhaps the nearest the boys came to that "Highland charge" by which schoolbook historians distinguished from time to time the behaviour of a Highland regiment in action was in the last charge from school before the summer holidays. It was a wild and furious affair, with a hundred throats cheering it on. The weeks had been counted. Then the days. And now the last day was over. Stormed at by shot and shell for a year, now they rode back, the full hundred.

There was never among boys any pretence of liking school. Scholastically it was a place of pitched battles, with certain subjects, like poetry, being vague enough to be a holy terror. Like old Gaul in the Latin lesson, poetry was divided into three parts: memorizing a certain number of lines; speaking them; parsing and analysing them. More or less successful efforts could be made with the first, and even with the third, if a boy applied himself, but on the second part, the delivery, every boy stoically foundered. To speak lines "naturally", with action suited to the word, to make such an exhibition of himself before his peers seated around in grim judgment — never! Better to face what might come to him now than what would surely come to him after. So in a high monotone, a sustained drone with a dip at the end, the words were spouted at a speed which abolished commas and other stops, except the full stop when it coincided with a lack of breath. And even when masterly irony was used to suggest that a boy standing on a burning deck whence all but he had fled might deliver himself differently, it made no difference. Indeed irony or sarcasm was the sure way of helping the boy to take in another grim hole on his protective circle. Not that the same boy, outside, wouldn't have rolled his eyes at the burning deck and even have flung a dramatic arm, if not two arms, at high heaven for the entertainment of all his peers. But that was outside.

Of the three parts of poetry, the boy himself preferred parsing and analysis. Memorizing was a hurried treacherous struggle, but parsing and analysis was in a way like arithmetic: once you got the hang of it you could get it right, though when authors left bits out and you had to supply them to make grammatical sense, it was not always easy. Here, however, the headmaster could all at once be helpful, throwing a new light on what the boy had misconstrued. When the boy suddenly saw it the headmaster would smile and between them for a moment there was an understanding that made the boy feel: dash it, I should have thought of that!

He was a powerfully built man, over six feet and straight as a board, with a tread on the floor that resounded. Nature had never designed him to suffer fools gladly and his wrath would flare up in a sudden and terrible way. His leather strap had three fingers when one would have been enough. Yet it was a real wrath, and the boys knew this even when it went beyond reasonable bounds. Like any other force in nature, it had to be reckoned with. There was nothing little or mean about the man. Even his roar was leonine. Yet the boys could roll up in the morning insufficiently prepared. So by and large the sense of justice did its work in a way that left no bad memories. Then suddenly, out of some good mood or whim or fancy, he could be arresting. On one unforgettable day he "took the floor" and delivered himself of a swatch of *Tam o' Shanter*. Perhaps he had been preparing for a Burns Supper. Anyhow, the boy hadn't time to think that this was poetry as he was caught and hurled along in the quickening tempo:

> *The dancers quick and quicker flew,*
> *They reeled, they set, they crossed, they cleekit,*
> *Till ilka carlin swat and reekit,*
> *And coost her duddies to the wark,*
> *And linkit at it in her sark.*

The schoolroom shook and the shivers went down the boy's spine. The culminating roar:

> *Weel done, Cutty-Sark!*

Then the awful drop in the voice:

> *And, in an instant, all was dark.*

Somehow the boy knew the sense of the more unfamiliar Scots words, though the change over from Gaelic to English in his district had been too recent for the old Scots tongue to have got a hold. Old folk still went to a Gaelic service in the church. Anyway, never again did he get the shiver from Tam o' Shanter's midnight ride as he got it then.

However, he was not asked to parse and analyse *Tam o' Shanter*, so poetry remained a school subject tucked inside Literature with its awful active respect called English Composition. How he hated English Composition! If school had to be endured, let it be in the guise of arithmetic, which a fellow could get dead right and so keep himself intact.

The first time he became conscious of being considered good at arithmetic was when the headmaster, after handing out problem cards to the others did not give him one. "You can help where necessary," said the headmaster, with the humoured smile of understanding. It was a hot embarrassing moment, but when he did get a signal or two of distress, how great was his relief to find that his help was genuinely wanted! That was a moment of revelation as well as of relief, and no fights followed. It was just accepted that he was good at arithmetic. But then arithmetic hadn't a "delivery" like poetry, or, even worse, taking the accent into account, like French. As small savages they naturally had rigid codes in their interpretation and application of *comme il faut*, not to mention *comme il ne faut pas*.

At school one had to be wary, it was so easy to be *touched*. Even the most stolid could be dumb in a cunning way, but so long as there was no *knowing* assault on the inner citadel, rages and thrashings could be borne, like rites in some mysterious initiation which all had to go through on the way to adult freedom. Even irony and sarcasm, these *knowing* weapons, could be countered by a smouldering rage and hatred, which drew the inner circle toughly tight. The malicious pursuit, the persecution, had to be persistent before evasions like truancy took shape; and when truancy was impossible, the nerves at last took over, turning a boy's stomach against morning food, until the second self became vulnerable and "lost" under the omnipresence of a fear more bewilderingly haunting than fear of the dark.

But all this may appear to give too gloomy a view of school, which after all was like a rough sea. A boy had to *learn* how to handle his craft. He knew that. There were continuous distractions, too, for girls were there, and though boys would have nothing to do with girls whatsoever, still the girls were there, and an unwritten code of behaviour was as uncertain in its exceptions as the fall of the teacher's wrath. Sometimes, too, when the wrath took a tangible form, some humour could be aroused, as when a boy, believing he was unobserved by the perambulating headmaster and instead of performing his set task was indulging in some private distraction, suddenly had the strap land on the desk in front of him and rebound against his chest. As the master had thrown the curled-up strap from a considerable distance, it really was a first-class shot, and all the boys, who were stone-throwers, quickly appreciated this. Even the headmaster himself thought it was a pretty good shot, and the boys agreed, "Yes, sir". There was no malice. Then one winter's morning, with the wonder of the first fall of snow and snowballing in full swing in the playground before the bell, out came the headmaster and gathering a fistful of snow let fly at "the big boys". For all of two seconds the world wondered, then it went into action. On the run the master did the full round of the playground, through a barrage of unerring shots, headed off, pursued, until he was plastered, until even the toddlers managed a loose fistful at close range on the last lap.

Formidable, uncertain as the weather, but with that smile thrown over his shoulder at the boy whom he had left with a difficult problem, a "teaser". That smile can still be seen. Certainly the boy neither played truant nor was put off his food, and deep in him knew that the headmaster was an extraordinary man.

So Literature took the form of penny dreadfuls. Not Tom Brown in his school but Indians on the warpath and Buffalo Bill in his saddle. This was the real thing, and therefore worthy of real emulation. Sides were formed and rules made on the spot, such a rule, for example, as forbade a dead man to get up and dispute his death, or, if he was only captured and due to be hanged, as compelled him — struggle permitted — to go through the motions of his unhappy end. Woods were the natural place of combat as they allowed the highest skill in stalking and surprise. But the hanging game was dropped after the enemy had been surprised before the hanging motions were completed and death established, for unfortunately the rope, which must never be tied, had a knot on it, and the knot caught in a fork of the tree, thereby tightening the noose round the victim's neck when the supporting arms were suddenly withdrawn; thus for once at least a victim was literally saved in the nick of time. The incident produced prolonged pow-wows and a very clear apprehension of the nature of responsibility in the ordering of human life.

The penny dreadfuls were never taken inside the home, so a loose stone in a wall was at once the cache and distributing centre. This itself was part of the game. Then somehow, in that early age, when a book meant a lesson, it was found that a book called *Deerslayer* was not a lesson. So Sir Walter Scott was in the offing; and even Tennyson's brook, that went on forever, could be spoken very attractively by a girl sitting on a bank babbling it to herself, with the monotony in the delivery curiously haunting like the monotony in running water on a summer's day. Not that it could remind him of a real river. Still, sometimes a girl had a way of making something sound gentle and nice and even strange. You could mock her of course. Still. . . .

Chapter 17

Games

Games were not an adventure, they were a passion; such games, that is, as constituted the "athletic events" at the annual Highland Games. Small boys tried to emulate the deeds of big boys and grown men, some of the men being very old, perhaps thirty or even more. Long jump and high jump, putting the shot and throwing the hammer — even if the shot was not an iron ball but a rounded lump of stone, and the hammer another shape in stone with a length of rope tied to it, so that it was advisable to stand well clear when it was being swung round his head by a budding athlete.

Two particular moments or skills gave the boy special delight. The first was in putting the shot, and can be easily enough explained, for the whole art of it lay in the rhythmic swing with which the athlete finally landed on his right foot at the stand and made the shot sail away. If he had caught the knack of this swing, the trick of it, he could easily beat a much stronger athlete who hadn't. Forcing the shot away, with an extra conscious use of the arm's strength at the last moment, was worse than useless; it could damage the wrist. Only when the ease of performance was perfect, when there was no consciousness of forcing anything, did the shot fly away from the body's rhythm. Not always could this perfection of action, of timing, happen, but when it did it was delightful, and the marking peg was shifted ahead and left sticking in the ground as a challenge, even to those who were a year or two older than the boy.

The second skill is more difficult to explain and it may even sound absurd. It had to do with the long jump, which meant you raced up to the stand and jumped as far as you could; or with the final leap in hop-step-and-leap, which describes itself, in that you hopped off one foot, stepped off the other, and landed on both.

Now the odd thing happened, while the boy was still in the air and trying to land beyond the peg, that his body responded to his desire by seeming to lighten itself and reach out — to levitate itself — for an extraordinary and even incredible moment and so get the extra distance. An extra oddity consisted in this, that whereas it felt like a pushing out of the feet before the body, so that the body on landing would be bound to fall back on its bottom and so "foul" the jump, in actuality, if the outreaching was somehow "right", the heels landed in front of the body but the body, in a little neat jump of its own, came erect out of the heelmarks without falling.

It need hardly be said that there were no such luxuries as a jumping pit and spiked shoes. Indeed shoes were not worn, only boots with tacks in the sole and a slim half-circle of metal round the heel. It was this metal that bit into the grassy turf and made the end of the jump so neat an affair.

The consciousness of having brought off a successful jump in this way gave a subtle and inexplicable pleasure. That it should happen to a boy under thirteen years of age suggests a source of delight that should now be considered on its own. All delight may ultimately be a mental affair but matter in its bodily realm of action would seem at times to have its inexplicable moments.

The more I looked into this bodily realm the more remarkable it became. Clearly it had a government of its own, but where the actual seat of government was or how its legislative, administrative and judicial systems were carried on, the mind by itself did not know and could not know. Not until something went wrong could the mind even become conscious of a hitch in the functioning processes of that inner realm, from a colic to a fever. As, in time, investigation revealed its chemical factories, its electronics, its mighty self-acting pump, the vast personnel of its repair departments, its hormones, chromosomes, genes and other gadgets of inconceivable complexity in action and inter-action towards a unified end, the mind could both be actually astonished and treat the whole as it wouldn't treat a dog; not to mention, of course, special departments, like the sexual, which produced urges and impulses of far-reaching effect.

What in a way was even more astounding was the conscious capacity of the mind to initiate movements in the limbs and elsewhere that in ultimate complexity grew wonderful enough but in the matter of sheer speed simply left the mind itself standing. The boy, for example, was fond of violin music, and even came to play in a fashion local dance measures, like reels and strathspeys, thereby acquiring a dim understanding of how a human hand could perform, on its own, truly astonishing feats — astonishing in the sense that if thought interfered for a moment the feat was destroyed, the tune was disrupted. Until the hand on the finger board and the hand with the bow could produce the tune as it were on their own, there was no tune.

Again something was happening here like the rhythmic swing in putting the shot or that extra lifting of oneself when flying through the air. When mind or thought tried to force the issue in a difficult passage on the tailpiece the fingers fumbled and even grew tired. Mind's command was like a brute command. By this time the fingers themselves knew the notes but could not free them properly. Then at some rare moment when the mind was not interfering, when one was not "trying", lo! the fingers danced over the tailpiece and the notes, distinct and bright as sparks, threw their pattern on the air. What a thrill of delight then! If a poet had told him that the stars were God's bright notes singing in their courses at least he would have risen to the analogy.

So if the inner body had its seat of government, so had the hand, and so had thought. In action thought was the slowest of the three and at times had to be told to keep out of the way and mind its own business. Logic and delight did not always cohabit, though logic had its delights.

Doubtless logic came into its own by stating that if three such realms did exist it was obviously in a federal system, for man was an individual, a whole, a unity. Where then was the federal seat of government and what exactly was it?

So philosophy got going, with thought, the born interferer, in full command. The creation of systems became a high and solemn pastime, if not indeed a grave duty, definable as "man's chief end". The boy's earliest encounter with systematic thought took place in the pages of a thin booklet called *The Shorter Catechism*, consisting of Question and Answer and proceeding from the simple to the complex, with "reasons annexed", in a way that manifestly had exercised profound minds. At an astonishingly early age, children could rattle off most of the Answers, word perfect, with a delivery not unlike that devoted to the boy on the burning deck or to Tennyson's brook. In truth, question-and-answer because it partakes of the nature of a game could at times become quite exciting. Question: *What is repentance unto life?*

Sometimes a boy (or girl) was completely stuck because he could not remember the opening words. This sort of frustration was painful. Sometimes he got half-way and foundered. Sometimes in the thick of it words might get transposed or even left out, and, though knowing he was thus dismasted, a boy would still valiantly struggle on, making for harbour with all he knew. But one boy (so often it was a girl) would be waiting with impatient anxiety for his turn and when it came the broadside was released with a weight and speed that emulated a Highland burn in spate rather than any gentle brook. Answer: *Repentance unto life is a saving grace, whereby a sinner, out of a true sense of his sin, and apprehension of the mercy of God in Christ, doth, with grief and hatred of his sin, turn from it unto God, with full purpose of, and endeavour after, new obedience.*

The boy's introduction to the Catechism began at the beginning with the first Question: *What is the chief end of man?* and the Answer: *Man's chief end is to glorify God, and to enjoy him for ever.* This introduction must have taken place at an early age, for the two words "chief end" sounded in his mind as one word "cheefend" for quite a long time. Indeed he might still have to make a deliberate effort to break the old hypnotic clinch, to separate the words into "meaning", so strangely attractive a sound is "cheefend". The accent landed on the second syllable, "fend". Yet because of all the words some overtone of meaning was doubtless conveyed, or if not of meaning at least of the atmosphere in which it tried to breathe. One got acclimatized in some measure to a country where great divines could putt the shot towards some very mysterious pegs. It was there, if only to be avoided like lessons generally, though that is hardly exact enough, for the other could *touch* in a way no school lesson could.

Being a normal savage the boy was able, with temporary defeats here and there, to look after himself, and the Shorter Catechism, far from doing him any harm, as tender humanists equipped with a knowledge of child psychology may nowadays fear, it probably did him a lot of good. There was something tough about it and thorough. However, no opinion is being expressed either on the profundities of religion or on the art of teaching. As times change new methods of instruction evolve. All that need be said was that when Thought was a tyrant in more than one guise, the boy found ways of countering him.

In systems other than religion a philosopher (the boy discovered in time) could use thought in a way that was not quite, as it has been expressed, like lifting himself by his own bootlaces into rarified atmospheres, but rather like keeping himself going through the air in a phenomenally long jump. As a performance it was wonderful, and here logic sustained itself with its own kind of delight.

However, this is not the place to deal with systems, religious or secular, nor with the appalling tyrannies that have come from a few of them. Each system has its own premises, or axioms, or bootlaces. Granted these, the system is enclosed and logic follows.

But the boy was not enclosed in this way. He was not one foolproof system but, as has been suggested, at least three different kinds of systems anything but foolproof, but all with their delights.

Thought as the infiltrating authoritarian has had so long an innings in our Western systems that it is extraordinarily refreshing to come, as I have just done, on a system which gives, almost literally, the hand, the human hand, its innings. What was missing from our logical systems in the way of delight is here found in a fashion the boy can appreciate. Now the whole of him is included, not the school learning part only. And it is rare, with that feeling of the rare which spills over so naturally into laughter.

Chapter 18

Zen in Archery

The very small book is called *Zen in the Art of Archery* and I hope I may be forgiven for describing it here in outline, not because of its background of Zen Buddhism, of which I know very little, but for the way in which it deals with the human hand in action. An Eastern viewpoint on what we are inclined to consider a Western characteristic or skill comes with a refreshing surprise. It is written by Eugen Herrigel, a German who (between the two world wars) took up, an appointment in philosophy in Tokyo University with the hope of studying Zen Buddhism on the spot, of arriving at a clear understanding of the Great Doctrine, for of course none of the Western systems had been able to formulate the ultimate mystical reaches of the Great Doctrine in terms sufficiently rigorous to satisfy the Germanic mind. Something had been left out, or indeed had never been included on the principle presumably that it either did not exist or was an irrelevance. And however much thought Mr Herrigel took to himself did not help. Here apparently was something that had to be personally experienced before thought could go to work on it. Even the most exalted kind of *a priori* considerations missed the boat, or, more precisely, could not find the boat to miss.

Consider, then, his astonishment when the famed masters of Zen far from showing any inclination to teach him were reluctant to have anything to do with a foreigner who thought he could learn from words. Words were not even tinkling cymbals (one can do things with cymbals), they were a weariness of the flesh, a bore; or as Mr Suzuki, in his short Foreword to the small book, puts it: "A Zen master would perhaps answer, "I eat when hungry, I sleep when tired'. If he is nature-minded, he may say, 'It was fine yesterday and today it is raining'." As the "answer" is by way of comment on a Zen "feat considered worthy of the utmost respect", it is not difficult to appreciate a certain degree of bewilderment within the Western intellect. But to the boy (father of the man), brought up among countrymen, the particular words in the answers are at once familiar and very promising.

However, Mr Herrigel was so genuinely and deeply anxious to learn that he pursued his inquiries until he found that there were certain practical ways of entry to the hidden country. For example he could take up the arranging of flowers, or making and handing round tea, or painting, or swordsmanship, or archery. Knowing about shooting, he chose archery, but again he was refused as a pupil, this time by a distinguished Master in the art, for the Master had had experience of foreigners. With outside aid, however, the Master's reluctance was overcome and Mr Herrigel became his humble and earnest pupil.

The rest of the book describes with an engaging lucidity the long and arduous struggle towards mastery of a bow and arrow. For, to begin with, the bow was over six feet long and to draw it the full length of the arrow and hold it before letting go required such muscular exertion and tension, with labouring of breath, that in the ordinary way it was quite a physical feat. Once more consider the pupil's astonishment when he was told that there must be no such muscular tension and labouring of breath; that in fact the muscles of his arms and shoulders should remain loose and relaxed; the hand must do it all, and almost as if it weren't doing it at that.

In any verbal argument on possibilities this is absurd, yet when Mr Herrigel is invited to feel that Master's muscles at the moment of top tension with a tougher bow, the muscles are in fact loose and relaxed. The pupil despaired, and then the Master told him how to breathe. This helped, but when the pupil asked a Japanese colleague why the Master hadn't told him about breathing earlier, it was suggested to him that telling wouldn't have helped before the difficulty became real. By the end of the first year Mr Herrigel had learned how to draw the bow.

It was in the next step, loosing the arrow, that the pupil was beaten. That he tried his best is painfully clear. To hold the "nocked" arrow and draw the bow, the right hand wears a glove with a stiffened thumb. The thumb hooks round the string and a couple of fingers hold the thumb. How to let go at the moment of utmost tension without as it were consciously or deliberately letting go is the difficulty, the "art". But until this can be done, until one can let go without letting go, until this very odd paradox resolves itself, there will be no perfection in the shot, the bow will wobble. This was Mr Herrigel's experience and it distressed him. Now it isn't as if he didn't know at least the general drift of what was required. He knew quite well that in firing a rifle the finger must squeeze the trigger slowly, gently, until the shot in its own last moment goes off. Simply to pull the trigger would make the barrel wobble, and however tiny or even imperceptible the wobble, the result at the target end would be considerable. Perhaps this can even be better illustrated in the case of the shotgun, for here every expert knows that when he is reduced to "aiming" at the moving object he is off colour or having a bad day. For perfection he must aim without aiming, make all kinds of allowances for speed and distance without consciously making them; and I should not have introduced this illustration if personal experience, too often of a defeatist kind, did not make it apt.

But pressing a simple trigger is one thing; unloosing fingers in a moment of high muscular tension, quite another, especially when the fingers have to act on their own so that the effect is rather as if the string of the bow cut through the fingers. Anyhow, at the point of highest tension the archer had to wait for the shot to go off, or, as they said, for the shot to "fall", as snow falls off a bamboo leaf. Unless this happened nothing happened within the art of archery.

At the end of three years Mr Herrigel was defeated; he still had consciously to let go with his fingers in a sort of explosive and shattering way. The shot did not "fall". It did not happen. "It" did not do it. And the Master replied, "'It' does it."

Now here was difficulty, particularly for a Western mind, for it "It" and "I" did not somehow coalesce, at least the "I" must be behind the "It". But apparently the "I", the intrusive "I", was the inhibiting cause of the trouble. The more "I" tried to think and do, the less "It" got a chance. To give "It" an innings, the "I", the ego, must keep out of the way. Only in a detachment that was selfless, egoless, could the "It" perform. "'Stop thinking about the shot!' the Master called out. "I can't help it,' I answered, 'the tension gets too painful.' 'You only feel it because you really haven't to let go of yourself'." Relax, leave go of the self. . . .

I am trying not to paraphrase too loosely, for clearly some of the fundamentals of the Great Doctrine are now around. However, let it be remembered that the moment for the archer is a practical one to the point of personal distress and he very naturally attempted to resolve it in a typical Western way. Far from stopping thinking he gave thinking a full innings. In brief, he took his bow home and practised releasing the shot by deliberately and gradually easing his fingers off the string so that at the point of highest tension the shot would *seem* to go off on its own. There would be every appearance that "It" did it. Further, he reasoned that this was probably what happened with the experts, the masters, only they had got so used to the performance that they no longer realized what was actually happening.

As a simple arithmetician I had every sympathy with Mr Herrigel, particularly when he became really expert at releasing the shot in this skilled Western fashion. And when he went back to the shooting hall, his first shot was a beauty. It made the Master sit up. "Do it again," said the Master. The second shot was even better. The Master turned his back on his pupil and would have nothing more to do with him. Towards whatever ends the art of archery was directed, they could not be achieved apparently by means of a "deceit" or trick.

Intercession was made, and the archer, chastened, was taken back. After many months of further practice, he one day by chance let loose a shot which brought the Master to his feet, bowing ceremoniously towards the target. "It" had at last done it.

But the worst was yet to be, for hitherto all had been a matter of drawing a bow and releasing an arrow. The target had not really been brought into the scheme of things. Now the archer had to hit a real target. And the way to hit it was by not trying to hit it. But whether the archer tried or didn't, the target itself, not to mention the bull's eye, remained uncertainly elusive. It was heartbreaking, and Mr Herrigel got more deeply involved in the "It" and the "I" than ever, until at last himself, the arrow and the target seemed so complex a system of interdependencies that in shooting at the target he was also shooting at himself.

Absurd as this may sound, something of the kind is not unknown to Western philosophy which has in its fashion struggled to find correspondence between subject and object of "identity of opposites", and suchlike mysterious entanglements. But this happens inside the Western head, in the region of thought, of metaphysics, not in the region of real things like bows and arrows.

At last the Master took pity on his pupil and privily got hold of a Japanese introduction to that philosophy which Mr Herrigel professed in the hope that he might thereby be able to understand and help. But apparently the vast concourse of words only irritated the Master to the extent of making him realize that it was no wonder the poor fellow couldn't hit a real target, outside him or inside.

Some talk of "I" and "It" there was, though clearly it never attained the height of a profound realization and acceptance of the vagaries of the weather. So one evening the Master invited his pupil to tea and proceeded with the real business which was not to "tell" his pupil but to "show" him. Now always — if the suggestion of comparison may be permitted in so exalted a context — this was what happened when the boy of the Strath wanted to tell another boy how to land on the right foot at the stand so that the shot was released and propelled to its farthest distance. The whole process of telling consisted in one remark, "Watch! I'll show you."

The light was switched off at the target end of the practice hall, leaving only a lighted taper thin as a knitting needle stuck in the sand before the target. From the bright end of the hall the pupil could not see the target. To use his own description: "The Master 'danced' the ceremony. His first arrow shot out of dazzling brightness into deep night. I knew from the sound that it had hit the target. The second arrow was a hit, too. When I switched on the light in the target-stand, I discovered to my amazement that the first arrow was lodged full in the middle of the black, while the second arrow had splintered the butt of the first and ploughed through the shaft before embedding itself beside it. I did not dare to pull the arrows out separately, but carried them back together with the target."

Clearly, as the Master observed, though the first shot might be considered "no great feat", in view of his familiarity with the target-stand, for the second shot the credit has to be given not to "I" but to "It". "Let us bow to the goal as before the Buddha."

In due course Mr Herrigel graduated as a master of the art of archery.

Chapter 19

The Dummy's Hat

While writing these words about *Zen in the Art of Archery* I remembered an experience which the boy had with a bow and arrow of his own manufacture that was anything but amusing at the time. But as it was possibly the boy's first introduction to "It", it may have its point. The boy would have been in age anywhere from eight to ten at the time. I find it difficult to date incidents precisely in these early years, and often it is a case of remembering the boy's competence to do this or that, as, for example, his ability to go up and down steps, with the feeling of adventure that accompanied this new experience (as on the occasion when his father warmed the boy's hands).

It is often thought that a small self-contained community with a long-established way of life, with actions and responses known and defined, must tend to produce an all-round montony which would even iron out differences in character. The boy knows that in fact the very opposite happened. It may be an exaggeration to say that the place swarmed with "characters", but at least each man had a character of his own, much in the way an actor has a character in a devised play. Here, of course, the play was devised by the playwright called "life itself" (or God, by the minister), so its next moves were often astonishing. Even the word "character" had its distinctions, so that when it was said of a man "He's a character", it meant that he was something special and odd and often incalculable in an amusing way.

One such man was deaf and dumb, very bright, quick-witted, short-tempered, and so neatly dressed that he wore a bowler hat during weekdays quite naturally. Children were so conscious of his existence that a few of them learned on their own the finger movements in the deaf-and-dumb alphabet. The Dummy's recognition of a child was always engaging, with some small trick for a smile, and the boy, who could converse with him in an elementary fashion, liked him.

Came the awful afternoon when the boy, bored with inanimate targets for his bow and arrow, saw the Dummy's bowler hat bobbing above the wall that confined those stone steps already mentioned. The Dummy was mounting the steps. Now the last thing the boy would wish to do was make a casualty of the bowler. Besides, to be able to do it was quite beyond his skill, so that in a sense he knew he could not do it. All he could do so to speak was to see how near he could come to it over so considerable a distance. However, there was no time for thought or reason because in a few more steps the face below the bowler would come into view above the wall and then the Dummy would see him. The arrow got "nocked", the bow was drawn and the arrow released within a world of action all their own. The arrow traversed the down-sloping garden with a frighteningly flat trajectory, pierced the bobbing bowler and sent it skimming. The boy turned, fled, and hid in the woods.

There were repercussions which no doubt defined badness and wickedness with some precision, for the Dummy very naturally had gone straight to the boy's home and left nothing unsaid, but the boy's real concern thereafter was not to meet the Dummy by accident. Once, at a distance, the Dummy's fist was raised in a way the boy was able to interpret fully. Then the inevitable corner produced the unavoidable meeting. To bring home to the boy his hideous guilt, the Dummy removed from his head his one and only beloved bowler, and exhibited the hole in one side, or at least where the hole had been, for the disrupted part had been wonderfully glued or ironed back into position. The boy was unutterably awkward and shamefaced and the earth as usual refused to open up. Nevertheless he did not fail to observe that the hole in the bowler was precisely half-way between its own crown and the living crown and between fore and aft. As a shot it had been miraculous.

This realm of movement, of action, where things could be done with skill, and occasionally with a "miraculous" skill, provided the utmost delight. It far transcended in this respect anything that thought could do in its realm. This may seem natural enough in a boy. But the refreshing nature of the Zen-in-archery story consists in the application of this naturalness to age. Doubtless age may sit and meditate and achieve the higher delights in such fashion, but it is not the only fashion; or at least inaction is not the only ground of commencement or initiation. The Great Doctrine, or any other doctrine, ideology, or system, remains susceptible in thought to any kind of criticism, for example to destructive criticism, to the charge that it is illusory or delusory, but the bull's eye containing the Master's two arrows was not an illusion. It permitted him to talk of "I" and "It", of a technique that after rigorous practice could so perfect itself that it transcended itself; and if the notion of transcendence were called in question, the Master could always bow to the target and plunk his arrow in the bull with certainty. If, on the level of action only, he taught that to achieve such certainty the archer had to leave go of himself, not to think, to become egoless, selfless, results squared with teaching, as Mr Herrigel found after he had exhausted his Western thought processes and skills. There seemed to be no other way. And if the Master should declare that his way was already "on the way" to the Great Doctrine, at least his experience had remarkable bull's eyes to its credit. The Master did not teach in words, he "showed" the way. Theologians or philosophers may dispute; the doer *does*. And it is this doing that remains an indisputable *experience*, on whatever level the doing takes place. Unless this doing has been experienced, criticism can only be irrelevant.

But the delight that comes from doing in a man's full maturity may be observed in spheres of action that have nothing to do with Doctrines great or small. At any celebrity concert, for example, the result in the way of music throws as it were the hand of the master violinist into relief. The music may be all, but if that hand had to "take thought" for a moment, Beethoven and his concerto would vanish.

However, more than enough may have been said of thinking and doing, of these two realms, from both of which characteristic delights spring. For the boy, doing was so essential that its importance can hardly be overstressed, and if, subsequently, he was assailed by a notion that a thought process was rootless it was in the sense that it was not rooted in experience.

But in the third realm, the body's own, what delights were there! To race and dance like a master's hand on the tailpiece of a violin — but that would need poetry, and poetry of the kind has gone out of fashion. Perhaps it would require too rigorous a technique; too rigorous for me, anyhow, ever to evoke the delight. But it was there. It had its wonderful moments. Even to this day the scent of a wood fire or of burning heather can do more in the grey realm of thought to dispose me to believe in Freud's "archaic heritage" or Jung's "collective unconscious" than any number of analyses.

Doubtless that is an extravagant statement. *Extravagant* — the word is no sooner uttered than extravagance becomes deflated and the poetry goes. How easy is this deflating, this debunking of the extravagant, the lyrical moment! With what malice, too, it so often achieves the stale and unprofitable end! Until at last one can do it to oneself by a sort of introverted trick; until one is hypnotized into the grey belief that life itself, the world, is going out with a wail, when in fact the scientific realities point to its going out with a very extravagant bang.

To catch the singing bird on the wing and to be the singing bird that is caught is far from easy. Even to get near enough to the bird to drop a few grains of salt on its tail can be a feat of rare difficulty. But however short the salt may fall, the bird indubitably sings. The bird does it and goes on doing it, and will — short of the almighty bang. This is both interesting and pleasant to reflect on, and in any case brings the mind out of its reflective lapse to the practical business on hand.

The smell of peat smoke was thick and cosy. It had a social warmth. A whiff of it today, caught as a car hurtles along a Highland road, is enough to evoke at once a whole way of life. Cottage interiors, with thatch to hold the smell lingeringly, and folk round the fire; and folk on the crofting lands, with an outside fire here or there and a great black pot, or a fire by a burn and women trampling blankets. The sun had time to lie on a man's hands, the small rain was ignored, and the storm found inside jobs long neglected in barn or byre. To see in the distance a man running would check the breath of expectant tragedy, until the revealed cow in the corn let laughter out. For dogs were kept to do the running. Haste was a dog's business, though the way an old collie could lie about in the sun, if the children let him, was notable.

The smell of burning wood or heather is another kind of smell. It comes from far off. It has distance, and, as in dreams, this distance in space is also the measure of time. If something like this were not experienced in dreams I doubt if I would mention it, for there is always something a little suspect in verbally juggling with time and space. Even as I write this I am aware that I am not experiencing the category of space in a way that includes — or, more exactly, excludes or eliminates — time, yet I can go on writing about it, because I know the feel, the sensation, the climate of the experience. Indeed as critics we can go on expiating on what has not been personally experienced in a remarkable way, so apt are words in weaving tissues of their own. Yet it is the characteristic of this experience, and of all experiences of a similar kind, to be so fine and subtle that it is extraordinarily difficult to re-evoke them, as difficult as the boy sometimes found it to catch with his hands a tiny eel or elver under a stone in the river, and often enough when at last he turned the stone over the elver wasn't there, yet he had seen it go under the stone "with my own eyes".

This scent of wood or heather smoke — and it has to be the right and natural clean scent in the open air — has stirred in me a sense of enormous distance into the past, or, as we say so naturally, of "distant time". And I cannot see how this could happen unless there was something in the unconscious that was carried over from primordial time, an archaic heritage of some sort. However, that is speculation. Of the sensation itself there is no doubt. And as the sensation gives a peculiar kind of delight let me try to be a little more precise about its mechanics.

As one gets caught in the open by this scent, preferably sitting down doing nothing, space *swells* in an ever-expanding circle until its remoteness in one direction takes in remote life, human beings in far days of the world, with a freshness that is as it were like the mornings of the world. Not that one visualizes the human beings in particular any more than one does when referring by name to a district or town one knows well. The people are simply there. Indeed to stop in order to visualize detail is to throw the sensation out of focus as stopping in order to analyse a bar of

music would stop the tune. The morning freshness may come
from some quality in the scent. I do not know, though
presumably the pleasantness of this freshness, the brightness of
sunlight on straths and foliage, must indicate an aptitude in the
mind. But the more one analyses, the more complex all this
becomes, while the experience itself is simple to the point of being
quite involuntary. The next thing has to do with the swelling of
the circle of space, and as the plane of the circle extends itself, the
freshness, the pleasantness of being alive, caught from the early
mornings of the world, may be found within any part of the
circle, now illimitable, and forward or back becomes a mere
momentary slant of the mind, until slants or directions cease, and
there one is, sitting without a thought in one's head, at home to all
time and space, and experiencing so rare a pleasantness of being
that "coming back" makes the body sigh.

How different the scent of honeysuckle! So immediate, so near,
that the bloom was held against the nose. How exquisite the
scent, how surprising, so that one wondered why one didn't hunt
it out and sniff it oftener. But one rarely did. It just happened that
here was honeysuckle, always more exquisite and more
surprising than one had remembered. Primroses had something
other, but what I can hardly say. The petals, too, against the face
had a cool softness. Girls picked bunches of them, and if you
asked for a smell and got it, you stuck your face in the bunch, or
she stuck the bunch in your face.

But for boys fire-raising was the superb delight. It came in its
season like marbles or bird-nesting, and its season was the earliest
part of spring, when the year was at last utterly withered and grey
and dead. Spells of bright sunlight in cold east wind dried the
ground until the winter's moss in the old pasture gave to the feet
like a fabulous carpet. The dead earth in the strengthening sunlight, in the lengthening evenings, in the shafting sunlight that
among the dead browns and the withered-grass greys found a
bloom on the bare birches rich as ripe blaeberries, had an elusive
scent of its own that yet was hardly a scent so much as an
intimation of one. In the stillness you could almost listen for the
scent; indeed it was while so listening, with eyes to the uplands,
to the hills, while caught up into this involuntary listening as for
a real sound that would come from somewhere, that the earth

scent and the nostrils had their moment of communion in a sort of grave anticipatory delight. Then it was as if spring would come over the hills, was already coming, and you listened for it, the advance guard of its presence being this breath in the nostrils.

These momentary pauses in life partook of the nature of the wild burning revel, had the same quickening in pulse and impulse. *Falishes* — that was the word for the fires, for a waste land of withered whins — that grey-brown tinder-dry spiky gorse — and of all last year's dead growths going up in flames, ever-spreading curtains of flame, crackling and roaring, until delight in the holocaust became a sort of ecstasy and boys jumped through or over nearby flames, over young fires before these caught up with the central roar. The flames tore into the air, great sheets of them, leaping tongues vanishing, with the boys roaring back at them, eyes stinging, smuts on their faces, and great black smuts in the air, like crinkled pieces of blackened burnt-out paper, looping and side-slipping in the hot convoluting air stream like demented peewits.

A Dyonysiac revel of sorts, sometimes complicated by fear, if permission had not been got to start the fires. If the waste land is not defined or confined, where will the fire end? But the urge to start them was powerful, so powerful that right and reason were consumed.

At any rate, it was like many other urges of the body, and if at some deep level it had to do with renewal of the body, the earth's body, that was never consciously apprehended. When reason or explanation interfered it always lessened in some measure the spontaneity of the fun. To rationalize Dionysus is to lose the mystery, and when ecstasy is gone with the mystery, the hungry body and its psychic stuff, under the new rule of law, begin prowling around for the old food. Destruction can happen then for its own sake and not at all for the earth's renewal.

The taste of food — how delicious that could be to the hungry body! A family meal had its ceremony, particularly the Grace before Meat, which was no hurried half-apologetic mutter to God in the fewest possible number of words, but the Grace from the Shorter Catechism said with reverence. Not a bite could be eaten until that was over. And meanwhile there was the great dish — ashet — of potatoes boiled in their skins in the centre of the table, the desirable ones burst open and laughing, and the boy knowing that his elder brothers had a way of helping themselves that though decorous was cunning. Having already eyed the helping of meat or fish on each plate and made comparisons which acutely tested his sense of justice, he now waited with impatience for the Grace. Would it never be said? Then it was said. To grab the best would be a lapse of manners, so one had somehow just to be quick without being quick. When all was well, or as well as could be expected, he could take his time. But perhaps the Strath had flattened his stomach too much too long, and taking time was not easy, especially with a hot potato. When a bit of the laughing prize burnt the tongue, the mouth, wide, had to breathe in and out quickly, and therefore noisily, drawing brotherly eyes of veiled laughter and hopes for a burning that would serve greed right. However, the seconds passed, the blasts of air were successful, and now the piece of potato fell apart and was chewed; it dissolved; its delicious flavour was released as it slid around, and over, and down.

Somewhere the philosopher William James has said that the mystical experience is distinguished by Ineffability. Let it be said in no light manner that taste has its ineffabilities also.

Scent, taste, hearing and seeing — how rich the body in what so miraculously is! The fifth, the sense of feeling, the fingers touching — the boy's hand on a rabbit's back, on a bird's closed wings. He has caught the bird under a cunningly disposed piece of herring net in the snow, the small exquisitely coloured bird whose song he knows, whose nest and eggs he knows, with its fine claws now digging into his skin, its beak having a real sharp peck at him, so that he cries out in a sharpened delight; and then, so that the bird will really be more astonished than ever, to throw it up into the air and see it fly off! . . . He belonged for a season to a society of three whose aim and object was to hammer any boy found harrying a bird's nest.

But what — or how — could body be without sex? When — or how — the boy learned "the facts of life" is forgotten. It must have been little by little from so early an age that no shock of discovery was recorded. There is an early memory of a widowed woman from the hinterland taking her cow to the Home Farm bull. Her clothes are dark; a dark shawl is over her head and caught round her neck before it falls over her shoulders. She is walking in front of her cow, pulling on a rope. Sometimes the cow stops to roar fearsomely and then swings her head around to get rid of the rope. The woman pulls on the rope but the cow won't budge; when the woman goes back to urge the cow on, the beast suddenly goes forward in a little run and now the woman is pulled. Then the original pattern reasserts itself, the woman leading, bent forward slightly, followed by the cow on the rope, like figures on an archaic frieze.

For small boys there was at once something ludicrous and fearful in the scene. The cow's eyes rolled and her roar reverberated. But the woman was not frightened; yet it was ludicrous, even somehow a little shameful, that the woman should have to do what was a man's job. The adult reflection: she has no man to do it for her, poor woman, was hardly allowed to touch the enjoyment of the ludicrous, for children love their own jokes, yet the reflection was known to them. She was just that strange thing called "a widow". Widows were always old, and if a widow was forthright in speech or action it was as if she had to make up for something. She could be a "character" when it came to remarks on the facts of life. But if she was "quiet and retiring" then somehow things got done for her. It was a queer lopsided house that hadn't a man in it, and worse when it hadn't a woman. No little boy wanted to belong to that kind of house. To think that his own mother might have to take a cow to the bull — but it was not thinkable. Just as it was unthinkable that a man should wash dishes — though what a rare joke it would have been had it been thinkable! To have been able to say to a boy, Your father washes the dishes: what an insult would have been there, what bloody noses! To have passed the same remark to a girl: how instant would have been her denial, the eye-flash, the scorn!

The man had his place in the scheme of things and the woman had hers. What happened when either was ill was a mutual affair of tenderness or decency that no joke could ever invade. Any discussion of all this, had it been conceivable, would have been tiresome. How deep the dismissive irony in the Zen Master's comment, "It was fine yesterday and today it is raining". A variation on this comment was in regular use in the boy's time. When one had put forward as truth what was incredible to the other, the other replied, "It's a fine day!" or, quite short, "Fine day!" That it may in fact have been raining did not lessen the irony. A nearer approach to the Zen comment was achieved when the other forecasted, "I think the rain is going to take off." That generally finished it!

In records of the most primitive tribes known, where a lack of certain skills is to us almost incredible, where even the act of coition was not connected with procreation, there was yet a very intricate system of marriage arrangements in force, with exogamic procedures and with prohibitions that carried the death penalty. So sex is as ancient a story as the gods. Its taboos were elaborate and clearly defined. That such taboos originated in the basic need for a healthy generation or renewal of life would seem to us obvious. Anyhow, breeding outside the tribe, exogamy, would keep human affairs going in a lively way, when inbreeding might not. Yet how could a tribe that did not know the significance of the first act in the breeding process enforce exogamy to the point of death? What kind of "knowledge" is here? Clearly not our kind of rational knowledge; yet there is no denying the value of the practical results.

For the moment, however, enough may have been said to suggest that in the matter of sex there has been a long record of taboo, and when it comes to taboos or conventions, children are extraordinarily apt pupils. Indeed nothing shames a boy to his marrow more than for his parents to do what is "not done" or say what is not said. To be the fond object of maternal solicitude could arouse an embarrassment as piercing as that aroused by the Dummy's hat. Parents must behave themselves properly, especially in public.

Children, of course, need not behave themselves like this. They are wiser and can safely go to lengths that would astonish their parents. They know so much better what goes on in the outside world and can keep their thumb on a whole lot. They never make fools of themselves whoever else does. Catch them! And they learn little by little some amazing things, and have urges of their own with which one thumb might not be able to cope if a taboo weren't handy. And there is always the inner self that is not going to be touched. This avoidance had its own flashing evasions, its turns and sheer-offs, not unlike the movements of a tomtit on a hanging coconut — a few swift pecks and a quick look round. The pecks are delicious but — watch out! The tomtit cannot help doing this. The inner urge of self-protection sees to it that it is not caught unawares. That "wrong" may consist in being caught may go vitally deeper — deeper for life's sake — than any moral consideration. When moral considerations complicate the issue avoidance can become very wary indeed, for now it is not merely a case of the first self, the social self, being caught in the flagrant act but of the second self being inwardly caught and invaded, secretly invaded. That way dark ruin lies — look out!

The facts of life had their inner mysteries, and the boundary between what was known and what could be spoken or even consciously thought was subtly understood. If a precocious boy wanted to show off his facts, an elder's look was turned on him; if that did not stop him, a clip on the ear did. The difference between a clean mouth and a dirty mouth was deep as a chasm.

A clean mouth could go a long way with the body, a long and comical and even rollicking way. As the boy grew and found himself on the outskirts of his elders, listening, old enough to be ignored, he could join in the mirth. There was one man, a "bit of a character", wise in natural ways, skilled with his hands, easy-going, friendly, who could describe, for example, the effect of an over-strong purgative upon his body with an objective regard and use of analogy that shook and doubled up his listeners. As one homely illustration capped another in his serious, slow-spoken, eye-twinkling effort to convey truths of astonishment about what this wonderful contraption the body could do when it got really going in an affair with Epsom salts, an element of wonder did begin to inhabit the rollicking mirth. In the exposition of his thesis that more kinds of houses than one needed a thorough annual spring-clean he was certainly never dull. And as one who had submitted himself voluntarily to the process, he had all of a scientist's care for detail that gained if anything in precision by the use of an epic note; until for the body itself, pursuing its mysterious inner ways, there supervened a certain affection. Look after it and it will look after you. "You may laugh, but I'm telling you."

Rabelais had his primitive forerunners, and among them D. H. Lawrence would have been understood in his concern to distinguish between the clean mouth and the dirty mouth. When thought begins to pry into sex, to destroy the mysterious taboos, something destructive happens in a region beyond thought's reach. Down there a taboo is not "man-made" but self-created for its own vital purposes. If sex has its own ecstasy, a certain kind of prying is a spitting on it, a "doing dirt on life" in Lawrence's words. If it has been critically held that Lawrence over-stressed the body at the expense of thought at least there was need to make the distinction clear. Puritanism can be as destructive as idealism when as *isms* they invade the wrong country.

Chapter 20

The Memorable

In the boy's experience, then, delight came from three main regions: thought, skilled movements, and the body with its sense and its sex. Each had a very large measure of self-government and in each the moment of delight was most exquisite when there was no interference from the others. If it were possible to imagine an individual in whom the three attended to their own affairs to the degree that produced an overriding harmony in the whole, then he would be a full man. But that is merely one of those ideal reflections which nevertheless may have some value if it indicates the way.

In looking over, or reading an account of, a life-span, how often the early part impresses more memorably than the rest! If the child has had half a chance to run wild among natural surroundings — natural in the sense that being primordial they exactly match the primitive in the child's self — then everything is perceived vividly in a bright air, with all the freshness of the first time, so vividly that the child's perceiving eye has been called by poets "the innocent eye". The innocent eye, the clouds of glory, and similar poetic expressions or insights by adults all mean pretty much the same thing and all indicate something quite real. That "the innocent eye" as a concept is unknowable to the child does not, for example, destroy the fact that an adult may find it in the child's drawings. It is possible for an adult to experience, however fugitively, a child's animistic responses. But all this generally means a "looking back" by the adult, and so nostalgia creeps in, a longing for the lost, for the brightness, the vividness, the direct "innocence". And because of this the reader of the life story finds the early part the most attractive, for he too is looking back.

Words like nostalgia, innocence, may be vague, even sentimental, but when this and more has been said about them, still they contain at least a pointer to the element of delight, to a state of mind that was in some degree experienced. And even if it were held that the child never experienced anything of the kind and that happy state is a projection by the adult back upon the child, the very fact that the projection can be so made implies a recognition of the happy state in some form in the adult mind. It is there; but, above all, what is there is its *quality*. The freshness or vividness has a particular quality, known as it were in the mind's suspension, as memory of the scent of honeysuckle or the bouquet of a wine is suspended, until in the moment of its encounter or recapture it becomes a reality once more. What was not and is not cannot be. However, an adult has only to look at a child lost and transfigured in his own dancing delight to know that any amount of vivid innocence is in being now.

What is more difficult to understand is why so much of all this should be lost to memory, so that the adult should question its ever having been, and question also words like innocence in the case of a child who can often be "a little devil". It need not be said that such words — innocence, nostalgia and so on — are adult words. The child's dancing delight is no more innocent than the scent of honeysuckle. It just is. The adult words are verbal definitions for a cerebral dance in another region. Philosophers have manifestly enjoyed cerebral dances of complete innocence. The more bloodless the categories the more agile the dance. Unless this distinction can be made, discussion becomes irrelevant.

The core of the difficulty lies in the remembering or the lack of remembering. I have had experiences so striking or unusual that I said to myself at the time I should never forget them. Yet I have forgotten them. How can I know that I have forgotten? Because I remember saying to *myself*, Now, I shall remember that. As far as I can gather this is by no means an unusual experience.

Something so mysterious and elusive is in and around now that we are probably getting fairly near the nucleus of the atom of delight. But as it is of the essence of this simple inquiry to avoid theory as far as that is possible and plump for experience, let me revert to the boy nut-cracking on the stone in his river. He never said to himself: I shall remember this. Had there been any use of

the will at all it might have been for evasiveness, at least in the
sense that here is something that has happened by chance so
peculiar that one is not going to talk about it. The will, anyway,
had nothing to do with its becoming memorable. In a way, too, it
was just one happening, like others of a somewhat similar kind.
The boy had been tree-climbing, using his thought and cunning in
getting the finest nuts, tasting, eating, exercising all his faculties
and skills to the top of their bent, and now is on the stone without
a care in the world, the sun on his hands and legs, the summer
wind fanning his face, slipping past his ears as the river water slips
past the stones; and it was then, while sitting there in that
mindless state of harmony, that the extra thing happened, that he
came upon himself. Here I am: it's me — here. There was wonder
but not an active wonder; surprise but hardly surprise; for
everything flowed past and away; and self-recognition, though the
nucleus of the rare moment, also flowed away, while it remained.

Words by their very bulk can overstress the weight of an
experience which in essence was slight and evanscent. It takes an
enormous amount of machinery and power to crack an invisible,
infinitesimal physical atom. That said, let me pursue the elusive,
this coming upon oneself which gives to the experience of delight
its memorable quality.

There are so many delights consciously enjoyed that any need
for *coming upon oneself* would appear more than a trifle vague. If
only irony could get rid of the difficulty so easily it would be a
relief! But the undoubted experience on the stone would still
remain, for whatever the nature of the delight it certainly had a
memorable quality that distinguished it.

Let me suppose that there are three kinds of delight to fit three
states of mind which have already been mentioned in these pages.
Doubtless there exists a psychological nomenclature that could
have labelled them with some precision, but for the boy, who had
no labels, there was simply the experience of racing away from
certain family or social entanglements into the freedom of the
Strath, from that first self into this second self, the first state into
the second state. As an experience it was not only quite clear but
so desirable that he achieved it when he could. Somewhere
between these two states there was a third "lost" state, like an
uncharted island, where memory forgot itself, or had abdicated.

Now the delights from the first state were many and varied, and indeed in the ordinary way include most delights, for in practice man is almost entirely a social and political animal. But as such he is dependent on forces outside himself, on other human beings, and his delights are conditioned by their dictation. A man in a happy or optimistic state of mind may open his daily newspaper and at once be depressed by its world news, by what some dictator or politician has said, by a new and threatening discovery in the exploitation of atomic power, and so on. Then he meets a political expert who says the picture is not nearly so gloomy as it looks, because the dictator or politician is merely playing his hand in a propagandist game, and if that can be countered — and so forth. Depression lifts and the original optimism is restored. In brief, the man's state of mind depends on accidental happenings. He is continuously at the mercy of what happens outside himself. In the social or business world, at home or at the works, a neighbour or colleague can depress him maniacally or lift him into happy laughter. Whether ambition rides him to glorious heights or is a poisoned arrow in his vitals depends entirely on others. That Pavlov should have experimented with behaviourism in dogs in order to get a slant on behaviourism in humans would here seem entirely reasonable, and his basic experiment was characteristically of an elementary kind. He simply had a bell run when the dogs were about to be fed, and when this conjunction of bell-ringing and food had occurred a sufficient number of times he found that when the bell was rung the dogs' mouths would salivate in anticipation of food that was not dished up. By judicious use of such techniques he could produce neurotic symptoms in dogs. Is it too fantastic to suggest that in recent years words like Peace and Democracy, when used by world leaders or groups, made our mouths water in anticipation, but that now they do not water so readily, if at all, while in many persons the mere use of the words by certain leaders produce neurotic symptoms? Where delight is so dependent on accident it can hardly be anything but rootless, and a rootless delight is a snatched pleasure, and pleasure, as the tempo of the accidental increases, becomes a snatched sensationalism. Pavlov did not succeed in producing the gayest of dogs.

As for the "lost" state of happiness, the uncharted island, that is possibly in its purest state peculiar to childhood. The child can get so lost in what he is doing, so part of a happy-dancing complex, that no particular feature of it stands out, and like a state of the weather it passes, to be succeeded by another state. There is as it were no reason why he should remember it, or try to remember, for it is perfectly natural. In his early years his preoccupation with himself and his doings, his insistent demands, his roaring self, his wild sallies and intense delight, can be such that an adult can hardly believe that a whole year of it will be wiped out leaving not a trace in the memory. Yet perhaps something does remain, some soaking through mind and memory as sun and rain soak through the earth to produce growth and a climate; and in after years, when life is a less vivid affair, it rings a vague nostalgic bell, or, more effectually, rediscovers its "innocent eye" in a poem or a drawing.

The third condition of delight is that in which the second self is engaged, and it is this engagement that gives it a permanent quality, for its creation primarily depends not on others but on oneself. Perhaps the simplest way to illustrate this would be by suggesting that creative work in the art is an outcome of such engagement. It is a commonplace that an artist so engaged can be distracted to the point of irritation if not of fury by the intrusion of the accidents of everyday life, the moods and happenings, that characterize the first self both in himself and others. His instinct is to fly from them, to get into some blessed corner he can call his own, where walls of some kind will shut the intrusions off. If in order to earn his bread and butter he has to do another or outside job, then however reputable the busy job may be in the world of social necessity it will yet be to him in his creative urge an intolerable waste of time; more than that, for he knows, and he alone knows, how it saps that vitality which is of the essence of the creative *act*. Deep in him there is this absolute knowledge, absolute in his own experience, and he knows also that he has only a certain limited amount of vitality for each day. To suggest to him, as is often done, that such distractions and the fight against them enrich his personality and so equip him better for his creative task would not be a tactful approach *at the time* when he is creatively engaged, for then his is known to refer loudly to the ill-timed arguments of idiots. For when it comes to distraction, to

accidental entanglements and passions of everyday, who knows
them better; who indeed can better imitate the bull in their china
shop, often to the extent of making a convention-abiding citizen
wonder how one who has created such beauty or uttered such
insights can yet behave so outrageously? This slipping back from
the second to the first self, from creative engagement to a disengaged hilarity, often expresses itself in surprising ways, as when
a child kicks his toys through the flower plots. But perhaps
enough has been said to make the distinction we are concerned
with clear. What the artist creates when his second self is engaged
takes shape and substance to our eyes or ears and so appears to us
as rooted and permanent, for the time being certainly, and
perhaps for all time, but in any case stands over against, in striking
contrast to, the accidental and rootless. Its ultimate value may be
the crucial value of the life or death of the second self, of the inner,
the creative self.

Perhaps death is too strong a word, inasmuch as the second self
cannot finally be destroyed by the onslaughts of the first self, if,
as was said earlier, it is implicit in the psychic stuff to search for,
to find, what lies beyond reason's reach. What lies beyond may
have been given the name of Art, or God, or Transcendence, or
the Absolute, but these words are so to speak sounds made by the
pyschic stuff in its search or on its way, and one of the most
inscrutable things is that it knows, has its own awareness of, when
it is on the way. As for the expression "beyond reason's reach",
it in no manner lessens or underrates reason's value or purpose,
which here is to catch up with the adventurous second self and
attempt to rationalize its workings and its findings and fit them
into a pattern or — and we are back at the old word — system.
Critics, ideologists, philosophers, theologians are forever trying
to do this essential work of cleaning up and arranging, confining
and stabilizing, and when in the first flush of success they have
made a good job of it, the second self finds freedom for a time to
pursue its search in a wonderfully creative fashion; but always the
system hardens as the theologians or ideologists take over its
active control and justify their rule by a use of practical force
towards a reasoned end, and as the second self now begins to feel
the curb of a system which has the first self in control — for that
is roughly what it amounts to — it begins to wriggle and want to

break through for it knows that the rigid confinement will ultimately stifle it. It has got to be off and away. It has got to be about its implicit business. But because of the potency of the business, and because it is at least latent in everyone, the rulers of the system fear its disruptive force and so have it crucified, or poisoned, or otherwise liquidated according to the manners of the time.

The next step from the engagement of the second self to that point where it comes upon itself, as in the case of the nut-cracking boy on the stone, is much more difficult and its significance very elusive indeed, yet it is just here that the quality of experience is most rare and memorable.

Many years ago I read a slim volume of selected poems by Rainer Maria Rilke, translated by J. B. Leishman (Hogarth Press, 1934). Years passed and then an occasion arose when I had to recall this book and at once my memory on its own evoked two experiences by the poet that were in the nature of highlights casting a sort of radiance over the rest of the poems even though those had not as yet been, or could not be, recollected. Here must be two of those unforgettable moments when the poet had come upon himself.

On looking up the poems, however, I discovered that my memory had forgotten some of the dramatic detail or at least had extracted from it a sort of final essence that it had accepted as the poet's recognition of himself, a profound self-awareness. And it was this essence that had presumably shed the light. But because the moments of experience were dramatic I now found, in one of them anyhow, that it was not exactly a case of the poet coming upon himself but rather of coming upon himself in the guise of another. It was as if drama interposed an element that is not present in the final experience of coming upon oneself, which is essentially undramatic, yet an element that brings it very close. It is the kind of experience that the second self feeds on.

But perhaps this might be made clearer if I mentioned one of the instances, wherein memory retained the picture of a figure standing very still, with bowed head, in the Garden of Olives, while the disciples "stirred uneasily". Here are the opening verses:

And still he climbed, and through the grey leaves thrust,
Quite gray and lost in the gray olive lands,

And laid his burning forehead full of dust
Deep in the dustiness of burning hands.

After all, this. And this then was the end.
And I must go now, blinder than before.
O wherefore wilt thou have me still contend
Thou art, when I myself find thee no more.

Now the picture my memory had retained was not of Christ standing there in the Olive Garden but of Rilke, even while, of course, I knew it was meant to be the figure of Christ. But my memory saw Rilke as if in some way it had followed the intensity of the poet's experience until it found *him* standing there, and not Christ. Yet when my memory assumed that something like this had taken place there was no offence, no suggestion that the poet by such an identification had gone too far. On the contrary, in some remote unanalysable way, the meaning of the Christian belief that all men are the sons of God was being made clear not in thought but in act, not in intellectual apprehension but in actual drama. By this interposition of the poet's self there was added an extra poignancy to the revelation of each as the Son, even while each knew that he was not the Son. Along this way Rilke had become aware of himself in the Garden of Olives.

Chapter 21

In Galloway

In his thirteenth year the boy left the Highlands for Galloway, where he stayed for the next two years, did not go to school, had a private tutor, and discovered for the first time that literature could be man's main preoccupation and delight. On an afternoon's walk up the Earlston way, where the scenery was varied and beautiful, the tutor would have a book of verse in his pocket. He was a small, slightly built man, very gentle, with a quick laugh and bright dark eyes. He wrote a weekly article on the countryside for the *Kirkcudbrightshire Advertiser* under the pen-name of Theodore Mayne, and occasionally would mention his young friend in it. He had been a tutor in Edinburgh to a well-known family, had arranged one or more art exhibitions, and echoes of this came back but somehow so unobtrusively that the details are forgotten, if they were ever precisely acquired, perhaps from lack of real interest on the part of the pupil, upon whom remote adult affairs would not have the same impact as, say, the immediate solution of a problem in geometry. Something of this background was there in the tutor's small study, along with books, papers, correspondence and litter of the kind, in a state of congestion remarkable for its precarious balance. However, if the pupil's chair had been invaded by volumes, for occasionally the tutor spread himself in a book review, there was always a certain amount of free space on the floor. The room also had its own atmosphere which an opened window could dispel in a paper storm if a wind was blowing. He was a bachelor who lived alone, and such domestic help as came from outside was clearly not permitted to do the study.

But this background, so novel to the pupil, was complicated still further by an attitude on the part of the tutor difficult to grasp. Perhaps he was sixty and beyond such teaching, though rather it was as if teaching, setting tasks, overcoming mental obstructions, had, for this gentle man, something sad and irksome at its core. That the boy sensed this was clear from the conscientious way in which he generally prepared his tasks so that there would be as few irksome obstacles as possible. Thus learning his lessons got a new slant, which bore him occasionally to new heights. *Oui, oui, m'sieu*, or *Mais non*, taught the tutor with subtle facial and other movements more or less direct from Paris. And *Oui, oui, m'sieu* or *Mais non* replied the boy with a grave mimicry that would have carried his former classmates through amazement into helpless mirth. Pleased, the tutor explained how naturally it came to a Scot to narrow the vowel in the French way and, freed now from the irksome, they went ahead in a pleasant discursive manner.

In geometry the pupil tilted the balance the other way, for he found no difficulty in learning the proofs of Euclidean theorems and generally managed to solve the problems or deductions based on them. But one night in his preparation he was stumped by a problem that required a straight line to be divided into two parts so that the square on one part would be twice the square on the other and, feeling that for once he could ask for help, he next day admitted his failure. It was then he saw the look of irksomeness at its sad best, directed now, however, at the geometry book, at the whole meaningless grey waste of mathematics in a world that, left to its natural self could be so gay and exciting with art and poetry and French. After staring at the tiresome problem for some time, the tutor said he would ask his friend, the professor in Edinburgh, to solve it for them, and though the pupil had been on the point of helpfully suggesting that it was obviously based on Pythagoras's Theorem, he remained silent.

This small incident gave the boy a curious kind of shock; an eye-opener into the adult world, into what had seemed in the realm of learning the infallibility of the master. But as this information involved the master he not only decided never to blab but also so to learn his geometry that no similar moment of embarrassment should arise again. It was then he discovered, consciously discovered, how beautifully neat a game Euclid was. Sometimes he would cover the proof of the next proposition with his hand and stare at the Euclidean figure seeking for the proof in his head, but his sloth or impatience was greater than his resolution, his hand would slip away, and then the quick glance down — of course! The flawless precision of hitting an empty bottle at thirty yards with the first stone. But how seldom one could do that! Euclid never failed.

Another insight into the adult world came through literature. It was a summer afternoon, warm and sunny, by the wooded banks of the Ken: as lovely a spot as any in his Strath, with a river and birches and ups and downs and overhangs with cushiony growths where robins liked to build, and here he was sitting listening to his tutor reading Tennyson. It was the age of Tennyson still, with all that kind of sensibility so difficult now to recapture. The tutor began reading "The Queen of the May", possibly because its moving story should be immediately intelligible to a youthful mind. However, as he read on he got caught by the pathos of the poem and when it came to the tragic note his voice broke — and he stopped reading. The boy felt acutely embarrassed. It was difficult to know where to look then, and as for saying anything, that was quite impossible.

But the tutor showed little or no embarrassment, as though that would have been an intrusion of the personal into a reality beyond all vanity of appearance. He was quiet, and the moments caught a detachment within which emotion itself thinned away, taking much of the embarrassment with it, until the pupil dimly apprehended the passing of the tragic into an aftermath that was curiously still. He had a suspicion that tears had come into the tutor's eyes, but he had not looked at him and did not, and as the book was closed they continued their walk and presently were freed into a livelier mood than before.

In all this it is very difficult to recollect the pupil's attitude, what he said or how exactly he behaved. Not only can nothing of what he said be remembered, but the impression is rather of one who never in fact did say anything. He was tall for his years, lean and athletic, and in memory walked around with the dumbness of one who somehow was not engaged. Yet some understanding of what went on must have been acute enough, for he certainly would never have dreamed of mentioning to anyone what had happened when the tutor read "The Queen of the May". That would in some way have been a betrayal not only of the tutor but also of the moment and he would have resented any kind of laughter. In this matter of loyalty when it touches the young he was presumably normal. But he must also have talked and even laughed quite a lot, for there was one final moment of embarrassment that in this respect contained within it a real shock of surprise.

Not to make the moment seem too personal would require an understanding of the tutor and of the Victorian atmosphere in which he had been brought up and lived. On one occasion the book of verse must have been Omar's *Rubáiyát*, for at some point in the talk he said that to him the saddest line in all poetry was, "That youth's sweet-scented manuscript should close". Now in the tutor's case this was not vague nostalgia, Victorian, Scots or Persian, because he was inhabited by a youthful sprightliness that loved the quick movement of a thought or a bird and was irked to a sort of helpless frown by the insoluble in geometry or the dullness of grammar. Certainly poetry was never invaded by parsing and analysis. And it is in this context that what he said to his pupil had its point. They had come to the end of their partnership and the pupil was leaving Galloway. Their talk must have been cheerful enough to make the pupil laugh for the tutor turned to him and said how he had always enjoyed that laughter. It was the first time he had ever been directly personal, and though doubtless the pupil tried to laugh it off, not knowing how on earth otherwise to behave, the tutor was not unaware of the shock of surprised embarrassment, for he looked away — actually towards the old walled cemetery — and into his troubled smile came something that the more profound reaches of poetry occasionally evoked, and he proceeded with his last essay in instruction. If only, he explained, flowers were presented to the living instead of being laid on their graves, what a difference it would make to the world.

An earlier parting was with a black retriever, a powerful dog, and though this was more naturally on the boy's level, still it, too, had its arresting end. The companionship of boy and dog no doubt started in the need for taking the dog for a walk, then grew into a mutual understanding where a look meant a lot. On their rambles they both knew exactly what off-and-away meant, but now the boy had to curb the dog whose hunting instincts were very strong. To begin with, the game of hide-and-seek became skilled and rather elaborate, for the boy, choosing the terrain and a moment when the dog was sniffing after scents, would slip out of sight, whistle, shift his hiding place, and generally do his best to "lose" the dog, for though in the ordinary way the retriever relied on his nose he expected to *see* the boy. A whistle made him look up. The dog always found him in the end and showed his pleasure in the game, gulping, brown eyes shining, tongue slipping to and fro over his teeth. Then one day the dog did not find him and the boy went in search of the dog. The real game scents had been so strong that the dog had ignored the whistle and when the boy at last found him a cock pheasant whirred up and away. So it had come to this, had it? The boy gripped him by the collar and told him just what would happen if anything like this occurred again. The boy's earnestness and anger lost nothing from the knowledge that the most likely thing to happen would be a charge of shot from a gamekeeper. However, the real hunting ground and pheasant coverts were on the other side of the river, so all was well for the moment. The boy walked the dog home in a severe manner and for some days they merely looked at each other, and though the dog tried in his guilty way to make overtures the boy would have none of them. Gradually restrictions were relaxed and when the boy went fishing — he had got a spoon bait for pike, a fish which he had never caught and hated the sight of when he did — the dog went with him. The tedium for the retriever was unendurable. All the delights in life came to him through his nostrils and not to follow for a little way the nearest rabbit scent was beyond his power. A little way led to a greater way. There were whistles and recallings and cuffs on the head. The boy did his best, for he knew what went on inside the dog, he could see it happening out of the tail of his eye, see the moment when the body could no longer lie still, had to get up, to sniff, to move off, not meaning to move off but just to sniff at hand.

A warning came from the proprietor who owned the estate across the river that the dog had been seen hunting there on his own. This was drastic news, hardly believed, for the dog had never been missed from the house. But the day came when the dog, having this time evaded the boy, started to swim the river, which was in full spate. The boy saw him, yelled at him, but the dog never looked back. When he got caught by the wide current, he angled his body to it, swimming powerfully as he was swept away. The boy followed down the bank but nothing he could do with shout or missile had any effect and ultimately the dog landed on the other side amid the sanctified pheasants in the holy of holies. The enormity of it darkened thought and the boy started running.

The way round by the bridge was about three miles and when at last he came on the brute his state of exhaustion was greater than the dog's but he managed to fall on him and for a while there was a sort of ineffective battle, where the world of primitive rage went dark and dizzy and at least the boy's chest was hurt in its gaspings for breath. They were where they knew each other, and that primal place is remembered.

This exploit could not be kept hidden and in the end arrangements had to be made to get rid of Sandy. By bus and train boy and dog set off for the town of Dumfries, where a new home had been found. At the appointed place two men met them and Sandy was handed over. The boy turned away, walking blindly anywhere; there was a shout and, turning, he saw Sandy coming, followed by the men. Sandy had broken loose for he was a very powerful brute. Yet on the journey, and even on the handing over, he had behaved with more than his usual good nature, which could be deep and fond to an inexhaustible degree. Now he came rushing right up to the boy and, rearing, got a paw on either shoulder and looked him in the face. His weight was staggering but all the boy saw was the dog's face, the brown eyes, not any questioning, but the awful fact that at last the dog knew. The awful "laughing" appeal. The boy shouted at him to go away shoved him off, pushed him away, and turned away himself.

After that the boy had found himself alone in a street, moving aimlessly and getting new smells, particularly the smells from one or two butchers' shops which conveyed a vague suggestion of crime. The whole outing had been a new as well as responsible experience for him. For of town he knew nothing. And though it might be supposed that the appeal of a town should be visual — the streets, the buildings, the shops, the traffic — actually what *touched* him came through his nostrils. He must have had some time to wait for his train, for presently he realized that he should eat and found himself in a restaurant where he studied the menu and decided he would have some lemon sole. The fish was golden brown and looked appetizing but when he tasted it his gorge rose at a flavour which had lost the first freshness of the sea. No doubt the taint was slight to the degree of being normal in most inland eating places, but somehow taste now went with the earlier experience of smell, and when he saw two businessmen adding a tomato-coloured mess to their fish, his desire for food faded out. The rest of that unfortunate day is completely gone. He tried to forget Sandy, whose capacity for scent was so infinitely greater than his. He can still feel the impact of his paws and see in his face that for which there could not have been any words anyhow.

Chapter 22

Blanks in Memory

The blanks in memory are numerous and often astonishing. Possibly the whole life is recorded in detail and filed away, and only needs a scent, a tune, a few chance words to bring the forgotten file, the lost experience, into consciousness. Indeed while writing here I have been assailed by memories that had seemed gone for ever. The mind rejects and chooses under its own constructive impulses, as coral polyps build under the impulses of the ocean. A resurrected memory, if looked at too long, may become an atoll on its own. For instance, the tutor's reading of "The Queen of the May", as I remembered it, evoked a much earlier Strath memory of a seaman in his cottage singing a tragic ballad of the sea. There were many in the small room and the fisherman stood erect, staring through the wall beyond which waves pounded on a dark shore, without a trace of expression on his weathered face or in his voice, *seeing* what happened in the dark stark ballad. It was hardly a song yet not altogether a montonous chant, and somehow by this very absence of melody or tune the starkness was emphasized.

Much in the same way, but this time *with* the melody, a Highland girl sings one of the traditional Gaelic songs of loss and doom without a trace of expression on her face or in her voice, and by thus becoming as it were abstracted from the song an element of primordial innocence is liberated in a region beyond the song where what once happened is now accepted and emotions are cleansed, yet not cleansed entirely for there is now this profound and deeply moving recognition of ourselves before fate. The intrusion of an active emotion, of a trained use of "expression", would destroy this ultimate effect, as the intrusion of the everyday, of the arts and graces of the social self, can dissipate those rare moments in that region where the second self comes upon itself and its mysterious outreachings.

But the fisherman recalled in particular the Strath tailor and a peculiarly complicated response to his one and only song which he produced at the New Year festival to a sweeping rhythmic action of the right hand that threatened to spill, though it rarely did, the contents of the whisky bottle which it used as a baton. For children this was a gay time, as the house was not only rich in bottles but also in a massive currant bun and cakes and other seasonal fare, and for the highlights of fun they had the visiting groups of men, each with his bottle of whisky. Footsteps outside, the rattling of the door — who were coming in from the darkness now? A voice, another voice — ah, here they were, the known, men from the district, from the far homes and the near, with gay greetings, a stave of song, dressed in their best, free in gesture and friendship, received by the woman of the house with the surprise of gladness, while the children stood back, all eyes and smiles, at once shy and acute as birds, noticing everything and in particular the fine suits, the handsome ease, of men whom they knew in the quite other and sober aspect of everyday. The glasses were there and each visitor made his offering to the adults of the household, and it was enough if the woman of the house raised the glass to her lips, for it was the blessings and the greetings that mattered, then back came the offering from the house to the guests and the jovial hubbub grew. The door would rattle — here was another group, but soon the first lot would disentangle themselves and proceed to the next port of call, and so it went on through the early hours. It was a season also of reconciliation, and two men who had developed any sort of feud during the past year would by an intricate use of diplomacy on the part of their neighbours in some secluded corner be brought to the handshake and raised glasses. To go beyond the stage of mellowness was bad form as well as loss of fun, and a glass from which a good sip had been taken could be topped up, for microbes or germs did not exist then among neighbours, any more than among lovers at most times, and germs would have had a difficult swim anyhow against the best whisky at three shillings a bottle. Man and beast were reconciled and the outpouring came from the heart like the tailor's song.

The tailor, who was not a notably robust figure, could carry his mellowness miraculously to the carefree distance where the song, after very little pressing, came forth adagio. The boy remembers only one singing line: "And her bo-ody it came flo-o-oating down on the silv'ry tide". So it must have been a very tragic song. But the children knew the tailor, had been waiting for his masterpiece with nudges of restrained expectancy, and when it began to issue forth and the bottle conducted the slow sweep of the tidal waves, their mirth raised almost painful internal convulsions, for politeness forbade outward manifestation. His elder brother, too, has that awful capacity for using a nudging elbow with solemnity. Eyes were veiled generally but his mother listened with calm appreciation and thanked the singer, complimenting him on being in very good voice, even while the children knew that a crow had better.

But somewhere deep in the boy a curious transformation in values must have gone on. In the first place "the silvery tide" was for him an exact description of what he had seen when a full tide filled the harbour under the moon and the boats rose and fell, creaking a little under the impulse of the sea. The heave of the water shone and glittered like liquid silver, with an eeriness in the night, in the creaking, a strangeness in the scene, a translation into that otherness that has to be watched, for it is uncertain and can drown. Keep well back from the harbour wall. The full tide brimmed and met the river, so that what came floating down the river was slowed up and in the moonlight a bobbing object at some distance could not be identified with certainty; it might be something of value or a dark drowned head. Articles of value were not lost easily, and this was a drowning place.

So, for the boy, the body of the young woman in the song came floating down the river to the sea, and he saw it just where the river became the slow-withdrawing moon-smitten tide. It was a vision as absolute and stark as what the fisherman saw when he sang through his cottage wall at the pounding waves, and nothing could be done about it except not look at it too long.

Then in a way that is quite forgotten the drowned figure of the tailor's song became in time Ophelia. A year or two ago I saw a remarkable production of Hamlet on the cinema screen, and when it came at last to Ophelia's drowned body, there it was floating down a rivulet, full length, buoyed up, beautifully dressed with fresh flowers in the well-combed hair, amid enchanting woodland scenery. That old-time sailor had his stark revenge on the old smothered mirth, for he quite ruined the pretty scene on me.

Chapter 23

Memory's Hat

In such ways, then, memory can produce some of its most surprising creatures out of an apparently empty hat. And though this can be understood when she is conjuring with the past on the principle that the rabbit though invisible is somewhere, I confess that for me her conjuring in dreams is quite miraculous. For example, in an instant, in one swift glance, the eye that does its work in sleep sees a human being, or a group of beings, complete in every detail, beings that have never been seen or encountered in waking life.

This apparently instantaneous creative feat mocks our waking notions of time; time as duration ceases to have any appreciable meaning, and yet meaning itself vanishes when we talk of things happening outside time. Nor does it help much to say that in sleep we have no way of measuring time, which may be shorter or longer than we literally dream of, because the same instantaneous creative feat is encountered, even by a child, in that region which lies just on the waking side of sleep and the unknown human face is suddenly seen on the dark air beyond the closed eyelids with a shock that so often terrifies. It is all at once so powerfully there that the child who cannot hide it, who knows it is *out there*, yells. The creative artist here is a sculptor of immense power for the face is not flat, it is solid, three-dimensional, in fact its sheer plasticity is such that it can almost be felt as part of its menace. If the child or boy were taken to an art exhibition and encountered that face on a pedestal in the entrance hall he would, if he could, turn and run. In how far symbolism in art is being used to veil that power while still retaining it, to dissipate the full shock in a veiled apprehension, or whether it is the best the waking artist can ever do on the practical level of doing, is an affair of speculation, with ascending ramifications, outside this simple quest from ordinary experience. But two considerations do call for some attention because in the rarer reaches of delight odd things take place both in the creative region and in the time dimension.

Apart from sleep where the creative act seems involuntary and instantaneous it does appear, then, that a creative process goes on all the time beneath the level of conscious thought. The tailor's song so to speak was already doing its subterranean work even while the boy laughed at it, dismissed it as a comic performance, and went on doing it long after it was utterly forgotten, and apparently still goes on doing it. Other lapsed memories behave in the same way, for any one of them accidentally recovered, provides its own significance in a similar fashion. But all these separates must have some balanced way of cohering together around or within some central nucleus or self, because at any moment — as in the case of Ophelia on the screen — a balanced judgment or appreciation springs into consciousness and thence, less nimbly, off the tongue's tip.

That this should happen interfered with a first early attempt to appreciate the essentials of David Hume's analysis of the mind's action with its succession of isolated *impressions* and their fainter copies, *ideas*, and in particular with the absence of a whole self which could sit and observe the succession and pass judgment. Since Hume's day, however, the exploration of that whole has taken us into some strange places. What are blanks to the conscious mind are too often far from being blanks down below. But tentative remarks of the kind may be overlooked, where the simple intention is to suggest that a creative process goes on in regions of the mind of which we are normally unaware, that it goes on whether we like it or not, and that accordingly it is implicit in the psychic stuff. To attempt to define "creative process" would raise difficulties, but they would be terminological difficulties. What happens is clear enough, as when the internal artist in sleep becomes a dramatist and uses all the arts from colour to sound in a supremely vivid way. For the needs of the psyche it does look as if an act by a creator is the supreme act, and this may explain why man gets rare quality of delight when he is engaged in making or creating. One tentative step further: the moment of rarest delight comes on the completion of the creative act, in that suspension of all the faculties in what is called a "timeless" way, in that transfusion of wonder and apprehension before and within creation fulfilled; and finally, if a nut-cracking schoolboy may be allowed his arithmetical progression, the wonder and apprehension before and within "all creation".

"Timeless" raises our second consideration. In a way that a schoolboy finds difficult to follow, Einstein arranged a time and space in 1905 which required a new kind of logical structure to house them. The concept of rapid *relative* motion can make one pictorially dizzy, apart from scientific clocks going fast or slow or lengths increasing or diminishing in mysterious ways. Not only are things not always as they seem but often quite otherwise. For example, down in the infinitely small electronic regions the boy's algebra, groping darkly, got a shock when he read that p multiplied by q was not the same as q multiplied by p; which came first made a difference that upset the old homely security of $pq = qp$. And what could happen in the way of speed made duration meaningless in so far as any possible apprehension of it was concerned. Time appeared to be a word with practical uses on the human level, but it took on the nature of a sign or symbol on other levels. What could happen on some of these levels seemed to be even more startling than an earthquake in everyday arithmetic, particularly when one got beyond arithmetic.

If coral polyps were to get a glimpse of the island they had created out of infinite digressions and see its coconut palms swaying in another kind of breathing medium, it would, one may assume, be a new and startling experience for them. Arithmetic could conceivably compute the number of polyps engaged in the constructive work but arithmetic would neither be the island nor the memorable experience of it.

Chapter 24

Behind the Wild Flowers

It was a lapse in memory that sent me in pursuit of memory, for how it came about that the boy went of an evening to the headmaster of the local school for Latin, whether the tutor was away for a time or did not know Latin, cannot be recalled, and anyhow whatever the lapse hides it seems unimportant, for the boy liked the headmaster and had fishing expeditions with him that brought back some of the old activities of the Strath. Pulling the boat against a strong wind back to the Head of Lochinvar was a tough and exhilarating business, then the drift, with not a moment to lose, the rising trout that was missed, the attempt to defeat wind and drift in covering it with a fly again, the golden glisten of the big fellow in the rough water, the landing net, quick! another capture before the end of the drift . . . but here is the end of the drift.

The contrast between headmaster and tutor was very marked. The headmaster met the definition of the solid intelligent Lowland Scot, but once that is said discovery begins. On the three-mile Saturday walk to the loch and the more subdued three miles back new aspects of the world were opened out to the boy. First there were those wild flowers, in their season, whose names the boy did not know and never had any inclination to know, for they had always been as common as weeds and too often were weeds on arable or garden soil. But when the headmaster rooted out the little yellow tormentil and they examined it together on the moor, it was astonishing to learn that from its threadlike white roots folk in the old days had extracted a substance that would tan leather. It was surely impossible! But in due course equally astonishing things were revealed in the way the people, his own people, used wild flowers and lichens for dyeing their tweeds, for, in fact, the bright colours of the tartans. They had nothing else to to get their colours from, explained the headmaster; and the boy thought: *they knew*. Beyond colours, too, in illness and disease — the knowledge of herbs — even for beasts — like the broom over there, so helpful to a costive cow when there is nothing else green to eat in the dead time of the year.

This kind of conversation was sporadic; it lit by chance on a new flower. The boy was not being taught, he was learning by the way from a grown man who knew the traditions of the tribe. And it was this feeling for a people *behind* the wild flowers that was somehow most strongly evoked; not the name of the plant but that *they* should *know*. This was what was new and remained when many names were forgotten. The people *before his time*, in the straths, on the moor, by the sea. The nameless folk who went back into time. The sensation of half seeing them without trying to was sometimes quite strong, and a moment's concentration could shape a few figures moving here and there, but when they came into focus they might be people he knew, the more personable men of the Strath, or remoter editions of them so that they were all but strangers yet with something known in them.

Nothing in this respect could be more different from the Tennysonian outing, from the sounding chime of the great name, from the world where people learned and got on, the art exhibition, the phrase in French, examinations, books, great artists, old Queen Victoria, The Queen of the May, the break in the voice, the sensibility, the antimacassar, the chime of the great name.

These figures of the Strath were nameless and for chime there might be an old bagpipe tune in the darkening in the distance, or a girl's face singing in the firelight in a way that drew all together and drew the hearts out of them, for what was told was the story of someone at some time, and the eye saw destiny last year, or last century, or any time beyond. A thousand years made no difference. Here where all might seem romance there was no romance, or very little. But there was an extraordinary warmth, a profound emotion shared in common, and the boy got the feeling that this profoundly mattered. This is the well from which the human tribe must drink or it will perish.

If some such thoughts were touched off in an elementary way by the headmaster, there were even more elementary matters brought into the daylight in a natural and pleasant manner. Here, he was not unlike the dry humorist of the Strath who described so faithfully the vagaries of the human body. There was no false modesty, even though the headmaster was decorous and modest, but there was a healthy appreciation of natural functions that worked well, and a word of gratitude for the delight that could accompany their exercise in natural surroundings of wild flower, and moor, and sheltering bank. There was also an antique humour that can still shake memory with its undefeatable human optimism.

On the way from the loch, conversation might take a more reflective turn, though here again the boy has no memory of his own share in it. Naturally enough, after sun and wind and exercise, the coming back to human institutions of any kind raised a certain detached, amused criticism of them. But the boy had no doubt taken it for granted that the master, who was precentor in the church, was very orthodox in his religious beliefs. His surprise was considerable when he found that this was far from being the case, in so far anyhow as institutions and observances were concerned, for on one occasion — the one that is remembered — he remarked, with the antique glimmer in his eye, that if he had a map with certain religious institutions on it he would ring them in red for danger. This was so striking and unexpected a picture that the boy could not help laughing. But it was probably the first time he had come in contact on friendly terms with an intelligent educated grown-up who could question what was normally accepted — or thoughtlessly avoided — as questionable. It made its lingering impression, and afterwards may have found its way into argument on rationalism and the rationalist press. Whatever may have been his ultimate beliefs, the headmaster had something of the pagan in him to which the boy responded, some of that primordial goodness which delights in sun and flower and life.

For all games there was now only golf, a new game. The boy leapt the garden wall and in a minute or two was on the nine-hole course. The holes may not have been long but they were rarely seen from the tee and then only from a height. It was as it were a half-visible game full of alpine surprises, and the boy in a short time became adept at it. Perhaps his devotion had some of the archer's in the East, for now all games were being crammed into one game, and certainly he discovered early that it was quite useless trying to knock the small white ball into the middle of next week. The more he *tried* to knock it, the more he *pressed*, the less the distance and the more incalculable the direction. If ever there was a game where one had to hit the ball a mighty smack without trying to hit the ball a mighty smack this was it. Here was Zen. Let the club hit the ball. When anxiety lifts the head before the ball has been struck what flies through the air is a lump of turf. When too mighty a swipe swings the body off its feet, intention is sliced and the ball swings the other way. Take it easy. Don't try. Let the club fall. Forget the hole and keep on the way, the fairway. And when at last the flag that betokens the hole is seen, now more than ever take it easy, relax, don't let the muscles lock on the club handle nor anxiety tie a knot elsewhere, but let the club head fall and swing through, and lo! the loveliest of all parabolic curves describes itself on the air and the ball, landing on the edge of the green, makes like a dancer its small bouncing bow to the hole, then runs slowly towards it with a beautiful and forever enviable modesty.

Once having hit his ball off the tee on "The Alps" with his mashie (irons then had names not numbers), the boy expected to find it on or by the green across the burn, but it was not there. It had astonishingly vanished. This was pure mystery. Then he chanced to look in the hole. It was there.

Possibly his "shinty stroke", as it was sometimes called, helped him in the beginning, for he was used to hitting any kind of ball with a stick. In truth the game of shinty as pursued by schoolboys in his native place had some rules of its own, including one which was concerned not only with how the club fell but also with where. When a player, ardently pursuing the ball in the region of the opposing goal, is obstructed by an opponent who faces his own goal, then such player may shout "Hoolum!" and deliver his club head in the buttocks of the obstructing opponent. Doubtless the shout was meant to warn the opponent and possibly give him a moment in which to reorientate himself, but in practice, so often a crude business, shout and club head were delivered as nearly simultaneously as made no difference. Too often discussion and hubbub followed, for no opponent cares to be accused of facing his own goal instead of the enemy even in a general way, and assaulted buttocks feel far from being general. There was no referee. Or at least the number of referees coincided with the total number of players, which had no limits.

Now in golf there were no such rules or distractions. Moreover the ball was stationary, not in motion and pursued by a score or more clubs each eager to be first to wallop it on the hop. The ball not only waited to be hit, but was teed up on a little mound of sand so that it couldn't be missed. When the boy had come to grips with this deceitful appearance, he won competitions and nearly got demolished by a lady player who was powerfully built. He had politely gone forward to a near hillock to command the line of flight of her ball, taking care to stand far to the left of that line. The ball hit him in the temple and felled him. After that, he rarely took the strokes of a lady player for granted. It must have been altogether a less distracted occasion when he equalled the course record, which was thirty-three. And this may have its interest, because never in after life did he play golf so well. But then never again did it compel the same devotion. The difference between the feel of certainty and the pleasure of a social game is very wide. All depends on where true devotion lies.

Chapter 25

What Next?

The boy was now about fifteen and wondered what he was going to do next, as though he had reached a resting place and must go on. This feeling of unrest had, as it gradually troubled him, little or nothing to do with what is called adventure or the adventurous spirit. It certainly never struck him that going away on his own and fending for himself would be wonderful or exciting. On the contrary it would mean coming up against the unknown in a world of strangers. Yet this is what he wanted to do and knew that somehow he would do it. He wanted to be off and away — if not now with the foreknowledge of racing into any strath of delights.

There is something here that may have to do with the vague feeling of not being engaged, of being the stranger never quite at home who must pass on. It is not that the stranger is looking for something he believes he will find somewhere, though there is that hope in it.

But the mind rarely goes as far as that. It stops short at the beginning, the going away. The boy can remember one of the young men of his native district on the morning of their departure for Canada, saying, "Ah, well, we'll see what happens now!" They were going to "give it a chance", "give it a trial". They were off. In some such mood the Vikings left their creeks. What would happen would happen according to the mood and the wayfaring, the world and its ways.

There always are "practical consideration", economic ways and means, involvement of others, of money, and when the thought of this becomes as irksome as geometry to the tutor it also becomes the private spur. Besides, others have gone, the world is broad, and once "free and independent" one can look after oneself.

But the only kind of longboat in the boy's creek was rigged

with geometry, parsing and analysis, and similar elementary gear of an unreliable kind and the only men known to the boy who were prepared to accept this craft on its merits were called Civil Service Commissioners. Advertisements of coaching colleges described the Civil Service as an ocean of opportunity where any boy without "influence" could ultimately rise to command one of many kinds of large craft. However, it was the first step that mattered to the boy so he wrote to the Commissioners in London about a clerical post in the Civil Service for boys over fifteen. In addition to an assurance that they were his obedient servants, they enclosed the results of the last annual examination for this post from which it appeared that whereas over one hundred boys had been successful some sixteen hundred had failed. He had about a fifteen to one chance. A few months later, without any coaching, he set off for Edinburgh and sat the examination.

It was a disillusioning experience in one way for he realized that he did not possess the kind of temperament that produced the best under the surveillance of an examiner and a clock. Things went wrong. He was cast down. The examination was spread over several days and he knew no one. There may have been a hundred boys in the hall and of these only six or seven would pass. This involuntary exercise in mental arithmetic did not help. The slips he had made, the wrong choice of questions, magnified themselves in his mind. For he knew that he could have done so much better, even believed he might have had a chance of coming within measurable distance of success, if only he had been coached in examination hall conditions. Nor was his gloom lightened when he overheard boys outside the hall laughing and saying how well they had done in this or that. All he could do was hang on to the bitter end; keep hunting the salmon that wasn't there. But one slip devastated him more than the others, for at the end of the day he discovered that he had got the wrong solution to an arithmetical problem. And it wasn't as if he didn't know how to work it out. He knew so well that he had hurried, and in his cancelling out of the final equation had in the mass of figures overlooked a 2 and thereby doubled what should have been the correct answer. The genealogy of John of Gaunt might wander here or there, for school history had never been congenial, but arithmetic! As a first real encounter on his own with the outside world it was such a levelling experience that on his return from Edinburgh he merely said he had not done very well. The amount of unconscious pride a boy carries around he realizes only when he has been floored; and even then he can still carry a little.

There was a long wait for the result, but it was bound to come, and it came. A boy has great soticism but his hand can shake when he flattens out a foolscap-size volume of many pages knowing that there will be one entry which will remorselessly disclose the number of marks he was awarded in each subject, with a total number which will fix his place in the long list. Now the Civil Service Commissioners with characteristic politeness publish only the names of the successful. They come in order at the top. After them appears only the distinguishing number which each candidate was given and which he put on his papers. The boy started at the bottom of the last page to look for his number.

His number wasn't on the last page. That was something, if hardly a breath yet. It wasn't on the next page. By the time he had scanned some five hundred numbers he began to swallow. By the time he had scanned a thousand he was little but a swirl about an eye, so his eye slowed up, for what if it missed his number? Page after page, and at last a page showing printed names near the top, the end of the successful list. His eye went up the numbers until it came to the names. It switched to the names and began to go up the names, until it came to a name printed in full that looked back at him for it was his own name. It was the first time he had ever seen it in print and, like first love, it held something he never saw in it again.

Chapter 26

London

Posted to London he at his first meal in his first lodgings got sliced tomato with cold meat. The tomato had a rank taste, reminiscent of those hollow hemlock gourds which as children they had used as pea-shooters, or rather as blow-pipes for red rowan berries. The room was dull and dreary and heavy; the paint had died long ago and the light, lingering, had lost its brightness. He followed the tradition of all lodgers by wondering vaguely what his landlady would think when she found the tomato uneaten. There was a stillness in the room from all that had happened and died in it. His wage was fifteen shillings a week and his lodging twelve shillings. Here he was and this was London.

It was notorious that Civil Servants had little to do, with accordingly plenty of time for study or even writing poetry. Not that the boy ever thought of writing poetry, but he believed that with further study he could keep his independence going in whatever direction might appeal to him. He had now realized that all candidates must make slips in an examination, and that perfection in knowledge was rare and perfect expression of it much rarer. So the future did not worry him, for the future belongs to the young. What worried him a little in the early days at the Bank was whether he would ever be able to do "the average". "The average" had been worked out on the basis of what could be done in a hour after weeks of trying by a boy writing full speed as he dealt with "warrants", "acknowledgements", and the addressing of envelopes for bundles of bank books. It went on for eight hours a day and four on Saturday, and was as near sweated labour as is no matter. One further dull point: four years was the total length of service, so at the end of them a boy was dismissed. His Majesty's Commissioners had not exactly arranged a picnic for the young.

But the boy learned to do "the average" and before the year was out was reprimanded along with a Cockney companion for smoking on the roof one afternoon during working hours. They had in a burst of speed got half an hour ahead of the average, and felt rather insulted at not being allowed to do what they liked with their own time, especially as they had been enjoying what they considered a rich joke. The Cockney was a pleasant lad with a natural reserve which the boy liked. As a free-thinker and experimental scientist he had for some weeks cast a covetous eye on a microscope in a pawnshop run by a Jew. There had been various hagglings over the matter of price which, between spells of flying work at their desk, the boys had discussed. Then last night Campion had gone into the pawnshop with a new idea which he thought he would try out and asked in an off-hand way if he might see that old microscope again. It was produced. Campion looked at it. "Thought so!" he said with disdainful dismissal as he pointed at the words engraved on the brass: *Made in Germany*. Reluctantly he turned back from the door as the Jew called to him, and he got the microscope at the figure which he had previously offered. Now the joke lay not in any question of meanness or haggling on either side, but in the realm of intelligence, for the Jew, who must be intelligent being a Jew, yet did not know that the best lenses were made in Germany. It seemed to the boys a superb joke that needed time and a cigarette for its full flavour. When the pompous boss began talking about discipline, or interest in work, or whatever his theme, the boys strolled back with every appearance of being unimpressed.

The boss was an elderly Civil Servant who appeared each day with a flower in the buttonhole of his morning coat and a flawless crease in his pinstripe trousers. But it was his wonderful pomposity that appealed to the boys and, in after-thought, endeared him. Sometimes this remarkable quality was dramatized in a way that shook the pens of industry to sprawling blots. A window cleaner is whistling at the top of a ladder in a manner appreciated by youth throughout the vast, bright, high room. Towards the cleaner's mate, holding the foot of the ladder, strides Pompus, after a preliminary long-distance survey, and coming to a tall halt gives tongue: "I should be obliged if you would inform your comrade at the extremity of the ladder to refrain from favouring us with any more operatic selections." And the mate cups his mouth and yells aloft: "'Ere, Bill — shut yer row!"

This kind of Cockney humour — the drier the flavour the better — had a particular appeal for Scots boys of whom there were a few scattered over various large working groups or Sections. Generalizing is the kind of bubble-blowing that this particular seems to have been designed to puncture, but, that said, there was something in the Cockney that the Scot took to, a carefree, happy-go-lucky living in the moment, with a bright eye and a laugh in the top locker. It had the ease of the music hall, where the gods of the Empire cost sixpence. Some of these young Cockneys could paraphrase the more risqué ambiguities of the reigning and luscious comedienne in a manner that made a soiled bank book bloom with flowers unknown to old Pompus's garden in suburbia. One, in particular, could pun with a genius that would have been an infliction if it hadn't developed an esoteric quality that needed, as in chess, two or three mental moves to get it. When he got the groan of acknowledgement he proceeded with his task of distributing work like a bright solemn conjuror. This universal quality was like London itself, unknown and inexhaustible.

But there was another quality that was personal and intrusive and could be uncomfortable. It was not like London, but it was English and had to do with schools and class distinction. It was subtle and searching and assessing. It went far deeper than any matter of snobbery, but to those who could never know its reality it was irritating. And even when they fancied they knew, and found traits of it in themselves, it was still, over a practical matter like arranging football matches, an intrusion, an infliction. The boy fell foul of C., a senior boy, over a football matter, and C. invited him out to the cloakroom where presumably affairs of honour were settled. The boy went, and was glad — in retrospect anyhow — that others were there to perform the offices of mediation, while keeping an eye open for Pompus.

The boy carried his point, which was a simple one: that C. and his friends who were the Section team last year in the inter-Section football matches should not take it for granted that they were to play again this year. There were new boys, not to mention boys who had never been asked to play at any time. There should at least be a trial game of last year's team against the rest. The boy's cool stand made it more difficult than ever for C. to "place" him. But fairness had its way, for the English lads saw to that, and a trial game was arranged in an amicable spirit. But it was fought out with tremendous spirit, and two or three players among "the rest", including the boy, got their place in the Section team, though the only goal scored in the game was against them. So all ended happily with no ill-feeling anywhere, and the boy found his new team-mates helpful and friendly, and did his best in the place to which he was allotted.

But this local spot of trouble had a still happier outcome, for one of his seniors in the Section, who played for a west of London team, approached the boy one day and asked him to join it. Diffident at first, in the end he agreed and played left back, with an occasional outing at centre forward. It was a private team in the sense that it did not belong to any league, but it had its wooden pavilion, its home and away matches, and its photograph at the end. So on Saturday afternoon the boy caught his tram and for twopence was hurled along Uxbridge Road to green fields in the west. Larger fares were no doubt a matter of careful arithmetic, but the boy knew he had a few pounds in the gladstone bag though he was also resolved to leave them there as long as that was possible, for a vague instinct warned him that some day he might have an urge to go elsewhere, the urge that feels itself coming before it is quite known, or even desired to be known. The idea of asking for help was the last or impossible idea.

He never realized how "impossible" until he first read an account of the life of Robert Burns, and came on an incident at the end that suddenly pierced, that was the real nail in the flesh, the cry. Despite the biographer, whose condescension seemed misplaced, Burns never lost his grip on life, even before the Kirk Session. Bawdry was a stone flung at empty bottles, and Burns knew his bottles. His poetic outcries, when misfortune got past his accountancy, distilled a sage advice of sound quality. When he went over the score himself he paid for it in a bitter currency of which he had more than his share. What got him in the end was a matter of accountancy in solid coin of the realm. He was ill and maybe dying, but to make sure he would die — as he did — medical advice dipped him in the cold sea. Knowledge does its

imperfect best and we are all mortal. But there was a haberdasher.

"Independence" was the magic word for Burns; it put its circle
round him as guard against the taboos. In a life that seems more
riotous and spendthrift than most, yet he contrived, while early
doing a man's work, to live within the few shillings he earned, not
for the shillings' sake but for the "glorious privilege of being
independent". This privilege, this human right, this rite. On his
two feet, come hell or Jamaican water, he could guard his cricle
and all of what was immortal inside it. But there was a
haberdasher to whom he owed some £7. And when Burns' feet
could no longer hold him up, the haberdasher struck and Burns
saw a debtors' prison in the offing.

Burns' cry, to the boy, was the last cry of agony, nor did it help
to make plain the inscrutable ironies of life that it should have
been a begging cry to a publisher from whom Burns had refused
to take any payment for his incomparable songs.

Chapter 27

Opening Out

London began to open up, or at least long vistas like spokes were glimpsed from its hub, which was Shepherd's Bush. Possibly no greater contrast to the Strath could be conceivable, yet there was little outward drama in the contrast, little of that wonder which the countryman is supposed to experience as he wanders open-mouthed looking at great buildings or, as in the Irish song, for the streets paved with gold. This myth of the golden city had probably another origin, and anyhow it must be difficult to grasp by the young today for whom even the fantasies of Hollywood in its Roman splendours are debunked at intervals. Then there was still a horse bus, and if you got on top and right behind the driver, you could with luck engage him in conversation over a long evening amble. Occasionally, too, London and the Strath came into focus in a natural way, as when an older Scots boy related the saga of a driver who had fought through the Boer War on his "near 'orse". Of all drivers' adventures in the heoric and incredible, it was the masterpiece, and its conclusion had the cool almost bewildered air of verisimilitude that pervaded the whole, for when at last the driver and his mate had chased two Boers over the veldt and into a house, they found on entering the house that the Boers had vanished. With bayonets at the ready they looked for them everywhere: not a sign. Then, said the driver, we looked for 'em under the bed and, gorblimy, there they was! Wot could a bloke do now? So he turns to 'is mate an' asks, Wot'll I do to 'em now, 'Arry? An' 'Arry, 'e says, Pass it straight up 'em, Bill.

As a piece of fiction it held all the attributes of a legendary story, and linked up with an early memory the boy had of a Lovat Scout returning home from the Boer War on his horse and riding it down a steep hillside that normally would never have been attempted. London and the Strath came close in a primitive, fabulous way. And laughter had its air of adventure through which a country lad wandered with a rare feeling of anonymity.

On fifteen shillings a week he could hardly have had much else; all the same, it did provide a certain detachment, an objective outlook, with a sense of freedom in it. This may be contrary to the fashion that finds misery in a small wage and horrors in the young being sweated, particularly by a national institution or Department. But the young did not feel it like that. They were alive, and that was enough to be going on with. If they can't afford a bus ride, they walk. When they paid a penny for a punched ticket for a chair in Kensington Gardens on a Sunday morning to watch the miniature yachts going through their paces in the Round Pond, they stuck the ticket in a waistcoat pocket lest they needed a chair on the night of the same day up at Hyde Park Corner where the band played. Not that they sat down then as a rule, because in the grand perambulation of the bandstand were those as young as themselves and as alive, and a crack Guards' band had all the technique of a haughty young beauty's glance. If a second ticket were needed it could be bought when the keeper came with his punching machine through the shadows cast by the trees. For a penny — or twopence — what a wonderful show it could be!

The arts were there in colour, sound and sweet confusion. Thought was at the opposite corner of the Park, by the Marble Arch, where the atheist, whose beliefs were very strong, was balanced by the theist whose beliefs were strong also, not to mention the anarchist or socialist, or the speaker whose creed was unknown, with a policeman or two on the outskirts or a man in plainclothes taking notes. How fluent these speakers could be! How it came out of them in spate! And time to the boys did not matter for with a latchkey they were freemen of the city.

On his first Sunday morning in London, standing at his window, he had seen his landlady come up the street holding something under her apron with balanced care, and it took him a little time to discover that it was a jug of beer. She was as warmhearted as that. But as he got to know other boys he shifted his lodgings and finally came to rest in one of those innumerable side streets of small houses so drearily alike, one beyond the other beyond the other, that they looked as if they had been arrested, permanently dwarfed, in the class struggle. However, the aspiration had been there and each was still its own castle, for the three Scots boys never knew who lived in any house other than their own, and in their own lived a solitary old woman who presumably made some profit out of them and would have made more if their appetites had been less healthy. She stooped slightly, had a thin damp nose-tip, and wore mittens permanently. Occasionally they pampered her by not eating too much — their politeness rarely faltered — but not too often. In practice the golden mean forgets too often the too little. The old lady had a way of opening a door as if she too anxiously expected to meet a rat that the cat had put up somewhere, for she was a widow and doubtless had had misfortunes in her time, but then her face would lift in a wavering smile like light in troubled water, before she withdrew to her inmost den where she cut buttered bread in a manner that all but achieved the Euclidean definition of a plane: length and breadth but no thickness.

Possibly it was Will who found the diggings for he knew of the daughter when her hearty voice resounded in the hall or at least in the dim passageway. She was fair, thirty, erect and full of a bouncing gaiety that was like the top of the morning to her mother's dewey eve. She was in business somewhere up in the City, and when, a week or two later, she came on another visit she brought two girls with her who matched the boys in age and one of them was more beautiful than the other. So there were politenesses in the chintz drawing-room and somehow it happened that two of the boys had to see the two girls home, and somehow it happened that the more beautiful was the one whom Will did not escort.

On his way back from Notting Hill this troubled the boy's conscience just a little but he need not have worried, for Will, home before him, had gone straight to his Tennyson, who had written a whole poem to his new love's name.

The best the boy could do to meet this poetic outburst (though outburst is the wrong word, for Will had a better ear for Tennyson than the old tutor) was, doubtless out of some appreciation of Will's boundless good nature, to refer to the quality of his mercy as not being strained. "The quality of mercy is not strained," he began, and surprised himself by giving Portia's whole speech without a falter, even with considerable "expression", blessing both him that gave and him that took. That he should have parsed and analysed Portia back in that Strath school at the age of twelve was natural enough, but that he should have remembered her! That he should have used her to put Tennyson on his back! High recompense indeed.

On sixteen bob a week (there was a yearly increment of one shilling a week) they occasionally did themselves proud, and it would be idle to pretend that life was not alive and full of astonishing surprises. Will worked in the Admiralty and the other in the Home Office so their range was wide as their status at the bottom was equal. Some day they would have to pass an exam, but that was not yet, though a certain amount of desultory reading was done.

Perhaps life's greatest boon is that dubious things, like ambition, can be forgotten. They knew it was within their powers, given application and reasonable luck in the draw of exam papers, to wear a flower in the buttonhole of a Pompus morning coat. But who wanted to be Pompus yet? Ever? It was the kind of sobering reflection that drove Will from Tennyson to Matthew Arnold when he should have been reading history. Many boys, of course, went to some Civil Service college, like Skerry's, in the evening and were thus already preparing themselves, not merely by acquiring knowledge but in learning those neat methods of its presentation that made all the difference in the final result, for two or three successful names were sometimes bracketed to the same total of marks, thus making one mark in many thousands of crucial importance. Moreover, as any kind of exam for permanency with prospects in the middle reaches of the Civil Service could not be sat until one was nineteen, it meant that a boy had only one chance, in the last year of his service, of being successful. Backing oneself was like putting one's shirt on an unknown horse in a vast field for the Grand National. It was more hopeless than that, if one wasn't practising at the jumps. Now all this should have induced in the boys at least an anxiety neurosis. They should have scurried to the cramming college and had nightmares over essays in English composition. Suffering from malnutrition and introspection, they should have seen acres of mean streets as haunts of seedy sins, but nothing quite like this happened. Even the prospect of being thrown on the scrapheap left them with a vague feeling of landing on their feet. Cats must have some such feeling for they are great landers on their feet, and no other animal lives so blissfully in the timeless moment.

Chapter 28

As for Sins

As for sins, London had every variety, conceivable and inconceivable, but "seedy" was a word not current then, and, as current today, seems to refer to sins which are indulged or enjoyed by those of a "class" different from the observer's. A chat and a pint on a Sunday morning — or any holiday morning — was the pleasant tribal custom. Occasionally it led to a brawl or a fight, but not often for, though great grousers, they were skilled in puncturing a grouse with the remark that restores hilarity. Two costermongers had fallen out and nothing could stop a resort to arms. If one was big and tough the other was small and ardent. So a ring was formed outside the pub and off came their jackets, disclosing a waistcoat on the smaller man of such startling checks that even a Highland boy's eyes blinked. In the set-to the small man was getting it hot, and as the crowd's sympathy was naturally with him there descended at a critical point a decided hush. Into this hush aspired a cry of lofty encouragement: "'It 'im wiv yer waistcoat, Bill!"

Will, who knew the City, had a lot of information about curious sins and Low Life. A visit to Low Life was more than a theatrical outing. One of the best shows at the time, according to Will, was the New Cut on a Saturday night. From midnight till one in the morning it was at its height, for by that time rotten oranges flew through the air, elderly females tore each other's hair to the music of barrel-organs, no vehicular traffic was possible, and no policeman walked alone. As the boy saw it at midnight it was certainly a lively and congested scene, but Will and himself were unmolested as they slid unobtrusively through the flaring lights and the cries, with a fair command of Cockney and heels that could be nimble in need. No pickpocket could remove what they hadn't got so they were wonderfully free to observe, and knew enough not to stand and stare. The initial absence of fights, male or female, and of rotten oranges as missiles, did not lessen the possibility of unimaginable outbursts, and they were careful not to penetrate too far too fast into the shrill riot. Where anything could happen at any time it was as well to keep some hold on a known way of retreat, yet the more they got used to the scene the more curiosity tempted them to go a little farther. Folks were certainly having a night out on their native terrain without a dull moment. By the time the two boys had walked back the endless miles to Shepherd's Bush in the small hours of Sunday morning they were all but leaning on each other.

Pictures of the kind had the effect, long afterwards, of impressionist paintings, except that the inner eye could focus now and then on a face, a gesture, the whipping sinews in a man's throat, dissolving laughter, a wild flare of light and movement in the build-up of a momentary scene.

Not that Shepherd's Bush at its dullest was without its surprising moments as the boy found early on, when returning late one evening from visiting friends. The visit had been so amusing that his mind was still happily preoccupied and when someone spoke to him the old country habit of stopping to return a greeting in a friendly way reasserted itself. She was a street walker and he was very green, but he contrived some further polite talk before proceeding on his way, she now following. Two side streets, a convenient corner and a quick sprint succeeded in shaking her off. Will laughed over the encounter, called her a hoor, and complimented the boy on his resource, saying he was lucky she hadn't grabbed him and called the police on the plea that she was being assaulted. A friend of his so grabbed had shed his coat into the lady's hands before winning free. Every foreign landscape has its dangers and diseases, and they got to know theirs with a sure life-preserving instinct.

There were many ways of making a living, and though some were very astonishing indeed, they all conformed to Herbert Spencer's first law of life, self-preservation. In the jungle Tennyson and romance came second. So said Campion, whose tribal gods had names like Herbert Spencer, Darwin, Huxley, and the Haeckel who unriddled the universe. How the boys contrived to take a header into this new jungle while doing "the average" was merely a wonder among others; and when the boy came up there was Campion's smile, never too complacent, merely assured as Reason or the pile of bankbooks in a pigeon-hole at eye level. Omar's advice to take the cash and let the credit go nor heed the beating of a distant drum wilted somewhat in this rarer air, or at least had its own air, which Campion admitted. In truth his humour could compliment the Persian tent-maker on having "seen through" all the gods, and the argument could be continued at lunch, for now the boy, who was finding his way about, had discovered the restaurant in the building where for some sixpence he could lunch richly on the food which Pompus ate. That he paid one penny for a plate of thick soup which cost Pompus twopence gave to this non-profit-making staff restaurant a tinge of that political doctrine which was concerned with giving according to one's capacity and receiving according to one's need. At least it gave it that tinge in the eyes of the boys, for Campion in his advanced Socialism and ethical humanism had transcended what he considered the illogical puerilities of class distinction. That those who conceived and then made a reality of the restaurant may have been dyed-in-the-woad Tories did not "alter the fact" (a favourite phrase), and further analysis merely disclosed how divertingly amusing the British were in so often achieving in practice what they denied in reason. No wonder Marx thought, possibly in despair, that they might even achieve a revolution without making it bloody! The humour of this was delightful, for the boy took to Socialism as a duckling to water; and if doctrines were new to him at least ducklings were not; in fact he still doubts if nature anywhere achieves a more exquisite surprise than that of a duckling, brought up by a hen, when it first meets water, tosses it over its head and paddles in ecstasy, while its bewildered high-stepping foster-mother croaks in anxiety by the dry verge.

In accord on Socialism, they frequently differed elsewhere, though Campion had the punches and often the boy was driven into the corner where all he could do was say that no one knew even what life was, much less God-or-no-God. It was a precarious hanging on the ropes, but it served for a breather, while all the time the boy had the deep down discomfiture, if not grievance, of feeling that somehow or other Campion had bagged his Euclid off him.

But in a more public way he provided laughter for the whole Section. He told the senior boys that he had never played cricket, not real cricket. However, his games reputation must have been high for they either would not believe him or believed he would make a show of some sort. Fielding was all right, but when it came to batting he insisted on going in last legs, on the principle of not making a fool of himself and his side too soon. The bat seemed unwieldy and the pads stiff, but when he got to the crease he was unaware that he was patting a tiny hollow exactly as he would address a ball for a golf drive. In short, he stuck the bat well out in front in what seemed to him the most comfortable position for a full swing. This unorthodox stance, this utter absence of style, was a sight for the English gods, but all the boy knew was that he had been unlucky enough to have to face the fast bowler. That bowler took a long run and the boy was aware of a darkish streak coming at him with vicious velocity. It was the only ball he ever encountered in cricket and the memory of it left him permanently with the impression that what seems an idle summer game has one unholy terror. To hit what can be seen should be within the compass of any youth, but to hit the unseen is another matter. However, he swung his bat at the streak and somehow hit it a crack. Like a good golfer in difficult country he was waiting to see where the ball would land when a yell of "Run!" made him run. They ran three times and he would have run a fourth but was told to stop. However, this meant that he had scored three. He wasn't a duck. And next time, knowing better what to expect, he might hit the thing for a hen and chickens. But there never was another time. The other bat now had to meet the bowling. Down came the fast bowler and off went the streak. There was a *snick!* and his fellow batsman, already haring towards him, shouted "Run!". Like a stag the boy bounded home — to find to his intense dismay that the other had been run out and the game was over.

On Monday morning on the Section floor the punster demonstrated how to hold a bat in the new style. A good time was had by all, including the boy. But, in addition to carrying his bat he carried a legacy which still prompts a profound sympathy for those who have to face in Test cricket a demon bowler, that Lucifer of the sunlight.

Of the great or famous in London — writers, artists, politicians

— the boy knew little beyond their names, and curiosity — it could only have been of a gaping kind — was not aroused. In a visit to the Tivoli — how he came to occupy a good seat is forgotten — he looked up at a box and was surprised to see ladies in jewels already convulsed with laughter in the pause before Harry Lauder appeared on the stage. Harry's Highland rig-out made the boy feel awkward, as though there was a limit to guying even in farce; but this secretive reaction he subdued, and when Harry appeared in another turn, dressed in trousers as a dusty half-drunken baker, the boy was held by what seemed to him so superb a piece of acting that he wondered why it was not this aspect of his art that was talked about. But apart from an odd outing of this kind, including a visit to The Mikado, where Will and himself had to stand in a queue, stand in the gods and, missing the last bus, trudge all the way home on foot, there was little commerce with the West End, and none with cafés which the famous frequented. It was not entirely a matter of cash, for in those days one could sip a coffee in the Café Royal for long enough. The two boys spent a bank holiday in Brighton and returned solvent, for one of them still had a halfpenny. They could contrive to go where they really wanted to go, for transport was cheap, and what they couldn't afford they didn't worry about. Where they went the ordinary folk went, the native Londoners, scattering drama and brightness around in an inexhaustible way, with, in places, the shadows and darkness of the almost incredible and completely unprintable. A wide knowledge of queer trades and unnatural sins did not, however, penetrate the inner circle, and in a sense made the "innocence" within it more untouchable. This was particularly true, it seemed to the boys, of the London young, for the girls could be as shy as any from a country village and even more naïve — even more romantic than Will, who reckoned that Herbert Spencer wasn't life itself, whatever he may have written about it. The dreary streets were far from being haunts of seedy sins whatever a writer from the high altitudes of the Café Royal may have imagined after giving them the once over. They probably still are.

Chapter 29

Rhythms

The boy was now launched and the far coasts of the sea were in the future, in time not yet reached, but they would be there when he reached them. Coasts and harbours existed already. They always existed. Kew Gardens was a foreign port. Birches, silver birches, on Hampstead Heath should not, he felt, be there. This kind of magic happened in the wrong way, against the sun. He looked at one of the birches and found the loneliness of himself. To him birches were the natives of Highland glens. His surprise was a vague resentment against London for having brought them there. They were not the real birches because virtue had been taken out of them, for what gave them their virtue was everything that was not there, from the salmon in the pool to the rose in the rock cleft. But more than that, from the cool freshness of the morning to the lazy songs of willow wrens tumbling down the silence of noon, to the anxious peewit on the moor in the night. Yet no romantic notion or even clear picture of any kind was evoked, simply a vague wrong; but the feeling of virtue being drained from himself, and he knew that there was a secretive place, far inside, that contained this virtue like a well. Draining of this well could be drearier than the dreariest streets, so stop thinking about it and go on.

Lilacs seen from the top of a bus, almost touched in passing and touched by their scent, were another matter. Flowers in gardens, loops of rambler roses, green fields, playing fields: these were for the traveller that went by, the anonymous traveller. This feeling of anonymity on the road was carefree and rare and reached the romantic level for the boy in Spanish folk song. Here the wayfaring was a daydream strangely active. He saw a Spaniard, tall and wearing a wide black sombrero, on a country road in Spain, voyaging on foot and coming to an inn, with the rhythm of the song in him like a courtesy, the grave gaiety of the song, the sweep of the hat in the silence of the song remembered. Why Spanish folk music from an accordion — at least that kind of it which contains his rhythm, the rhythm that even as it is being heard is already known — should have had this effect upon the boy cannot be explained. Perhaps a legacy from those Iberians who in the shadows of prehistory came by sea to his native land? Perhaps a northern longing for a southern sun — though this familiar supposition is difficult to maintain in the face of other folk musics from sunny countries. But it was always known, had in it some ultimate grace of being alive, not passive but sun-bright and positive, on the move, to an inn, a resting place, on the way.

Sometimes, too, this rhythm — it can hardly be called a theme, though yet it contained all the themes of its kind — could be come upon in the most unexpected places, as when, many years later, he found himself listening to a symphony by Sibelius. But perhaps that need not be pursued.

Too much critical analysis of a specific experience can drain its virtues away. This realization always comes with dismay, often an intense dismay. Reason's noise. One who makes too much noise will never see a fawn in a glen. But there are fawns in glens.

Folk music gives its ancient background an immediate reality, as though its forms of life run through primal glades and can still be surprised there. The waves that swing to the rhythm of an ancient Gaelic melody are the waves of the sea that swing forever, but now a known sea in a known place, where a man pulled an oar with his fellows and sang to the swing. Countless generations have winnowed the songs that have most of the sea in them and all that the sea meant. After that, let sufficient notes be whistled to establish the rhythm, let it be introduced anywhere, in any circumstances, in any composition, and at once the response will be out of all proportion to the brevity of the means, much as the click of a switch will light up a picture gallery, familiar before the pictures are yet seen or focused — as they can only be — one at a time. And even the pictures in the shadows at the far end that cannot be focused, that may never have been focused, are potently there.

Folk music has this kind of extra-musical magic, which some-times works quite involuntarily, as when out of a mood of weari-

ness or depression the mouth on its own hums or whistles some
snatch of it and in a strangeness of familiar surprise transformation takes place, the subtle change from the dreariness of woe to
the honey of woe and then, with luck and a little effort, to the
recognition of an ancient strength.

So folk music can be as potent as a scent in touching off delight,
and indicates again how unexpected, even unknown, the touch-
stones can be. A conjuror can take things out of the empty air and
present them to an amazed boy. Grown-ups smile believing that
the things were first secreted on the conjuror before they
flourished on the air. Then the grown-up, so often the conjuror in
spite of himself, finds himself taking things out of the vacant air
that he is not at all conscious of having secreted anywhere. The
old ambivalent conjuring is at work. The lasting marvel is that the
empty air should be so full of things. Some distinguished
astronomers believe that the total universe is expanding and that
new galaxies are being spontaneously generated. It is the kind of
conjuring that is "very like the thing". Plucking galaxies out of the
vacant air is in the tradition. At the thought of it we feel on the
way. The heart lifts up, the song is sung, and off comes the
sombrero.

London had much of this wayfaring. London was an immense
digression in the sense that all life is a digression. Man is on the
road because the unknown is round the corner. He never comes
to the last corner until he comes to the last corner. So he keeps
going. A platitude was in the going until it stopped short. It is the
milestone that sits on itself because it is tired. The real milestone
is always a digression. It is off the road or by the way, but in some
mysterious fashion what its wonder illumines is the road itself.
This kind of conjuring is always going on.

Will read Tennyson when he should have been plucking dates
off the genealogical trees of English kings. Other boys had other
diversions. The cult of the body was strong with many and swung
its Indian clubs or stretched its elastic sinews or whirled its
skipping rope until the biceps rose and the calves danced. All
muscle and no stomach like Sandow. This was an austere dream:
the boxing ring, the rowing club, the racing track, the cross-
country lope, the piston-elbowed walk that ticked the minutes off
the milestones. It helped, too, to keep the body from dreaming

other dreams. Campion had his microscope and a detachment that played tennis as a smiling diversion. He was a cool oasis. Donald born in London of a Highland father had a brother who was all for Wagner. This amused Donald very much, so much that sometimes he wrote the same name and address on successive envelopes. His writing was a swift splurge, a flat-out race, and he thumped the blotting paper as he turned his head to finish his sentence. His knowledge of ongoings in the world of highbrow concerts was wide but he was not a Wagnerite, though he had a pen like Siegfried's sword. He was dark and gook-looking, but his brother, who worked elsewhere, had fairish eyebrows already like solemn thickets guarding the vision on the way to Valhalla. Donald's gossip would not have amused him. But already he was the death of many envelopes. The boys chuckled and glanced at the clock.

But the digressions from this maw of the wastepaper basket were too many to be numbered, though always at the end there were those who studied, who were like a conscience, who fed on the dates of kings and who proved that gathering nuts in May was absurd because it was impossible. With Campion's wit they would have been tolerable; without it they now and then set up a short wave of the awful feeling that they were right, that life was a gaping wastepaper basket for torn envelopes.

The boy was not a natural student. He only liked to study what he liked. Will, if anything, was worse. So the boy tried to reform Will. Reforming someone else always creates a good and warming feeling, so good sometimes that it makes one already a reformed character. In this high mood he tackled Will, who had other ideas about life and its particular delight at that time. However, he downed him in the end, and the following evening, when Will was tied up in equations, he quietly purloined the bicycle on which Will rode to the Admiralty, and went for a spin into the city. He had not been on a bicycle for a long time and then only on country roads, but he soon gathered confidence and by the time he was sweeping past the Marble Arch on the way home he even thought he could overtake a motor bus. But the faster he pedalled the faster the bus went on the down-slope, until he saw another bus coming up and realized that he was going to be crushed between them. It was all going to happen at top speed in a couple of seconds and nothing could be done about it by anyone. Fortunately for him he didn't try to do anything. A touch of the brake, an infinitesimal wobble, and he would have been mincemeat in the mechanical sandwich. The cavern walls on either side seemed to brush his shoulders, but presumably they did not actually touch him, or, if so, only just. As he was taking a breather by the kerb the thought of what might have happened to Will's bike helped to steady him.

Notting Hill after that looked friendly and a drayman wiping his moustaches more than he seemed. Shepherd's Bush Green was one of the old familiar places. Had Will still been swotting the boy would have remembered it as an astonishment. So it may have been his lady love and her with him on the road to Spain via Hammersmith — or was it Kensington? For the boys did not have castles in Spain, just a road. So ended the only serious effort at being a schoolmaster.

Chapter 30

Poisoned Moments

All this may seem light and irresponsible and not the true picture of the actual way and the life. But truth is difficult and the whole picture impossible. Even for describing a few moments in the dream of an erotic woman a writer of genius needs endless reams for his paper boat on the stream of consciousness that cannot pause even for a comma much less parsing and analysis. And even then, though memory be whipped like a top, she is still selecting impressions, and ideas from impressions, and so on. "So on" means memory cannot exhaust them, and if the writer had another go at swelling his stream he could swell it. What stops him is lack of staying power all round. But this lack is not an end even of the stream, for consciousness of the lack sets up a counter stream of contrary impressions, ideas, and so on, as in those ever-whirling gyres which Yeats invented in "A Vision".

Memory, on her own, selects what she likes and there it is. If the picture is a pleasant one she obviously prefers it that way. This may look nice and simple until it appears part of a great mystery, all the greater when memory behaves quite otherwise.

There were dreary spells as dreary as the streets, anxieties and frets and miseries and fears and conflicts and temptations and illicit desires and obsessive sex and the rest. The old bundle of faggots. Or should it be the old stream that was not always Tennyson's babbling brook? *Mais oui*. And to make light of it in a moment's lightness is not to forget the moment that was poisoned, even the irritation — the disappointment that in a few minutes could become, for such as Keats, a drama by Sophocles. Keats could be a sparrow pecking about the gravel before D. H. Lawrence was. The body and its inhabitant have their fundamental ongoings and needs. This is known by the inhabitant even when he cannot stop memory whipping herself masochistically, even when he artfully uses the performance to get his own back on someone else, even on the public. This stream of consciousness has no end, like the fabled race between Achilles and the tortoise. In that race (handicap) Achilles, having given the tortoise a start, must forever through infinite subdivisions of space be arriving at the spot which the tortoise had just left. Here is the ancient story which, as succession, Hume attempted to analyse and Joyce to synthesize. The old Greeks did not miss much. Reasoning can become as narrowly obsessive as a poisoned moment. But immediately the eye of attention is lifted from the reasoning to the racers, from that which is *about* them to themselves, it sees Achilles overtaking the tortoise with the greatest of ease. The tape of reason's infinity is burst without bother. When the poisoned moment is gone the world is fresh and wide.

In some such sense, the frets and the worries did not matter. The body itself has boils and abscesses, but not always, even hardly ever. The boy had a short spell of heat spots and wondered what on earth was happening to him. It was far from a laughing matter. Another boy developed a constipation of a remarkable objectivity. It was no laughing matter to him either, and even his friends stopped laughing when a horse pill failed. But boys, who worship the body, are full of lore and skills, and one of them said that green apples never failed. So green apples were bought and the afflicted boy partook of a few. They were certainly the Achilles to his tortoise. He all but died. No story by Rabelais provided such mirth in the aftermath. Nor did the boys go on to think that the apples in the gardens of the Hesperides were green. There might be a tree or two of them, of course, in the scrutable wisdom of Providence.

The poisoned moment that exists on its essence can become a cult like any other, and by the nature of it an exquisite cult. Some modern French literature knows this. Curiosity can stick a knife through a palm and examine the wound from time to time to see how the gangrene grows. To be aborted or not to be, that is the woman's question, and a man moves beneath his lowering skies like a hen in thunder trying to achieve the indifference of a bootless cock. Here is the tragedy of life as it exists and communicates itself in the essential now. The agony is so agonizing that it curls upon itself and would lick its sores if there was any point in licking its sores. But there is no point, not anywhere. All is pointless. So the sores grow and violence is an ever-present help, for it can rapidly make them grow bigger, and the bigger the better for the more readily then can they communicate one with another. Where all is one living sore, plotting sore points becomes a metaphysical exercise. In a metaphysical exercise pain is no longer present as felt but as an idea. The greater the brutality the richer the field of ideas. More scope; opportunity widens. Fascinating deviations appear. Some cry to the dumb sky; others kick the sky in the belly; still others just kick the belly. Integration is in the hermaphrodite. Man ceases to love his fellow woman and loves his fellow man in a revised version of an old commandment. But always it is the fellow who has the brass tacks in his boots and kicks the other chap in the belly who is the key character in the basic story. Refinements upon this story provide an infinite complexity for the exercise of a subtle and penetrating and exquisite art.

But that is a highly civilized art, city art. There are those beyond the urban walls who live in the depths of the country. From their dark dens they stalk, inarticulate, across the sombre landscape of the regional novel. The old barbarian is the new moron, and the new moron is the peasant, the archetype of the brutal before the brutal got brains. His hunger is in his prowl, his covetousness in his eye, his greed in the dark impenetrable intricacies of his bowels where all that matters is digested until the plot requires indigestion. With flawless art he is observed from the manorial house in its walled garden, that outpost of civilization, with sins that would not be seedy if only they flowered in Paris. Escapes to Paris, excursions and alarms, but alarms that are curiously soundless, for a carefree ordinary sound would be a flaw in the art. If Rabelais appeared in the midst thereof and laughed, the landscape and all that it contained would vanish.

To return to the green apples of London. In those early years of the century just before the first world war London was outflung in a sprawl of side streets with a life of their own where little shops of every known and unimaginable kind kept open to all hours. An elderly Cockney warned the boys against pickpockets in Petticoat Lane on a Sunday morning. You wouldn't believe, he said, how these light-fingered gentry could take things off you under your ruddy nose and you wouldn't feel nothing. All kinds of tricks. A little disturbance — put-up-job — on the side, see, and you shoot your neck forward to see what's happening, see, and at that moment your little all is gone. So the boys buttoned their coats and tried not to forget themselves while refusing the goods of the world so urgently thrust upon them by expert salesmen. They came through, but the elderly Cockney, like a good countryman, had his wallet pinched. His ginger moustaches, though worked overtime by a self-conscious hand, would never live that down. He loved giving advice, but his old woman would be bound to say, "Just 'ark at 'im!" This unexpectedness of humour, this individualism in its infinite variety, was caught finally by G. K. Chesterton when he said that a small grocer standing at his shop door might be contemplating suicide or a half holiday.

That was London. Memory has the boys wandering in and around but coming in a welcomed way on the brightness of green grass in parks. The works were a barracks that loomed in a cold morning and a boy kept his right hand warm in his pocket so that it would be ready for writing. He clocked in by signing on before the time line was ruled off by Pompus. And there he was, though he was never all there, for this would pass. Where the boys were going was elsewhere in another time, but this was particularly so for the boy who did not belong to London. Though involved he was forever a spectator, so memory sees him as curiously anonymous and in this anonymity there was a freedom so intangible that it could hardly be touched. It was like the air in the park, the light on grass. There were ducks in Regent's Park and animals at the Zoo. But the boy knew wild duck, had glimpsed a fawn in a strath, red deer in a corrie, fulmars with unbeating wings against dizzy cliffs. The Zoo was full of interest and he gaped with the rest but could not laugh easily. He was not aware of any morbid thoughts as he watched a lion treading its mill before the iron bars, but he has never forgotten the beast. He never went back to the Zoo. Many years later he was taken to another zoo, in Munich, and in particular to the edge of a waterhole where a sealion could be observed going through its endless figure-eight.

So he stared, dumbly fascinated, until the brute paused for an instant and shot out a stream of water. It hit him in the fork and the light grey flannel all round turned dark with wet as if he had suffered from a sudden and considerable incontinence. His German friend grew helpless with a laughter that could not but attract the attention of bright young women in summery dresses. Still, the memory of that zoo has helped to redeem all zoos, for at least there was once when an animal got its own back.

Anonymity has a wandering freedom. The boy depended on himself and no one depended on him. Memory selects a certain aloofness in its reconstruction as if the boy were never really engaged, never committed to anything. The frets and the worries did not matter, because what mattered was elsewhere. Yet what was elsewhere was unknown and what happened was here and now.

Not to have ambition increases anonymity. Total anonymity would be nothingness. So something else must have been going on. And it is the something else that matters, though it cannot be known, cannot be plucked out of the air; yet intimations of it may suddenly be conjured — or conjure themselves — from airy irrelevance. It is not abstract like an "ism". The road in Spain does not lead to an "ism"; it leads to an inn. One can only get so far at a time on this road. An intimation is that distance.

The road that leads to nowhere is the road that once upon a time led to somewhere. Somewhere becomes nowhere in a new mood. Literature becomes nihilism in a new fashion. The primal serpent twisted so far round that it caught its tail in its mouth. The living serpent never actually did this but prehistoric man did it for him in order to stop him, to put him out of action, to get him to eat himself up, starting with the tail. Or at least early man may have had some such idea in his head and drew the picture of what he hoped for. But the picture was a circle and a circle has neither beginning nor end. The picture of the endless serpent became the symbol of eternity. The Chinese added beauty. Beauty in a jade dragon ring is without beginning and without end. So it trundles down the road through the milleniums with man after it. A road in Spain or a road in China, a child's hoop or a jade ring. It is man's eternal game. The "isms" and the poisoned moments are the hazards. But no hazards have stopped him. How could they if the game is in his psychic stuff?

Perhaps, like a puppy dog, even a living serpent may go round after its own tail in a joie de vivre that, cold-blooded, may have the exhilaration of a frosty morning. The boulder that bounds down a hillside develops a remarkable exuberance. Einstein played a new ball game with Newton's gravity. We always come up for the next round. There is no end to the pursuit that takes us round the corner even if, as sadly happens sometimes, it only takes us round the bend.

All of which is about as elusive as what happens to a boy for whom an imaginary road in Spain may be less transitory than Petticoat Lane on a Sunday morning. Who is to select what he fed on: sliced tomatoes, the odd glimpse of the spectacle (the glimpse hardly consciously observed at the time, which yet becomes the glimpse for all time), Westminster Abbey of the lofty dead, living girls circling a bandstand at night, the unending comedy of 'Arry and 'Arriet, the Savings Bank on fifteen bob a week, the landlady's nose, ethical humanism, the socialism that fancifully gathered all the little grocers into one great grocery store, thereby with flawless arithmetic giving them several half holidays a week and a long weekend (perhaps in Paris) *and* everyone else cheaper groceries, the dialectic of history and the almost equally difficult (as a feat of memory) history of John of Gaunt's relations, the Wars of the Roses, Catholic emancipation, and so on by way of Shepherd's Bush Green where a pub flashed its great electric sign CLAYMORE, which is the English spelling of the Gaelic word for a great sword?

If only that were all! But the boy, it may be remembered, raced from the first self to the second self, from the engagements of everyday to the Strath. The race that once was so simple becomes obscurely involved, but it is the same race. When he encountered the birches on Hampstead Heath he saw them all in a moment, from within the circle around the second self. That kind of seeing is never lost. It may seem to be lost, then instantly it is there. Where all is food for life, this is food of the living tree. The tap root of the tree is watered by the well, with the circle around it that the serpent made. In our most modern moment we are back in the Garden where the Devil entered into the serpent and broke the circle.

How then can one select out of such inifinity what made the

man? Can memory be trusted? What artist is behind memory to give the selections a true pattern, to shape them into what is called an autobiography? Can this happen? It will happen in its fashion as a man knows himself. But "know thyself" is about the oldest and most difficult of all injunctions. It is, but there is a self, an abiding self, which every man is aware of as himself; there is a self to know. But what artist bothers about himself when he sets out, say, to paint a tree? Nevertheless the artist writes his autobiography when he paints a tree.

Chapter 31

Anonymous

But perhaps the boy has been followed far enough in time to establish the main, the original points of happenings. For a happening is not something that happens and there is an end to it; even the happenings that don't matter serve by implication to suggest that something else does matter; more than that, for the mind on its own refers them to happenings in the world or the universe outside and even uses them in judgment.

Take that word anonymity, for example. As applied to a boy it seems peculiar. Yet small boys are adept at assuming a mask, say the mask of innocence. The accuser, looking at that innocent face, may be pardoned for wondering where the real boy has gone. The boy leaves the room, taking the face with him, and may even wander around or sit in an attic with it, lost as it were to himself while he is still strangely there. The dog nudges him, then stands back in wonder and the tail subsides. A stray cat is assailed by no more than his incurious eye. He is not at home. If he remains not at home when the dog chases the cat, he has made a tentative entry into anonymity.

Later, in his early teens, he wanders around a city and this detachment comes upon him, the feeling of not being engaged, of not being implicated in all that is around, including his future or fate. But now, because he is on his own two feet, he becomes more clearly aware of himself, of the self that is on its own, and suddenly this detachment has an air of freedom and in this freedom there is a fine delight, fine as air and as pervasive. He hardly knows himself, yet knows himself more intimately, within the experience of wandering around anonymously.

Yet in that last paragraph there are no less than three difficult words: freedom, detachment, self. (Delight is never an important enough word for serious discussion.) Let us consider them in relation to the boy.

Here we are not concerned with what is difficult in reason, but only with what happens, what is; in short, with the boy's actual experience. And his experience will always and involuntarily sit in judgment on the three words. As a definition of freedom approaches his own experience of freedom, so will it seem to him a good definition. The more it departs from it, a worse. If, for instance, someone says out of a current ideology, "Freedom is the recognition of necessity", he will have the sensation of being assailed by sound, by a jumble of jargon with a wild humour in it, until in a moment or two he realizes that here is a matter for thought, not for the experience of freedom itself but for thinking about it. This is quite a different affair and argument starts. Thought has its own delight and paradoxes fly around like the balls of a conjuror. Parallels shoot their grown-up lines: music is the recognition of the necessity for scales. Opposites come into their own: man is born free and is everywhere in chains; recognizing he is born in chains he is everywhere free. You pay your verbal money and take your thoughtful choice, unless you want to start it all over again by asking, but what is "free" and what "music"? For always at the back of the mind there is the freedom that has actually been experienced, and the music.

Detachment, not being engaged or implicated: here the involutions become even more involved when adult thought sets about them, all the way from art for art's sake to *la littérature engagée*, with pilgrimages to Moscow. But for the boy the experience of detachment seemed spontaneous and simple and quite natural. That other boys experienced something of the sort was also clear to him. Even collectively they could experience it in some measure. A phrase could disengage them from the poisoned moment or from the restrictive forces of predestination personified in Pompus and all the Pompuses beyond. Oh to blazes with it! or Oh to blazes with them! And at once there was levity in an air of freedom, laughter as a matter of choice. Having won free they could take a bus ride or bust a tanner for a seat among the gods of the Empire. And if they had pence for neither they could always walk to the Round Pond and watch yachts sailing the high seas. For doubtless one man's road to Spain is another man's voyage to the coral islands of the Pacific. Once a blue yacht, a lovely craft, was caught by a clap of wind, a gale in fair weather, and up into it she came, gallantly, riding the sudden seas, and though others came futilely about, making for nowhere like wounded swans, not she, the beauty, not she, and there she was, there she was, as the peak of the storm passed, falling away on her true course, saluting the waves as she trod them under her forefoot, her foot of grace, with all her canvas spread and from the wonderful look of her not a wet inch in the lot. She was a lady, that one. Her owner-skipper, a grown man, strode to the far shore like a high admiral among raw ratings, and we looked at him as he passed. He was detached.

In some such fashion every individual has his moment of being withdrawn. The bubble of the self discovers itself floating on the stream. When it thus discovers itself, comes upon itself, consciously realizes that here it is despite all the hazards — this is me, intact still — the feeling of fine delight is born. It is the irreducible moment, from which all moments start out again on the voyage. This is the reality, the active certainty, the direction and the way. By bus and train and steamer the cooped-up pigeon is carried into a strange country. Then it is freed. It circles once or twice until it has found itself in its freedom, then it finds the way. It presumably does not reason out the way. The way is already in it. Man is the pigeon that has lost its capacity to find the way, that has lost even knowledge of the capacity, until in a moment of detachment a vague apprehension of it is recovered, an intimation.

Man may be some sort of half-sublimated homing pigeon. In the evolutionary process from the warm and comfortable slime he passed through the homing pigeon and a gene of the bird stuck to him, as a burr in a hedge sticks to a leg of his trousers today. It may be. But of course. In his passion for explanation man is prepared to argue not only the homing instinct out of a pigeon but the hind leg off an ass, and so on and on and up and up in the evolutionary process until he is hay-making with ethics and religion and in windy weather has a dry harvest.

An argument may not be a homing pigeon but it does a lot of flying.

Chapter 32

Further Steps

Happily, as has been said more than once, we are not concerned with intricate cerebral exercises but only with the simple experience of a moment of delight. This has to be said over and over until the moment of delight, like the hedgerow burr, sticks. For we can hardly believe in it, as the young student of Euclid's geometry hardly believes that the axioms have any importance. Then he comes to that Theorem called "the bridge of the asses", and is surprised when he falls off.

Now for the next step. From this delight in being free and intact, he sees his fellows more distinctly, more in the round. They are separated from him, with peculiar habits of their own. That he should have got hot and bothered with so-and-so over what really didn't matter a hoot was, he now realizes, quite absurd. How one can get worked up over nothing! Out of his airy freedom he smiles, and part of the smile is already for reconciliation. He sees both the other and himself amused in a light eye-glancing joke about it and about. The old affection takes on a new warmth. And the people he passes as he wanders by are all individuals hurrying on their ways. They are real people, he observes, with faces. But this does not occupy him much except in the sense that he is detached from it, for all the time he is on his own way. Yet this detachment helps him to understand better those whom he thought he knew well. When thought falls on them they are seen in the round, no longer distorted. Something delightful about this, because now they cannot touch him, he has won free of them, need not think about them, and in the next moment doesn't.

This account may have an optimistic air in a time when optimism is rather indecent. As in Victorian times a well-brought-up young lady would swoon at the mention of words like trousers or legs, so today are those who get a sort of morning sickness at the sight of words like good or kindly or decent. Times change, naturally enough.

But delight remains a condition of mind like any other and its nature is to spread warmth around, around its own mind and then outward. It is radioactive in this manner. This is the axiom that should stick like a burr. When delight happens in the time of detachment, it happens. Any effort to take the trousers off it is quite another and rather adolescent affair.

Let us take a further step in detachment. And as it leads to the remarkable, let us look at the boy again, experiencing his carefree moment, intact, his circle around him. Here I am. It's me. And this me is like a self that he has come upon with some surprise. The self, complete, here, now, and those things there, the road, that person and that person . . . trees, rocks, grass.

Let this glimpse of the detached self be as brief as no matter, the air of freedom comes around it and the self steps on like the traveller in Spain. Or sits down, and in a daydream the self passes away, and Spain; nothing is left but a listening as for some strange wonder. In this half daydream there is yet such a sense of well-being, so utterly desirable and yet held so briefly, that awaking from it makes it as it were not. The sigh of awakening while it affirms almost denies it. But its air lingers.

However tenative and elementary all this may be on the boy's level it may still be enough for him to appreciate what may happen on a different level.

For example, what may happen to a sage, what may happen to the man who went out into the desert, or up into a cave, or who just sat under a bo tree. Here is deliberate detachment, an effort not only at surprising the self but also at communing with it. And here, as history relates so often, the sage strives to become completely disengaged from worldly affairs and his fellow men, to become totally detached, so that he may discover what this self is truly like and thus *know himself*.

Somewhere there has been an inner logic in it all and here at last is one man who is going to find out. But before the inner logic there was the inner urge, in the psyche. Whatever the sage may find there is no denying the urge to find. In his attempt to find, he knows accordingly when he is on the way and when he goes off it, much as the mouth knows what is sweet and what sour.

Than this hunt for the self and urge to commune with it nothing apparently could be more egotistic. Than this detachment what in fact could be more selfish?

What happens is quite other. The sage comes back from sitting under his tree and, knowing himself, knows his fellow men. He sees them in the round. Reconciliation is in his mind, and a profound desire to tell them what matters and what does not matter, for this, in his detachment, is what he has found out. All men have an urge to know this. Who should know the urge better than he? But who among them knows the years of finding, the hunt that did not let up until it had hunted the self into very thin air?

But esoteric knowledge of the self and the not-self is not for the moment the matter. What is remarkable is that he comes back, that to an utter detachment has succeeded a profound engagement. Gautama Buddha was so concerned to tell his fellows how to get on to the way that he apparently did not even reply when asked if the universe is infinite and eternal and if a wise man exists after death.

Now all this is far beyond any tentative traffickings which the boy may have had with himself and others. It may seem absurd or absurdly naïve to grope for a parallel here or there. But as the nature of the quest is to find the beginnings in the end, or the end in the beginnings, the absurd is neither there nor here.

How can one kill the self, become selfless, and yet become more of a self than ever? Short of there being at least two selves, this would be difficult arithmetic. The boy was conscious of racing from this first self into his second self, from the entanglements of everyday to the nut-cracking on the stone. Does this give him an indication of an answer to the question, an intimation, however transitory, however uncertain, of at least the direction towards the sage's way? Would this way have any meaning for him at all without the early intimation?

The trouble with questions is that they, too, starting at the beginning, rise in ascending order.

Let it be supposed, then, that the boy never had another experience of this kind, that it is the only evidence he can use in an effort at understanding the issues raised, from the sage and his way, the self and the selfless, to eternity and immortality. Can so slender an experience, to which recording in writing gives more body than it possessed, be used with any conviction as a kind of measuring rod? The answer is: it is the only one and nothing stops its being used. It will use itself willy nilly and measure God and all else that comes its way as naturally as a child asks awkward questions. This goes on from the beginning. This is the mode of the self.

At the end of the race what makes the boy feel he has come upon his second self? Actually, of course, he does not think of a *second self* but of his real self, the one he comes upon. He can go on acting in the world and not come upon it. It is as if, unaware of impersonating a character in a play, he then meets the character. But who is the "he" that does all this, behind the scenes as it were in which the characters play? Does this "he" go on to meet a third self and so on? No. Whatever may happen afterwards, at the moment when the boy comes upon himself all is suspended, achieved. "He" and the second self fuse. There is no going on or going anywhere. He is here, himself, now, and it is rare and delightful, so delightful that it has the sensation of radiating away while it remains, of going into farness and, in the going, of thinning the ego away, of dissolving the clot, so that what is left is the essence of being, in the act of being, now. Accordingly, from this simple experience, retained by memory and worked upon unconsciously (as was the tailor's song), the boy will in the future have his apprehension of states of being of this kind, however or by whomsoever spoken or recorded.

To take the next step. Supposing, when the boy is enjoying this rare moment, someone approaches him and asks: Do you believe in God?, how would he feel and react? Presumably as he felt and reacted when a stranger did actually ask him: Are you saved? He felt embarrassed and did not obey, possibly out of politeness, the impulse to take to his heels. By the native or Strath standard the stranger was intrusive if not bad-mannered. Had the boy been asked about God as he sat on the stone he would have been trapped. But if he could keep God outside his circle in church, he would surely fail on the stone. It was fairly easy to keep God outside the circle. You merely turned your eyes away and, in the face of persistence, went anonymous.

Accordingly it might be thought that the boy's experience

excluded God, and all the more certainly and permanently because it was delightful. For God and delight did not go together. It was all very well to preach that joy was next to godliness. But such joy — even when it broke into song, shouting "Joyful, joyful, joyful" — had a falsely bright, lugubrious sound. If you didn't look out something might come out from under it and *touch* you. That really was what it was for, and you knew it.

But (to step up once more) would this one and only experience in fact permanently exclude God or any conception of God? How did Buddha come by chance to be introduced above — because he, too, avoided talk on eternity and immortality? Not altogether, I fancy. At that moment interest lay in Buddha's experiment in detachment and in what he had to say about it when he came back. Manifestly Buddha's experience so transcended the boy's that any kind of comparison is absurd, yet while taking this into account the boy cannot help using his own experience, which is his knowledge also, in attempting to apprehend, get a glimmer of, that which is so far beyond him.

When Buddha came upon his second self, what a coming upon must have been there! thinks the boy. The way, the Eightfold Path, the valleys of the years, the final coming upon and dwelling with.

The boy's mind gets lost in this complexity. But even while it gets lost, it cannot repress the involuntary surmise as to how Buddha felt when the disciple asked him about eternity. What could the disciple be told of eternity when obviously in himself he had not met the timeless? Where questions are being asked out of the wrong category what is one to do with the babbler? Was Buddha bored?

That last youthful question springs spontaneously from a feeling of the absence of delight, perhaps because all that can be *told* had to do, not with achievement, but with the teaching that must precede it. Over and over again the Zen master of archery had to instruct his pupil just to go on pulling the long bow, to practise and yet again to practise, until the pupil became familiar not with delight but with despair. If this could happen in the simple matter of archery, how much more so in the complexities of the Eightfold Path; until at last a sort of Eastern quietism of defeat, of grey despair, spreads outward and seems to invade the whole, to include the end, whereas in fact it includes the teaching only and the trying to learn.

The Zen master grew impatient more than once with his pupil who not only wanted to be able to hit the bull's eye with every shot but to know straight off what bull at the same time was being scored in the ultimate region of philosophy or godhead or meaning. So he was told that although it was raining today it might be fine tomorrow. As a perennial topic of conversation the weather has proved useful in many lands.

I have read somewhere a story of Chinese who trekked across Asian country to receive, by order of Buddha, a copy of the scriptures. On opening their copy they found that it contained no writing. When they showed Buddha the blank pages, he smiled. They were wanting it in writing even then.

Now all the boy has to go on is his own simple experience of nut-cracking on the stone (not to mention his archery, such as it was, or flying through the air). But somehow he is left with the notion that delight is found in the moment of achievement; that Buddha had achieved so rare a quality of it that it was quite incommunicable; and that perhaps even ultimate questions about eternity were so contained in the incommunicable that they answered themselves, in the sense that question and answer coalesced and were no more there. But delight would have been there, perhaps the Delight that sits on its immovable stone in the eternal river cracking its nuts. And if that is too youthful or pagan an image still it at least serves to keep the way open for youth, to suggest that a gleam of the way is in the beginning, that it was and is implicit, the radioactive atom, in the psychic stuff.

Chapter 33

Satire and Music

Why this feeling of continuity, of being part of that which was in the beginning and forever goes on, should give satisfaction is difficult to discover; and possibly it might give no satisfaction without those moments of delight when the whole process seems balanced or suspended in a wonderful manner — wonderful because not balanced in a static way but alive. The living moment; the livingness of the moment. The lightness of thistledown. The light, around and above. Could anything be further from deep thought? Yet only at such a moment can one appreciate most the words of the poet Hölderlin:

> *Who most deeply has thought*
> *loves what is most alive.*

Or, perhaps, *after* such a moment, when one comes back to life in its various guises and regards each with that detachment which sees more precisely, more intimately, than ever before. The movement of a squirrel or bird, a girl's face, a boy's swift feet, a man's hand. How exquisite then the vision that flashes back and finds again and sees what the Greeks made! Here is the love that is not for possession but for being a part of. The vividness that runs over laughter like a wagtail over a lawn; the entranced silence wherein the stone-deaf composer heard — and composed — his last quartets.

All part of the going on, whatever chance mood may like it or not. For a chance mood may not like it, may want to shoot it. Satire. Malice. Why? Because an apparent optimism offends? Because there is no nonsense about a shot bird? Or does it go deeper than that?

Let us glance at satire — in its common form, the book that

satirizes human relations, beliefs, institutions. At once it is seen that the book would be pointless unless the author had notions of superior relations, finer beliefs, a better institution; but he rarely or never hints at these, because if he did he would in turn be exposing himself to satire. So his higher standards and beautiful thoughts exist by implication, and the author knows that the reader knows, and what either doesn't know he vaguely feels. In a sense the satirist is the shyest of all birds. He is the wild duck that covers up her eggs before she leaves the nest; the bee that seals up holes in the hive with a substance resinous and waxy. After that he can fly high and wide describing sins and perversions and horrors, for he is having a day off from the eggs and the honey. This is notoriously the case when he has acquired a new religious system. The ferocity of a satirist is never much to go by, for he may be either wildly exhilarated or morosely suspicious. But it may be as well not to suggest to him that he is a secret hatcher of eggs or addict of wild honey; and above all not to imply that he is a jealous guardian of the true way, for now you might be touching his marrow.

The satirist who destroys for destruction's sake is a very different bird and on the whole not too common. He rarely runs to book length, but may be found here and there as a critic or reviewer of other people's works. Between creators and critics there is an old warfare, but this is understood, and can be helpful to the creator when he sees that the critic understands the creative intention. But there is a satirist who destroys for the fun of exhibiting himself in a witticism. He is usually expert at finding the sensitive spots for the neat squirt of his malice. And if he can't, at a glance, find them in the author's or artist's work — he hasn't time to waste in a tiresome search — he can suggest their presence and then perform. But even *his* aim is to be diverting. Every creator has encountered him at least once and thinks him the lowest form of life. This is possibly an exaggeration.

However, without going into all its dimensions, satire on the future as well as the present, into all the forms of destruction of all that man had made or built, individually or collectively, in art or artifact, belief or institution, one may conclude that always the worst is done in the name of the best, and even when the name is not named, when the best is not specified, it is understood, taken for granted, it is implicit.

It all starts with each man and starts in his beginning. A man may run most of his course without consciously discovering what most affected him long ago. For what has most affected him must have affected him in his essence; but this essence is very elusive, and only rarely self-aware. Otherwise those who have researched far into this matter would not have come away with the final winnowing; know thyself. Even as a joke it would be pointless if we all knew ourselves, as we so confidently believe we do. Some of us, indeed, believe we know ourselves only too well, though here perhaps there is a first tincture of the humour of humility, the first indication that someone inside is looking at the show the self is putting on and not thinking a great deal of it. If this someone were the second self looking at the antics of the first self some sort of pictorial meaning could emerge.

Books have been written, systems created, on the esoteric difficulty of knowing the self. Very few beings apparently have attained this knowledge; and even, it would seem, as the knowledge is being attained, as the self is being apprehended, so, in inverse ratio, is the self thinning away, passing into that which is greater than itself, though of the same kind.

But the curiosity in the psychic stuff has its urge to find out what so strange and paradoxical a performance amounts to. If it hadn't there would have been neither the books nor the systems. So it casts about among its experiences for some sort of intimation, or analogy, or direction, and lands, let us say, in music, the music that most deeply moves, the concert of its choice. The opening theme, the profound familiarity once again, the stirring within, the expanding as the musical statement expands, expands until it is creation, and the self is caught in it as in creation, and expands with it, passing away with it, circle beyond circle to the utmost vanishing circle of all creation, in the silence beyond which what has been heard goes on.

In brief, as the self is borne away, as the central ego or clot thins, so is the self more profoundly and centrally enriched. This is a common experience. It happens. The wording, the analogy, may be matter for debate. There is no doubt about the happening, about the feeling, the apprehension, that in these minutes one was with one's real self, and also with that which was beyond the real self but yet of which the real self was part.

To take a more simple musical analogy. As has earlier been suggested, those brought up within the region of a distinctive and still active folk music are sometimes susceptible to qualities in it that seem extra-musical, as though the simple traditional tune carried racial characteristics, was archetypal in the Jungian sense. What can actually happen — did actually happen — is something like this. The time is the dusk of evening and the place a Highland sea loch; across the water comes the music of a traditional lament. The theme is stated — that awful terrible familiarity of the theme — until the head bows before it, as before what can hardly be borne, and the theme repeats itself with the inexorability that has in its simplicity, its final cleansing, all that can be said for ever, and the body doubles over like another boulder on the shore, egoless and faceless, and bears the wind of time from all of the race who have gone before.

This effort to defeat the paradox, to find the self in the losing of the self, by practical illustration is open to all who have had experiences of a similar kind, whether by a Highland sea loch, on a road in Spain, or among the Fiji Islands. There is nothing peculiarly arcane or dubious about it. Let us try to take it one step further.

When the self gets lost in the music, classical or folk, the nature of the experience is very difficult if not quite impossible to define. For at its most intense or most profound it is pure experience, and as such devoid of pictorial or literary images. This, I believe, is generally accepted.

By now what appear to be similar states of mind though in different circumstances, in other environments, swing into focus, and as it is in the nature of man to go one step up, and then another, step after step into the unkown like a scientist, let us look far and select the East, and, to make a long story short, that vision of the East wherein as an ultimate step the wise have found God, not as an image, not as form or shape, but as pure experience.

It may be difficult to ask any further question now, for a last step is a last step, so all the mind can do is wonder if there is anything in analogy. When Western man gets lost in music is he approaching in any degree the condition of Eastern man lost in God? Is this that which is not the same thing and yet "like the thing"? Is the pure experience of music *on* the Eastern way, in the Western sense?

As there may be something diverting in the questions, whether they make sense or not, let us consider this aspect of God. The word mystical I have never quite understood and therefore cannot comfortably use. For the same reason possibly I find I have not used words like soul and spirit. God is a much more definite word if only in the sense that the boy was taught in the beginning that man was made in God's image. So the image of God as the bearded patriarch coming down the straths of time is familiar. He could all at once be there, like the gamekeeper. A person in authority could suddenly *appear*. This was something learned; it had meaning. It was far from being theoretical.

In much the same way — and at the risk of further reiteration — any quest for delight must have some element of experience behind it to give it meaning. But these elements though primary, like Hume's impressions, give rise to ideas or reflections, and as these distinguish man from the other animals they have their importance in his sum total. They have to be brought into the count. They have to be brush strokes on the canvas, however "impressionist" the canvas may be. Further, when one feels that an impression may be unique, an exclusive experience, one can always test this by looking into literature or talking with a friend. Usually one finds it is not unique but shared. This is normally a delightful discovery.

That said, there is one further distinction before the Eastern or imageless concept of God may be considered. How words convey meaning and how much meaning they convey, with all that is thereby involved in use and wont, is a speculative matter beyond our purpose, but that only some part of meaning can be apprehended at certain times or in certain conditions and discussed with uncertainty and imprecision is a matter of ordinary experience and therefore much to our purpose. Often what is dismissed as vague and woolly in a thought process is of real and even vital importance in the life process. Logical speech may proceed from a tidy mind but often the mind is untidy and unsusceptible of being formally arranged and arrayed. It cannot so to speak find at times its braces or even its buttons. To condemn it for this would be like condemning it for being naked instead of in tails and a white waistcoat. You cannot tie a white waistcoat to the button of nudity. We have got so used to applying formal reasoning to every state of mind as a test of its "reality" or "truth" that it has become automatic as a piece of mental behaviourism. But both formal logic and informal logic seem to be able to exist at the same time, and on remarkable occasions to cohabit, as, for example, in the boys' thought of Pompus going for a swim in his morning coat. This "impossible" conception they could entertain without difficulty. Indeed, as a sort of final "truth" about Pompus, it rocked them with delight.

Chapter 34

Buttons and Braces

Axioms and premises do not exist in nature any more than buttons and braces: they have to be manufactured and used for a system or a suit. Outside system or suit, as inside, the buttonless proceeds, the unaxiomatic makes hay. This is not to decry the value of buttons. Far from it.

Western theologians use a lot of buttons to tie up their almighty conceptions of God the Father. But when it comes to the ultimate concept of the East, the apprehension of God as formless and imageless, where are the buttons now and with what shall they be tied? Here the last metaphysical button fades upon the viewless air.

Nothing is any more except what is now, and what is now has been called light, love, harmony, integration, participation in the all or the absolute; indeed many variations and combinations of such terms have been used by those who, having had this experience, have wished to communicate it, to share it. But although the actual experience cannot be communicated to those who have never had it, yet there seems to be something apprehensible in the way, or along the path, of the happening or experience that can, however vaguely or informally, be caught by all.

Not to repeat the musical experience here but to go a step beyond: it can happen on occasion that one is taken far further into music's creative region that one had anticipated. This is not only a memorable but an astonishing experience. There is about it an air of the incredible: that this farness of creation should have been revealed and that I was there! Of course, afterwards one quite naturally *talks* of the greatness of the composer, the remarkable qualities of a work that opened vistas, plumbed deeps, or performed more esoteric feats according to one's skill in using critical counters on the current exchange.

Now the odd thing about the real experience, about finding oneself with a selfless wonder at the heart of the creation, is that though it astonishes it yet does not astonish, it has the familiarity of something that has always been there waiting to be found, or of something that, lost long ago, has now been come upon with delight. Expressed otherwise: in the heart of the farness of creation, when one should be overcome by the fact of being there, of having accomplished so remarkable a feat, of having gone far beyond one's knowledge and power, one is overcome by something quite other, namely, the wonder of discovering oneself in this strangely familiar place. What should be a vast presumption is in the actual moments of experience a wonder, a delight, so final that it is pure.

That something like this happens in music is well enough understood. I have never, for example, met a person who said he experienced presumption in appreciating Bach. Such a statement could be made but only as an afterthought, in the realm of thought after the experience. If it connoted a genuine humility, a deduction might follow to the effect that the appreciation had been profound. But this is thought applied to the experience, not the experience itself.

To take an earlier slant on this elusive matter. It may be remembered that in the discussion of totems and taboos, it was understood that man could find a spirit in a stone or bush simply because he had first of all and quite unconsciously projected it there, much as the boy had projected it into the solitary bush when with his brother and Angus he was hunting for the salmon in the dark. In our realistic way we are satisfied that in fact there is no spirit in the stone or the bush. It is all quite clear to us now, and that's that. But it is not quite so clear when it comes to Bach's spirit being projected into another person, because now the other person can in fact get charged with Bach. He does; he sings Bach; he has even been observed to waltz around under the impression that his impoverished movements expressed holy joy. That Bach is dead and gone these two hundred years makes no difference, nor will it in two thousand. If music were all creation and Bach all music, there would be those who would call themselves the sons of Bach.

Is it too fanciful to suppose that what thus happens in the part (musical creation) provides an indication of what happens in the whole (all creation)? Not entirely, if one may judge by the expressions used by the Eastern religious, whose self gets lost in a greater Self. It may be no more than an indication, an intimation, the merest apprehension of "something far more deeply interfused", but it would seem to be of that kind, susceptible to similar modes of expression, and on the way so far as the mysterious journey of the self is concerned.

Now comes a rather more difficult step, for, as we are told, the Eastern religious who experiences the total harmony participates in the Ultimate or the Absolute, in the Godhead. Those of us who have not had this experience can once more but approach it in an analogical way. This may amount in practice to little more than an attempt to apply reason to what has not been experienced, or, more familiarly, to argue about what one doesn't know. It may even suspiciously look like tying the white waistcoat of formal logic this time to the umbilical button of the Absolute.

The Eastern religious experiences participation in something outside himself, in something which is greater than he but which includes him, and he calls it God or Unity. He gets "lost" in it as a listener gets "lost" in Bach. Bach's music is not a projection by the listener upon the vacant air; it is a direct projection by Bach upon the listener. The listener participates in the musical creation. When his participation is at its highest, the experience is pure in the sense that it is imageless; and in this respect approaches the imageless apprehension of God by the religious. At whatever point the analogy is considered, it conveys at least some meaning; except, of course, at one point: whereas we all believe that Bach existed, not all believe that God exists. By many this is considered anything but a small point. Let it be looked at.

Chapter 35

Does God Exist?

If God does not exist, then what is happening to the religious who experiences God? In ordinary language, we say he is just imagining God, he is having a delusion or illusion, or, in accord with terms already used, he is projecting God upon the vacant air, just as primitive man projected a spirit into a tree or bush. As the process is unconscious, as he is totally unaware that he has done this, he finds his consequent apprehension of God very convincing. Why he should go to all this circuitous trouble in order to get the feel or apprehension of a spirit inside him may seem obscure, but is far from obscure to those psychologists who have studied the mechanism of projection, particularly in a world that from the beginning was — it still is — full of mysteries.

Man has been given to this sleight of mind for a long time and accordingly God may be no more than a man-made creation. Assuming this to be the case, let us consider what it signifies, or, at least, let me, for I am probably full of prejudice, having remembered the boy who was always as it were evasively careful to keep God outside his inner circle. This may in some degree have been a matter of fear, which was probably not lessened by momentary glimpses of a smoking sea of brimstone that, being hell, was bottomless. But this fear must not be overstated. A boy's capacity for taking evasive action is prodigious, so long — and this is the important point — as his second self, his individual essence, remains intact. It is this desire, impulse, to keep his real self whole that keeps God out, that keeps everything out that might *touch* its wholeness, its independence, its freedom. For it is here that freedom and choice operate as elements of a living whole, of a livingness that is the creative entity, and as such are inseparable from the act of being alive and thus beyond logical analysis, as life is beyond it. When something like this is experienced then any outside authority or power that threatens the wholeness of the second self is evaded, just as a disaster on the physical level is evaded by the body. When authoritarianism breaks into the second self and orders it around, freedom and choice and the creative element are its immediate victims.

Now anyone who has empirically arrived at some such findings may be inclined towards the assumption that the religious person has deceived himself and that God is man-made because, to the end, he himself would rather suffer no authoritarianism even on the highest level. This need not be enlarged upon, so long as it is recognized as a possible factor or prejudice in the assumption that God does not exist. Thus recognized, there is ease in the air (for such as the boy), a feeling that now one is quite free to look with positive interest as the deception which the religious has unconsciously practised upon himself and see just what it may signify in or beyond itself. For when the second self is not threatened by authority, it delights in adventuring and finding and doing. I'm off! I'm away!

Now the first arresting thought is the extraordinary nature and quality of the deception, for as an experience it contains the most subtle, profound, elusive elements that the mind is capable of hunting. How can this be known by one who has not experienced the deception? By reading carefully those who have and who are admitted by the initiates to be the great among them, and by analogy from one's own experience whether in music, archery or cracking nuts. The more the experience is appreciated the more astonishing it becomes.

Out of this astonishment starts the opposite or counter notion: that at least it would be simpler to grasp, more a matter of common sense, if God did exist and by communicating with man at the utmost stretch of man's intellection and capacity for enlightenment, at his deepest capacity for pure experience, give rise to what would no longer be a deception but a direct cause-and-effect affair. This would so to speak clean up the whole business and do away with any further bother. In the universe there is an intelligence higher than man's and on occasion a man can get in touch with it. Call this intelligence God and there you are, ready now to receive even formal logic in full dress.

Mathematics thrives on its laws of probability; indeed in the new statistical reaches of physics among infinitesimals it behaves with the flawless art of the conjuror. So there seems to be no particular reason why an ordinary inquirer should not have a crack at probability in the non-statistical reaches of man's communication with a higher intelligence.

This at once takes us back to earlier remarks on what (in a verbal emergency) was called "psychic stuff" and its chances of existing elsewhere than on this planet. I confess again that at every effort to make it an element or manifestation peculiar or exclusive to this earth I have the feeling of offending against probability in an ever more embarrassing way. If only all the physical elements of this planet were peculiar to itself — not found elsewhere — then, it seems to me, one might with some face, even with mathematical relief, conclude that the psychic stuff was a function — or, anyhow, a manifestation in its fashion — of these elements, and as such only to be found on our planet. But scientists know that our physical elements are common to the starry systems, that hydrogen atoms are daily fusing with explosive effects in the hearts of suns. That this psychic stuff, which we salute as the universe's marvel of marvels, has appeared only on this earth is surely stretching probability, to put it mildly, beyond its usefulness in mathematical practice. Short of a "special creation" by Someone, it seems fantastic to believe that this "crowning achievement" should have exclusively appeared on so small a speck in so unthinkably vast a whole — and a whole that throughout hangs together in such order and harmony.

This may be a special pleading in favour of one's own concept of the absurd — but not, I think, altogether. When the earthly claim for the sole possession of psychic stuff falls away into the larger or astronomical harmony one is at least set in an order of creation that seems reasonable and without *special* favours. When stripped clean, whether for a bout of boxing or a bout of thought, man wants no special favours and an impartial referee.

If, then, as a matter of probability psychic stuff is elsewhere in the universe, it is reasonable to assume, as was earlier indicated, that here it is "higher" and there "lower", even as we use these terms on earth. The boy experienced a certain harmony when nut-cracking on the stone that is very "low" when compared with the harmony achieved by the Eastern religious. We have at least that range here. But when we assume the existence of a higher intelligence outside our earthly scheme of things then we have to consider the probability of man's getting in touch with it or it with him — as in the physical instance of cosmic rays from outer space, which scientists on mountain tops are now trying to understand, with a devotion not unlike that hitherto given by another order of inquirers to psychic or spiritual affairs. It cannot be said with certainty that to get in touch is impossible. One finds oneself expanding into the creation of Bach. There are those short intimations of other conditions of being like breakthroughs from the normal. Indeed nothing characterizes the nature of the psychic stuff more distinctively than just this tendency to break through from the normal, to get rid of fettering custom, to disrupt the rigid in ritual and old rule and be off on the new hunt. This is what happens, so the urge is implicit and active, as if it were the radiant element in the psychic stuff that no curtain of custom ever quite succeeds in effectively screening. Indeed we call that civilization the higher where the curtain screens the less.

Experiments are going on with thought transference, telepathy. In this silent realm at what speed does thought travel? Or is "speed" here an inapt concept, taken from the physical world to measure the psychical? Concepts within physics itself have changed in recent times, at least in the sense that they have expanded to include a wider apprehension of reality, as quantum mechanics includes the classical mechanics as a special or limiting case. One may need a concept other than "speed" or "time" for a telepathic communication. The psychic stuff is not unused to such a notion, indeed it has been stirred by apprehensions of the instantaneous or timeless from the beginning.

Such tentative considerations can expand verbally, speculatively, in an endless way, so let probability simply emerge with its natural air and see how the short argument runs. The psychic element exists outside us, beyond this earth. Communication in one form or other takes place between psychic entities. The Eastern religious in a "high" manifestation of the psychic stuff finds himself in contact with a "higher", which he calls God or the Absolute, whereupon communication completes itself in communion. The Eastern religious is not now "projecting" God, any more than the listener is "projecting" Bach. God and Bach are higher manifestations of the psychic stuff in their respective creations. Cause and effect operate in the old familiar way.

Yet scepticism remains reluctant to accept any intelligence higher than what we know. This reluctance is like the boy's reluctance to let God inside his circle. It persists, and in some measure must forever persist, for what is really being protected is the second self, the need to keep the essence intact if one is to continue to be and know oneself, and particularly if one is to continue to come upon the highest delight in being alive.

But however attractive this scepticism to many of us, what it stands on must also be looked at, otherwise scepticism cannot be wholly enjoyed, for it does hold the suspicion of merely being the opposite to acceptance, an "attitude" like any other. Let this attitude be phrased as undogmatically as may be, "in the light of all we know" and so on, it still contains the assumption that the psychic stuff in all its manifestations is exclusive to this planet, that man is the sole manifestation of it in the total universe. In view of the marvellous nature of the stuff *that*, it has earlier been suggested, is a rather staggering assumption. It begins to look as if man does not want to give up his pre-eminence, either from fear that he may not be able to cope with the "higher" or from the power and glory of being himself the "highest". The one and only. Said the fond Scots mother as the regiment marched past: "They are a' oot o' step except oor Jock." The total universe is a considerable regiment.

If one could free oneself from old associations, verbal and other, and consider the alternatives from the standpoint of probability, it might be more difficult to see man's intelligence as the only intelligence in the universe than to see it as a manifestation of intelligence which may be of another order or level elsewhere. From evolutionary notions in science to the participation of the Eastern religious in the greater Self, there would seem to be some kind of ascending order, or order of development, which has been generally accepted, if not with certainty or finality, at least with a sense of direction. It is the kind of order within which man has fruitfully worked. It is the direction in which he has found out things. It is forever on the way to apprehension of the next mystery. On the material side, only the advanced scientists know how deep the mysteries are and how some of them must remain permanently unknowable to any exercise of our normal faculties or senses.

Let it be said again that this book is not concerned with religion, ethics, scepticism, though words like these may have to be used in a quest for the orders of delight. Perhaps, therefore, it should be made clear that an expression like "Eastern religious" was used for simple convenience as it readily denoted a kind of imageless participation in something bigger than the normal self. But of course it is not peculiar to the East. The Christian religion, even in its most anthropomorphic phases, carried the same participation by its saints or mystics. In fact, if the participation had not this attribute of universality it might be suspect as some sort of neurotic development of a local unbalance. But the whole point of the discussion here is that it is not simply a universal matter of religious experience but a universal matter of secular experience also, and that adults who have professed no defined religion have experienced it at odd moments, and that even children — but now we are back once more at the boy nut-cracking on his stone, back at that which is implicit in the psychic stuff whether we wish to believe it or not, at that coming upon the second self when at once an intimation of it is apprehended.

This may have the air of light irreverence to the deeply religious; it misses so much, its ignorance is so vast, that it may well be spurned. The sceptic may find in it something so slight that it is a light irrelevance. The psychologist may find a simplification of his science to a first self and a second self so undefined that it may be lightly dismissed — or recognized as a sort of ogham script by a primitive. To make matters worse, the very thought of such judgments induces a light and possibly irreverent delight in the boy as part, if not father, of the man. It is not the ten commandments that worry the boy when he is cracking his nuts. In fact nothing worried him then; which is the simple but real point; just as, he assumes, nothing worries the saint when he is in communion with that which is greater than he, but of which, in the actual moment of communion, he is part. This comparison may seem a presumption that out-tops irreverence, and admittedly there is a wild extravagance in it, but again an extravagance that (before analysis begins its devitalizing business) induces delight as light as foam on the river water. This happens, and the smile is there on its own.

Chapter 36

The New Dark Night

The boy keeps cropping up as if he were driving a flock of unruly geese through too many holes in too many hedges. But to go beyond the boy and his hedges would be to enter new territory, where the geese would not be quite the same geese and the outgrown boy would on occasion mistake one of them for a swan, and not always a living swan like a woman but a thought-up one like an ideology. New experiences would require a new record, so, for the light-hearted present, let autobiography stop in its youth.

And doing so may at least have this interest — if this writing means anything — that in the beginning are intimations of all the different kinds of ends. The boy at his very earliest recollection, in the darkness beyond the gable-end when hurrying through a simple function, experienced the "imageless and formless" in a memorable manner. True, what he experienced then was not harmony but its opposite, fear. In the air beyond him was that which would grab him if he did not bolt back. That this was a simple case of finding in himself what he had first unconsciously projected upon the vacant air may seem clear enough. The vacant air was probably innocent of any grabbing intention. But at least the boy had the fear in himself. There was this element of fear in the psychic stuff, and it was related on this occasion not to what was known, not even to what was imagined, but to what was imageless and unknown. This is the simple experience, and it has got to be held if possible for a clear couple of seconds — though that is a long time for reason to contain its desire to rush in and explain it away in terms of archaic heritages from wild-beast eras, Jungian archetypes and similar simple myths and symbols from psychology's fascinating kindergarten.

This nameless imageless fear became, then, the basis of all

apprehension of this kind of fear. It grew enriched in its subterranean quarters (as the tailor's song grew enriched) for all the world as though memory working out of sight on its own had the habit of looking over the record and adding to it, bringing it up to date, without altering the theme itself — the enrichment, the addition, being a matter of quality rather than of quantity.

In course of time the boy comes on the expression "the dark night of the soul". It affects him strongly, like a powerful line of poetry, but with something added, something of fear and struggle too real for poetry, beyond poetry, where what happens is terribly more than what is said. The sound, the rhythm of the words may have beauty like a drug but it is *about* what is beyond beauty. In fact it is in that place, that dark night, which had better be turned away from, not stared at too long. And youth can turn away. Indeed it can turn away repeating the words like a sombre incantation — *the dark night of the soul* — enjoying them while keeping them imageless in a meaningless way, half wondering without approaching the wonder, and then, because of the seed of disaster in them, shutting them off.

Now the boy never, of course, consciously connected these words with his own early experience of the darkness beyond the gable-end. Such a connection presumably comes only after adult thought and reflection, and not necessarily then. For it is usually startled into conscious thought by some curious chance. Besides, how could a very small boy's simple happening have any connection with the saint's or mystic's "dark night of the soul", that awful experience of the going out of the light, of the darkness in which God has deserted him, and his cries are answered no more, and communion is no more, and he is now only at the beginning of his agony?

Even the grown man wants to shut that off, and to shut it off in a mood of avoidance that is not unlike the boy's. Before thought, or the making of comparisons which is thought in action, can get going, the climate of the mood is there. Between the beginning of a road and its end there may be a great distance, but it is the one road. Some say there cannot be meaning until it is expressed. With considerations of that kind we are not here concerned, but always and only, first, with what happens, with the experience itself, and the mood of avoidance is experienced before it is expressed, indeed by its very nature it does not desire expression, if, further, expression were possible. In this mood those who have had different degrees of the same kind of experience — such as fear in the dark night — may meet, if only to pass or overtake, like ships in the night.

But as we are now dealing with fear, with the opposite of delight, perhaps it had better be considered further.

When the boy had his experience of the darkness, he knew that behind him was a safe bolt-hole, his home, and he could hardly wait to finish what he was at before bolting back into it, for if he were not quick enough something might come out of the air and grab him. Grabbed, carried away, smothered, destroyed — something like that, but again not clearly imagined. Away, away, carried struggling away *from his home* to what would be the end of him.

In the soul's dark night there is no home.

The struggle is the struggle against being lost. There was a home, but the home has vanished, as if a satanic necromancy had removed it, and this necromancy is now the only reality, this emptiness of the air through which the cries pass, this darkness which shrouds the ever more desperate struggle to avoid — cast out from God, lost — the unimaginable end. And to some mystics at least "the dark night" was not just an emptiness in this terrible sense, for the satanic necromancy charged it with its own devil-shaped creatures.

The ordeal, the agony, varies in its manifestations according to the sufferer, as the evidence tells. Yet however it may vary in the individual it can pass, it seems to me, through two phases: from the active struggle to find again what has been lost to the endurance of the loss.

In the active phase the cries reach for the blessedness of what has been lost, the recapture of the communion, the love, that is gone, and the cries are a release of the agony in its terrible effort at finding again. But in endurance there are no cries, no release, and what is endured has the appalling premonition of ultimate disintegration.

To make this premonition of disintegration more than a form of words might again require an experience behind it, but this time possibly an adult experience, for disintegration is more than a boy's word. Let me therefore relate the following incident.

Chapter 37

In a Country House

I was paying a short visit to a family living in a large country house. The man and his wife were my closest friends and our relations were never shadowed but, on the contrary, lively and delightful, on a basis of real understanding. I was in my late twenties and they were a little older. After a varied and happy evening I went to bed without a care in the world. My bedroom was in the southern wing of the house and, as it happened, I had the whole wing to myself. As usual I went to sleep at once and normally would not have awakened until I was called. But some time during the night I not only awoke but awoke so swiftly that I was actually sitting up in bed before the opening door had come to rest. The smooth swiftness with which I accomplished this act held no sense of flurry or real fear but only an intense awareness. I saw the finishing movement of the white door in the dim light that pervaded the room, dim as bright starlight. After watching the door for a few moments and listening intently, I got up and looked along the pitch dark corridor. I could neither see nor hear anything. I shut the door quietly and it remained firmly shut. I was used to sleeping alone in solitary places and therefore not given to being unduly upset by odd sounds or happenings. The weirdest night effect so often has the most ordinary and amusing cause. But in certain circumstances I possessed that sort of animal awareness which could explain well enough how, without any conscious volition, I got sitting up in bed, wide awake and ready.

Back in bed I tried to work it out and decided that in shutting the door after entering the room I could not have pushed it firmly enough to engage fully the wedge-shaped end of the sliding bolt (the bolt that the knob works). If a gust of wind had come along the corridor it could have shoved the door open, and at the first motion of the door the compressed bolt would have clicked. The click had awakened me and before the door had finished swinging I was sitting up.

As explanations go, that seemed about good enough, even if I could not hear wind outside. As far as I knew, the old house had no reputation of being haunted. I had not heard, anyway, of a ghost, and though the blasted heath that Macbeth traversed was not many miles away, it was far enough not to trouble the familiar countryside. Certainly I had no definite feeling of an alien presence and I heard no mysterious sound.

I have had to mention all this because in some inscrutable way it may have been the cause of the unique experience which now followed. I was lying on my back in bed thinking of the incident before getting to sleep again — I was deliberately going to turn over in a minute or two — when I became aware of being attacked by something that existed outside the room. The bedroom windows were unblinded and tall and through them I could see the night and get the impression of immense distance. I don't remember being aware of the sky and stars, but then a wooded hill rose a little way off, there were trees in the park, and anyhow what I distinctly remember is the dim-blue darkness in the windows that suggested vast space. It was through the top part of one of these windows that the rays or whatever they were began the attack. At first I was merely uncomfortable and moved my head and body, but then my eyes went back to the window for I was not just going to accept this absurd feeling of being attacked. And it was absurd as this — for this was the feeling — that from somewhere far in space the rays were being directed at me, not so much by some controlling being or intelligence as by some intelligence in the source of the rays themselves. This may not be very clear, but clear enough perhaps to suggest how impersonal the attack was, how indifferent though yet knowing, without any feeling, with an effective coldness and precision. I am certain that I thought of the rays at the time, and not afterwards, as "black electricity". In the physical realm this description, of course, means nothing, but it had some sort of meaning for the psychic realm then, and I remember deciding that it was apt, for I was interested enough to try to think analytically of what was happening, to find descriptive words for so new a sensation. As the discomfort became a trifle too much I had to shed this detached (and possibly protective) attitude, for now it grew clear that the attack would continue automatically, like an electric current switched on, until my body was disintegrated, or, to give the precise picture, until the increasing power of the rays shivered the flesh from the bone, one organ from another, and so annihilated their common life. It was an attack on the body not on my mind, and the devilishness of this was extraordinarily subtle, though in a way I can hardly express and would not care to try.

I took deep breaths, turned over, strove to get back into my normal world. The time comes in such a conflict when the panic point first arises. It is the moment when man realizes he is vulnerable. He literally swallows it and takes an extra grip with the will. The will is a wonderful weapon, and man is a good fighter, a bonny fechter as the Scots tongue has it with its suggestion of exhilaration in the fight. And in a physical fight there is an exhilaration, however deplorable this may seem to the pacific mind. But in the kind of contest which I am indicating there is no exhilaration, there is its exact opposite, and that opposite is without colour, quite stark. Here, at this point, even mental agony would have colour, colour and warmth, as an outburst of despair has something of relief, yet its indulgence now would be a treachery to the will, for the moment of such indulgence would be a moment of relaxation through which the disintegrating force would slip in and complete its business. At such a moment one dare not enjoy the luxury of agony.

But I need not over-dramatize the incident. I came through it and probably fell asleep, though my memory is vague on the immediate aftermath, except that I did not mention the incident to my hosts or inquire about nocturnal hauntings, for when it comes, on departure, to leaving something behind there is no substitute for a blessing.

Chapter 38

Disintegration

The phrase about the premonition of disintegration thus takes on a certain significance. The attack was more than an attack on the body though it took that form; it was an attack right through the body and its interactions with the first self to the circle, and through the circle, that guards the second self. It was when that inner circle was touched that panic reared its blind serpent-head.

As there may be something here fairly central, let us consider it a little more carefully. And first, the issue of death. It is one of the obvious facts of his history that in a bodily fight as in one of his more desperate games, man is prepared, normally with an uplifted or exhilarated feeling, to take a risk on death. Climbing mountains or racing motor cars, primitive feuds or global wars. Even in boyhood: the dare, the foolhardy act, the slip that would have been fatal. Two duellists, inquiring courteously about mutual friends, while fencing for the fatal opening. But most people some time or other have been saved by the skin of their teeth, and afterwards laughed in wonder. Twice, in the simple matter of drowning, I was carried over hope's borderline and once had time enough for the drowning dream. But possibly we have to go back to early man, the hunter, in order to realize — if realization is still possible — a sense of relationship in death even between man and beast, whereby the hunter stroked the slain animal in affection as his dead brother. Here the game of chance with death may assume the name of Necessity, for the hunter hunted in order to live. But rationalizing or analysing an act is not the act itself but a comment on it, as has been said before, and if a comment does not, for example, include an apprehension of the affection it is to that extent inadequate, and if it misunderstands completely the full nature of what was experienced by the hunter it is worthless.

However, enough may have been said to suggest that when man is out on his game of desperate chances he accepts death as an element in it *so long as he feels whole*. So long as he is knit together, integrated in himself, he is prepared to take a chance on death and, in certain circumstances, has been prepared, as we know, to take death, to accept death, if the alternative meant signing his wholeness away — the breakdown, the disintegration of his wholeness.

In everyday existence this may amount to the feeling that, though a risk is being taken, death is not going to happen to me. This is but another way of saying that within wholeness there is no room for death, hardly even for the remote thought of it.

Now this wholeness is something that mind and body strive to achieve quite involuntarily. Ordinarily it is accompanied by a feeling of fitness, of health, of good humour. It is the happy norm of the psychic stuff. This is what the stuff is like. It is known from experience. And it can be so positive in itself, in its moment of fullness, that it hardly has standing room for negation.

Let us take this simple experience an extra step. Supposing the realization that death can happen is driven into the wholeness of a boy or an adult, say in the form of advice — what happens? We all know how often such advice was ignored and the chance taken, even when our case fell far short of other and extreme cases, as of the parent who rushes to save a child at almost certain risk of death or the man who refuses to leave his stricken comrade though by doing so he might save his own life.

What does doing this feel like as an experience? It feels like a movement of the whole person towards the chance. That is the simple, uncomplicated, unthinking picture. That it may be infinitely complicated as a harmony of mind and body does not take away from the simplicity of the picture, and certainly not from the simplicity of the feeling. Here we are back at the Zen Master telling his pupil in archery not to think about how he is to let the arrow go. The shot must shoot itself. The hand, the body, the mind: when the three are in balance the arrow lands in the target's centre.

To hesitate for a moment now and wonder just what kind of feeling is aroused at the thought that death may in fact be encountered. Almost involuntarily, before the event, there is a feeling that at least one would first do one's utmost to counter death, to give it a run for its money. And beyond that feeling, another quieter feeling that one would go into death's darkness whole; as if by this wholeness one were defeating death or making its triumph arid.

But all this, while the wholeness is whole. Let the wholeness be flawed, let the climber doubt on the cliff face, the mystic lose his way in the dark night, and what a change is now!

Fear, disintegration, horror.

It is difficult to isolate the operative factor in this swing between the opposites, to be sure exactly how or why the horror is aroused. But attendant sensation is something like this. As has been said, quite involuntarily one has the feeling of death as of something that one goes towards or encounters, a dark veil, a blind wall, an active enemy. It is external, objective, and has an infinite variety of means for achieving its end.

Disintegration is internal, happening within, not as objective death but as a subjective and horrible breaking-up. Colloquial phrases like "going to bits" or "going to pieces" hardly convey an intimation of it, though the words have somehow contrived to get the taint. The realization that disintegration is happening, that the will may not be able to stop it, that it is getting the better of the will, that one is being driven back and beaten down, the inmost fibres of the mind being taken apart, the inmost core of the self being smothered, the last cry of hope or aspiration being choked like an animal cry, this is horror, and horror tainted with a horrible shame, for it is happening within, happening to oneself, and one cannot stop it.

Whatever the cause, whatever the means driving the self upon such an end, the last cry of the self, while the self is still whole enough to cry, is for death to come and wipe the horror and its shame out, to wipe the self out and make an end. In the thought of the self being thus annihilated there is the last relief. No immortal self, no saving God, but an end for ever. The uttermost relief. It is finished.

In between the extremes, the opposites, there are all kinds of tenable conditions from optimism through irony to nihilism. That may be understood, just as it may be understood that the extremes tend towards either transcendence or annihilation.

The simple concern here is to spot as a matter of normal experience what first arouses the feeling of horror, and whatever the immediate cause — for that varies — the effect that first brings the feeling into consciousness has to do with an apprehension of the beginning of disintegration. Thus it would seem that to feel whole is a primary need of the self and comes in importance before any consideration of death, immortality or God. Indeed, as has been seen, a man will take a chance on death, and in our age, as likely as not, he believes neither in immortality nor in God.

To translate this into the simple terms of the boy's experience: so long as the second self remains whole he will adventure, take a chance, cunningly avoid or evade, break the rules, spontaneously run his fantastic risks, until he comes to the stone in the river and cracks his nuts.

Disintegration is the loss of this wholeness, and it is hated and feared beyond any other loss, because it alone is ultimate and irreparable. When the will fails here it fails for good, and because its exercise is under one's control, and control implies freedom to choose, its failure is always accompanied by a sense of dark shame. There is no shame in death itself because it is inevitable. The failure of the will is not inevitable, or so one feels, and, feeling so, one is bitterly ashamed.

Chapter 39

Freedom

In the apprehension here of wholeness — in being, at work, on the run to its own delight — we have probably the clearest possible picture of freedom in action. When the boy's acts are fulfilling his wholeness they have the spontaneity of complete freedom. This is freedom itself, the very breath that wholeness breathes. Spontaneity in action is freedom in being, unaware of restrictions. Now freedom *is*.

Any attempt to define this actuality of freedom is an attempt to translate it from being into thought, from the level of wholeness to the level of analysis. An analysis of a living speck of protoplasm reveals all the chemical elements of which it is composed but does not reveal its life. Life eludes the analysis. In fact, the analysis kills the living speck.

Freedom under analysis has a similar end. That is not to deprecate analysis. On the contrary, it is to make clear how wonderful and revealing a probing tool it is. But it has its limitations and by its very nature must work within its limitations, its rules and measurements. Earlier, mention was made of a materialist definition of freedom as the recognition of necessity. But necessity at once introduces the idea of rules and restrictions. And spontaneity by its very nature operates beyond rules and restrictions, is unaware of them, and — if the paradox be allowed — ceases to function when it becomes aware of them; just as life ceases to function when analysis has done its delicate and wonderful best in taking the living cell of matter, the amoeba, to bits.

Now this has to be said in order to make clear once again that the concern here is with something as simple and normal as a boy's experience and the feelings and apprehensions that accompany and arise from such experience, and particularly the feeling of delight. This delight comes from wholeness and is absent in disintegration. As wholeness is experienced spontaneously, in freedom, so is the delight pure; as disintegration proceeds fear takes delight's place, shame leads to horror.

Analytic machinery is always waiting to drag one in and grind one small like the so-called mills of God. Abstract words open its throttle. Freedom, mysticism, dynamism, perception that has by-passed the senses, yoga, the miraculous, second sight. Not to mention the fakes and the fakirs, the cults and the crystal balls. Who can blame reason for doing some pulverizing in the course of proceeding to proof, and enjoying doing it? The thought is refreshing. Reason has its delights, even if they laugh beyond reason. Laughter's response to reason can be specially delicious, like a cultivated palate's to a dry wine.

But though reason may give rise to delight like the exercise of any other faculty, in itself it is not delight. When reason goes beyond its bounds it becomes a cult, a mystique, like any other. This is the point that has to be made. When reason gets going, for instance, in that realm of freedom which spontaneously produces delight it introduces a concept like Necessity, shores it up with syllogisms, adds superstructure like a top hat, until it becomes the new tribal god which explains and orders all from art to economics, and must be worshipped totally. All cults that go grey and puritanical in this fashion ultimately go ruthless. As analysis becomes all it passes over into disintegration.

Thus delight can so easily be overlaid or smothered by cults and mystiques, analyses and techniques, that one has got to take a stand against them and say: This is delightful and that's that! If the word irrational is hurled like an epithet one may reply that the taste of a nut is neither rational nor irrational. However, if it is really an absurd game the hurler wants, then join in with pleasure, for there can be much delight in the absurd; but if it is a disintegrating hunt, then look out!

That most of us can argue at great length about very little is a commonplace. This may even have to be demonstrated further, because two main considerations have for some time been trying to get a final word in edgewise. The first concerns his "wholeness" and the possible dialectical nature of what underlies it. The second concerns the tendency to revert to boyhood, as though the present can always be explained in terms of the past; more than that, as though boyhood (the past) held something happy and glorious which, had it managed long to rule over us, would have made adulthood a different affair; even more than that, as we see in the Freudian concept of religion as a regression to infantile security; and even further than that, until we are swimming in a pre-natal security where the self is part of a greater self in an ineffable manner.

All this looks, and indeed is, extremely complicated, but the normal boy rushes in confidently where the angels of analysis have long lost the fear to tread. His ignorance is bliss and bliss is our subject. So let me say the worst by doubting if there is any underlying dialectical process in the concept of wholeness. It is very tempting to pose integration as thesis, disintegration as anti-thesis, and then combine them in a new synthesis or higher wholeness. It is tempting because it seems to explain progress in terms of history, or history in terms of progress, and anyhow feels ideologically comforting.

Let us take the body by way of simple illustration, and let us take it first in its state of wholeness, in that condition of physical well-being which made the boy race on his toes into the strath of delight. Introduce disease to the body and disintegration sets in. Health and disease (integration and disintegration) fight it out and, let us suppose, health wins. The body is in due course restored to wholeness. But it is not a different kind of wholeness, not a new synthesis, a super-health. It is, with luck, the old wholeness, the physical well-being that raced on its toes, the old blessed feeling — I'm off! I'm away! — once more. There is no "progress". There is the restoring of the wholeness. Any third or synthesis factor does not enter into this eventful duel.

In the psychic realm things seem more tricky because less obvious but the parallel is good enough, if, in fact, it is not implicit (body and mind being of all entanglements the most inextricable). The boy's bliss nut-cracking on the stone was a wholeness for him which was the measure of all wholeness. The utmost that could happen to him in the trials of everyday was to have it restored. Any attempts by his elders at inducing yearnings towards "higher things" vanished at the actual prospect of being off and away to the known place of delight, where salmon were salmon and nuts

nuts. There was a wholeness that was good enough for him and that did not progress in any synthetic manner.

Now — and, of course, solely from the point of view of wholeness — was it very different with the saint in his soul's dark night? Briefly, what the saint desired was to recapture the beatitude which he had lost, to find again Him, who had deserted him. In this beatitude, in God, was the ultimate and unchangeable wholeness.

Accordingly it would appear that the "whole" is in some way more than the equal of its opposite, as health is "more" than illness. Health can as it were so absorb illness within its system that it gets rid of it and thus becomes itself once more. The longer one thinks of the implications here the more elusive they become, until wholeness appears as something permanent and all-pervasive, having bits of itself so to speak at war now and then with illness or disintegrating elements, but overall holding its universal balance in equipoise. That disintegration may itself be a function of integration whereby the "whole" is kept awake and dynamic instead of asleep and dreamless is the kind of dark if lively speculation that can keep thought, in good company, awake to all hours.

However, once it is felt from experience that the ordinary dialectical process is not actually at work, how does it come about that there appears to be progress in the concept of wholeness from the boy's nut-cracking experience to the saint's beatitude? If opposites have not been fighting it out and achieving higher syntheses on the way, what has been happening?

Chapter 40

In the Beginning

Once more we come back to the second self, for only in this coming upon oneself, as earlier described, is the apprehension of wholeness, of harmony, experienced. Perhaps this second self is what others have described as the essence or the soul. I am not too sure. And I have a strong urge to stick to "self" as the only thing I can be sure of. Its recognition partakes of the nature: that I am here now. And the test: that the self does not become self-centred or egotistic but on the contrary expands into wonder. It apprehends a whole greater than itself, but of which itself is part, and in this apprehension is delight's essence.

Now this experience in any life may be rare enough (though every life has experienced it however fugitively) but it is the only kind of experience by which the second self can develop. It may find it in painted pictures and Bach's music, in a running stream or in a raging storm, under the stars or in the room of a house. But — and now we come to a crucial point — it may stop short at nut-cracking on the stone, it may not find itself thereafter, and accordingly there will be no further development or enrichment of it. No experiences of the first self in its contests with everyday affairs, no victories or defeats there, no acquisition of facts or techniques — of worldly knowledge, as we call it — will in themselves have any effect upon the second self except an obscuring effect. This is often quite obvious as in the case of a man of outstanding learning or acquired knowledge who in certain circumstances behaves in a childish way. Such unexpected behaviour, petulance, desire for a childish gratification is always astonishing to those who expect distinction in learning, politics, business, to carry with it a corresponding development in human understanding or wisdom. But that this does not happen is a commonplace, and has in fact from the earliest times been recorded in proverbs and sayings. Sounding brass and tinkling cymbals are familiar epithets.

It may seem, too, as though that which is not developed cannot remain even at its childish level but will tend to atrophy. The experience of the nut-cracking will grow fainter and fainter. But though this has been maintained by wise men from more airts than the East, though the second self does appear to become stunted and malformed and useless as a vermiform appendix, what actually happens, I suspect, is that the early experience of the second self becomes obscured as it sinks into lower levels of the psychic stuff. A man's individual essence is never wholly destroyed. And this can be seen in the familiar case of the worldly adult who suddenly and spectacularly gets "converted". What was obscured now flares up and in its light so much is revealed to him that he experiences "revelation". His behaviour and public utterance will seem wildly extravagant to those who have never been so affected. Presently it may appear even more extravagant and quite shameful to himself as the flare dies down and his first self reasserts itself in its ordinary world. In such a case the experience of the second self from long ago was not strong enough to stand up against the forces, the mass effects, of everyday life now, and its glim was doused by them. But if the second self had gone on developing coincidentally with the first self, then neither the extravagance nor the dousing would have happened, and if anything in the nature of revelation were experienced it would be a permanent enrichment of the second self and as such charged with a fine delight. For where the second self goes on developing in its own sphere, after its own essential nature, then it can make fruitful use of the knowledge acquired by the first self in its world of practical reason, for always and at once it knows the food it thrives on. And it must have food to thrive on.

But possibly it is unnecessary to illustrate this from particular instance or experience, for it is a matter of ordinary observation that a man may have all the book learning in the world and yet be a fool and, conversely, that without book learning a man may be wise.

This leads to our second consideration, to that tendency to revert to boyhood or childhood when the world has become too

much for us and security is craved. This is a familiar picture in all
kinds of mental illness, and psychoanalysts have specialized in
brushing in the detail. Literature, too, has its varied record of
golden boyhood, or of an earlier childhood that railed its clouds
of glory or had its "innocent eye": a nostalgic looking back to an
age of innocence, of wholeness, of bright security, and thus, by
implication, a record of what the adult has lost. The
psychoanalyst, in his thoroughgoing way, takes in the whole field
of human consciousness and unconsciousness and finds that
religion itself is but a craving for this lost security, a regression to
infantilism. In the child's world the living father provided all the
answers and the security; in the religious world the adult created
an Almighty Father to do the same for him, and inevitably created
Him in his own image; and so on — until a semblance of the lost
wholeness has been recaptured.

But even further than that. For how is one to explain that
mysticism which has got beyond the anthropomorphic stage to
an imageless concept of God, to an imageless Godhead of which
the mystic apprehends he is part? The simple answer runs: the
mystic is going back beyond childhood to the foetus in the womb,
where he was in fact part of a whole, where his security was
absolute, and all his wishes were fulfilled. Could any explanation
be neater?

I confess I find it impossible to test this tidy explanation in any
empirical way, and as the empirical is at least always the starting
point here, I can do little about it except say that I have no
memory of what happened in the foetus. Reason boggles
somewhat as the notion of all wishes being fulfilled there, because
unless at least one wish was unfulfilled there could be no
consciousness of wishes at all. And if we extend the reasoning,
consciousness itself seems to vanish. That leaves
unconsciousness, but where there is no consciousness, unconsciousness becomes the reverse side of nothing. However, the
Unconscious has a technical meaning, and even though it cannot
be known to exist until it is brought into consciousness, still there
may be something of it lying doggo in the foetus waiting for
consciousness to be developed after birth when it will be given a
chance of popping up into the said consciousness in some
mysterious or irrational manner; and when later on this cons-

ciousness has developed to a very high degree, into the conscious-ness of the mystic or saint, and had its transcendent experience of communion with God, of being part of the Absolute, all that is really being experience is an unconscious "memory" of the secure and happy condition of being a foetus in the womb.

When we were very young we used the critical comment: If you believe that you'll believe anything! And I confess as I write these words there is an absurd humour about of the order that uses a steam hammer to crack a nut.

However, psychic affairs during foetation may for the best of us be vague enough to permit delightful fancies, but it is quite another story when we come to childhood, to those earliest years of which we can remember quite a lot, if not (by the testimony of neurotics) too much. It is not a question here of doubting the findings of psychoanalysis, but it is suggested that the normal person must find his own feet in the realm of their interpretation or all will remain meaningless to him. That there is no normal person (that mythical average of uncertain human statistics), that we are all abnormal at times or in our fashion, is true, but that very truth helps towards meaning and understanding on the basis that a slight abnormality is an "intimation" of an advanced or even terrific one. Otherwise novelists and psychoanalysts would never have started up in business, not to mention the creator of Hamlet. Children play at being great persons, actors impersonate them, psychotics are them. A great actor embodies his "intimations" with superb physical tact. So, in this matter of assessing the experiences of childhood, the normal person may be allowed his viewpoints.

And the first thing that strikes him is that the psychoanalyst is rather having it both ways. Childhood is such a secure period, with a mother like a cornucopia and a father like God, that its memory in after years unconsciously creates a religion. When the adult has become a battered hulk of sin he regresses to the lullabied comfort and sweet innocence of childhood. But there is a second and somewhat different picture wherein the child is sometimes characterized as a little monster of iniquity, particularly in the matter of sex where he earns the distinction of being a "polymorphous pervert". Far from looking upon his father as God, he regards him as a rival for his mother's favours, and on occasion acts as obstreperously as any other principal in a sex melodrama of any age. He does things of which he is so ashamed that he pushes them down out of sight within himself, as he might push the household kitten, which he had "inadvertently" killed with the poker, into the deepest ditch he could find. Subsequently the sin, like the kitten, may stink, and thus guide detectives to the right spot, whereupon cleansing operations ensue. The unconscious is a very deep and capacious ditch, capable of stowing away any number of forgotten shames or sins and of carefully preserving them, though in a fashion different from that of a deep freeze. When necessary, as it were, the shames can "go wrong". They stink with psychic intention.

But all this is familiar ground. What seems less familiar is the picture of the normal child, that child of whom we are just a little ashamed nowadays, he is so unfashionable, for he doesn't sink into his ditches but takes them like a lively colt, with the independence of a little gentleman or promising gangster or filibustering buccaneer. He can rage, smile, bawl, wheedle, dance with the pounding foot action of primitives upon mother earth, hurl himself into chairs, kick his toys over the hearth, chew them if they are chewable, sing them to sleep, and say his prayers at the end of a perfect day, the little angel. Far from appreciating the security with which his normal parents provide him, he is continuously concerned to outwit them in order to get his own way. From minute to minute he knows what he wants and he wants it in absolute freedom. Security regulations are the bane of his young life, and the cunning with which he attempts to circumvent them is so subtle that his mother, in a simple first move, has been known to interpret the laws of probability fairly accurately by shouting, "Stop it!" As years add strength to his legs, he is off, he is away, as fast as they can carry him, from that paradise of parental security into the strath of freedom. In after years, realizing what good parents he had, he may regret that he did not show a little more appreciation of their patience, forbearance, understanding, kindness. He might have done this for them and he might have done that. But alas! he didn't. And it is too late now. How sad, how very sad! And that is putting things at their best. If the parents were dull, unimaginative, cruel, punitive, selfish, how much less than ever would an early security be recalled from the deep ditch and seem so like paradise that it metamorphozed itself into a religion, with God in the guise of the earthly father!

In this matter of religion, mysticism, God, I should doubt, then, if it is wholly a conjoint affair of the foetus swimming in the altogether and early childhood lapped around in parental security. Such psychoanalytic literature as I have read on this matter has always left me dissatisfied, though satisfied enough with particular case histories or regression to an earlier frame of mind.

But I should find little difficulty in being satisfied with an explanation of mysticism which used as a starting point some such experience as the boy's when nut-cracking on the stone. That would at once seem "very like the thing". The boy would appear to be on the way towards an ultimate experience that though very different in degree or density is still of the same kind. That he never achieved such a degree need not invalidate the contention, any more than being unable to compose a simple tune invalidates appreciation of Bach. Being moved by a simple tune and then playing it on the violin is, perhaps, a little farther on the way, to an appreciation, so to say, of a great violin concerto, inasmuch as it includes the acquired skill of the hand beyond the impulse of the body. But enough may have been already said in this connection to permit the suggestion that the mystical experience has its roots in an early actual experience rather than in any hypothetical "experience" by the "unconscious" in a floating foetus.

Analysis of course will always find a little of something in everything, for its aim is to analyse back or dissect out as far as it can. At the moment it has got as far back as the nucleus of the atom or those cosmic rays from outer space now being studied in elevated laboratories. So, as it were, why stop at the foetus? Why not go back to the amoeba that is not only all on its own but is lapped around by the security regulations of the universe, and, moreover, by the simple act of fission enjoys with luck an eternal existence? At least — no death. But why stop at the amoeba? Why not go right back to those electrical particles that constitute the atom and in the attraction-repulsion method of their behaviour provide rather startlingly an indication of the pleasure-pain principle of our master psychoanalyst?

But Freud stops short in the infinite regress, as we all have to do when dealing with human experience. Even Kierkegaard, that artist of Despair, decided that the Hegelian "concrete universal" was a cloud-palace not meant for living in.

So let us get back to living, which at the end of all talk is the sum total of what we can do; and in particular, with so much philosophic despair around, let us extract what delight has been left in the living act, and if that means extracting or creating God out of our delight at least it is a change from creating Him out of our despair. Changes, according to the best old women, are lightsome, and some old women appear nearer God than the philosophers whose systems are either closed in the grand old style or systemless and wide open in the existentialist new.

Chapter 41

A New Adventure

In the act of living we know what happens, what gives delight and the kind of delight it gives. Any philosophy or ideology that attempts "to argue us out of it" is by that very fact suspect, for it switches us from the actual experience to its analysis, to quite another kind of game.

If the boy's experience on the stone gives him an indication of the nature of the mystical experience so may it also of the nature of religion generally and, in particular, of God the imageless. Let this be considered a little further, for there is an ambivalence in the actual process of the experience which provides, in the normal way, the all important sense of balance or wholeness.

Far within, the boy comes upon himself. Surprise, wonder — here I am in this place; me — here. The me is hardly imaged at all though its form, even perhaps the expression of its face, may be "glimpsed". This may be regarded as the introverted movement from the everyday of the first self towards the deep centre of the second self. A whirlpool on the surface of the sea or on a pool in a river has its central vortex going deep. But once the second self is come upon, the rare delight of the experience sets up a counter motion outwards and upwards. In the old Gaelic myth, the small whirlwind that picked up the dust on the roadway was the passing of a spirit or soul. That vortex of air widened towards the sky. The outward motion of the second self has this feeling of extension, extension within that which contains it. The double motion towards centrality and towards universality balances itself in a conscious experience of wholeness and therefore of delight.

The description of the mechanics of a psychological experience, even with the use of words like introversion and extraversion, can at best do no more than provide an intimation or indication of what actually happens. But perhaps enough has been said to permit the suggestion now that as the second self becomes self-aware and thereupon passes outward into that which is greater than itself but of the same kind, at that moment an apprehension of the universal nature of religion, of the imageless God, is born. Any particular religion, any specific form (conceptual or anthropomorphic) of God may be an "accident" of history, but only because that which creates such forms is implicit in the psychic stuff. Whatever our attitude to communicating the incommunicable, even to ourselves, there is always that which by its nature must forever make the effort. Both the extent and the density of the effort will depend on the second self, but whether the second self is at the nut-cracking stage or at the saint's stage, the experience will be of a similar nature, will be on the same way.

I am aware that all this, in view of the tragic complexity of life, may have the air of a too obvious simplification, that the use of a boy's experience may seem little more than a trick for by-passing that complexity. Whereas there may be something in this, it should also be remembered that Freud resolved some of the darkest adult complexities by searching out their roots in childhood. We are not concerned here with psychic abnormalities, but with the normal in its moment of delight. Where that delight tends to get smothered by the complexities, the rediscovery of it becomes a new adventure and necessarily an adventure in the first place towards its source. Where the complexities involve, as they do today, a questioning, tacit or otherwise, of old standards — in religion, philosophy, art, literature, in all that the individual experiences and feels — then the adventure becomes more important than ever if delight is to be saved and, in the process, some clear recognition obtained of the smothering forces.

The nut-cracking on the stone has been frequently mentioned in an attempt to keep an involved matter as simple and clear as possible and not because of uniqueness in itself. I should fancy that an effort by any memory to "think back" into childhood or early boyhood would provide moments of a similar kind. If at first blush this should seem a startling notion, it is no doubt because in the first moment of entertaining it a certain startling does occur in the hinterland of mind or memory, an undefined flurry as of invisible wings around an invisible dovecot. Did one or did one not have such a tranced moment of delight when one found oneself there in that place? And even if one cannot think all at once of any particular moment or place it is yet as if the vague hinterland were stirred with wings.

Baulked completely, one may call this an absurd deception, a poetic fancy, or just sheer nonsense. But in doing so one merely gives the measure of one's distance from the hinterland, for the first self in its interactions with everyday can overlay the second self so densely that little or nothing comes through. Some esoteric philosophers think that the second self (or essence, or by whatever name they call it) can become stunted or atrophied like any other unused faculty, though it rather seems to me, as has already been said, that it sinks out of sight, beyond voluntary recall, in the psychic stuff; in any case, that it never withers away entirely, but, elementary as it was (like the nut-cracking experience), continues to remain so, and in some strange or unusual circumstance — as in "an act of grace" — may erupt through the everyday crust of the first self with startling effect.

But is there no method of checking by observation this question of deception? There is, by simply watching any child having his own way. Now the fascinating thing about the normal child when acting high and handsome, when spontaneity and freedom are one and the same yet never anarchic because the action is towards the attainment of delight, resides in this, that the *total* child is engaged: the mind, the body, and the skills that parts of the body have learned. Here is a wholeness that hasn't to be thought, it simply is, and when it thrills to its highest achievement its delight is absolute. As we have seen, this three-in-one can be broken down in the adult world into the skill of the hand as in archery, of the mind as in Zen, and of the body generally in sensual delight. But the child has not yet attained the reflective or analytic stage, there is no consciousness of any need to break down; which means that his second self, the essence of him as an individual child, has not yet been overlaid. The three-in-one finds delight not in reflection, but in action, in an utmost expenditure of energy, recalling Blake's line, "Energy is Eternal Delight".

That something like this happens — and more than this — is a matter of experience. It is not a deception. Any question of deception must be searched for in what goes to make memory defective.

Again, this matter of deception can so to speak be checked in reverse, as the pupil found when taking lessons in archery from the Zen Master, for the fascinating element here is the approach to wholeness (to total engagement, to Unity) through the skill of the hand as an extension of the "wisdom" of the body, and not directly through the exercise of the mind in austerity or contemplation. Here the three are being reintegrated into the child's three-in-one *on the adult level*. This is not a regression to childhood but a deliberate and very difficult effort to achieve wholeness among the "broken-down" or separated elements of adulthood. In direction it is not a passive sinking back but an active going on. And the wisdom of the Zen Master, I suspect, consists in refinding some measure of the wholeness of the child or the boy in action as an indication of the onward way for the adult. *Reculer pour mieux sauter* is a normal procedure for the athlete about to take a jump or putt the shot. That the fast bowler recoils upon himself quite a distance before rushing and even hurling himself forward is a fact which the expectant batsman does his best to observe. If I dare speak from my solitary experience, the aim of the fast bowler is to make the ball invisible to the batsman. Great batsmen have been clean bowled. The attempt to make a round, hard, fierce object invisible begins to approach metaphysical if not magical categories, particularly when viewed from the Zen angle. For example, a great batsman could hit for six a ball which an ordinary batsman would, as we say, never have seen. Yet if their eyesight, muscles, playing experience and so on were tested no material disparity might be found between them.

The best writer on games I know, J. B. Pick, recently summed up this matter by asking me: What would happen if a Zen master bowler was faced by a Zen master batsman?

At once the body took over and hit thought out of sight for laughter. Somehow the humour seemed richer than in the schoolmen's difficulty over the number of angels that could stand on the point of a needle. Its hinterland is dark with mysterious illuminations. After all, the Master did hit the invisible target in the centre of the bull, and to prove it wasn't a fluke he split the first arrow with the second. When the light was switched on, the target with its two arrows was examined with a physical particularity that could not be applied to angels. "It" did it, said the master; and whatever kind of ultimate wholeness or harmony "It" may be, at least the thing was done. And the pupil, having seen, began to learn the way. By comparison, the visible needle and the invisible angels present a mixture of categories on the road to nowhere. Even as a game its humour grows thin as the point of a needle, and at the back of a child's mind there might be some compassion for the angels' feet.

But discussion on the practical Zen level becomes inexhaustible. We found it delightful, fantastic, surprising — and even understandable that the Master should be bored by it — though we were possibly getting a bit ahead by that time. For clearly discussion of the how and the why never adds up to the "It" that sticks the actual arrow in the target. No amount of analysis, no exercise of determinism based on statistical elements of things past, will help here.

Possibly "It" partakes of the nature of that spontaneity which contains within itself the notion of freedom. Freedom may be an ambiguous word, but its nature is at least indicated, as has been suggested, in the spontaneity of the whole child in achieving its delight. Without consciously thinking or striving, "It" is achieved, spontaneity comes into its own, the arrow lands in the bull. Musical composers, scientists, painters, writers, know how in the midst of their striving "It" takes charge, strife ceases, and the "marked passage" is born. In that moment of delight freedom is known; as, not to be high falutin, its rare moment is known in archery, cricket and putting the shot, not to mention the way a rosebush looked at the boy when he had landed his fish.

The future remains open to this kind of freedom. Through freedom the adventure continues. The way goes into the future, and the end of it cannot be known. One can know it only as far as one has gone. Freedom has its growth like the second self, and along with the growth of the second self.

Chapter 42

Words and Reason

All words concerned with the second self and its growth must in some measure be ambiguous. "In some measure" because the ambiguity will vary according to the stages of growth. Thus among those of about equal growth it will be neglible; between those at a distance it will be considerable. The words of one who has gone far in development will mean little to him whose second self was overlaid or sank out of sight at an early age. Then, again, before the words are used at all they are saturated with the past. Thus there can never be exactitude here, as in mathematics, for even if an attempt were made to define the words precisely, the meaning of the definitions themselves would vary according to the development of those entertaining them. There is no way of getting past this difficulty. Even when one tries to help towards meaning by devising a fairly concrete term and giving it direction over and above, like "interiority", it will convey much more to the introvert than to the extravert. To the extravert it may signify an unnecessary brooding or abnormality; to a Kierkegaard it may open up a subtly inexhaustible and attractive underworld of dread and despair. I find, for example, that I may appear to have used the words mystic and saint as if they were interchangeable, whereas on each occasion I have been prompted to use them by my own apprehension of them. An attempt at defining this apprehension would disclose the saint as one whose second self has gone on growing, such growth being always a growth in wisdom, and the mystic as one who has had his experience of wholeness or Unity without (necessarily) an equivalent growth of wisdom. To wisdom comes naturally an apprehension of wholeness; to the mystic it comes sporadically. But even already I am running counter to some accepted meanings, both East and West — as in the case of the adolescent who having had a mystical experience is canonized by a Christian Church as a saint.

But my single intention in such rough word-play is to suggest that any philosophic system, or closed system of ideas, purporting to explain the universe, does little more than intimate the nature and degree of development of its creator's psychic stuff. But there *is* this intimation to those who according to their development will apprehend it. Despite verbal ambiguities, communication is made, and any communication from the second self is always potent as an experience. Similarly in music and the arts communication is made, though its nature here is non-verbal, and possibly most potent at its most wordless.

Thus any closed system will tend to lose its absoluteness as the second self feeds on it and passes along the way to which there can be no end, although at any given moment of experiencing whole-ness, there is "an end", which is yet an intimation of "no end". This may appear paradoxical, a fusion of opposites, of time in the timeless, and so on in the high metaphysical manner, but *as an experience* it is quite normal and perfectly delightful. Once more — it is the experience that matters. And every man has had his "perfect moment of delight". The rest is talk — and in its way can be delightful too *if* the talk illuminates the experience, for the experi-ence is as it were thereby given density, the second self is enriched, and the chances are increased of another moment of delight farther on. If, on the other hand, the talk is an analytical exercise of reason then its tendency will be to explain away the moment of delight, to say "That is all it is" — and the delight may well vanish, as life from the analysed amoeba. For analysis of this kind tends towards that disintegration which we have earlier considered.

Admittedly, the talk that illuminates may also be a kind of analysis in that it may single out elements or attitudes in the delight, but it does so always as active elements or attitudes in the continuing whole, and if perfectly done would evoke the delight itself. In this sense the talk is creative, not destructive. Thus to be evocative is art's high aim.

That there should be "no end" to the way is obviously a worry to many, including philosophers who would like their systems to enclose, to explain, the scheme of things entire, to have all ideas in the Ideal, to achieve Perfection in which are no loose ends.

But why should "no end" be a worry? In the ordinary way of life far from being a worry it is a spur or inspiration. To do better than one has done in a game, in art, in scientific research, in business, in growing roses or breeding canaries, gives "a zest to life", makes "time all too short". The real worry is that there is an end. If only one could live long enough to make the extra discovery, to find what is round the corner! For clearly there are remarkable discoveries ahead, some startling finds round the corner. "No end" is a rich country, with life still its enigma and death its mystery. One can give up or go on. It is one's own choice.

After the choice is made, it may be contended that the choice was inevitable, that it was predetermined. But determinism is always wise after the psychic event. And being wise after the event is tantamount to saying that it happened because it happened. If determinism were really omniscient it would be wise before the event. But determinism, as a rational process, cannot be wise before the event if the event embraced the exercise of non-rational factors, including those incalculable upsurges from the Unconscious, or from the intromissions of archetypes in the Collective Unconscious, not to mention ongoings in weird realms where perceptions are extra-sensory in a way that would have shaken Hume to his Edinburgh roots and may yet produce another kind of smile on the face of a physicist. To provide for all this (and the still unknown more) determinism would have to be omniscient, and omniscience of this order is as unknowable as God, of whom it is accordingly postulated as an attribute. The materialism which makes use of determinism finds itself, if taken far enough along its own way, in ideal country.

But the simple point here is that any system of thought must be limited because it is achieved by rational means and man is more than reason. To despair because we cannot prove the existence of God, the certainty of immortality — or because we cannot disprove them — is to despair because reason cannot do more than its limited best. Does one despair in a moment of delight because the delight is experienced without any exercise of reason? This is not to disparage reason or intellect and opt wholly for the dark gods, the irrational flesh. Once reason's sphere of action is clearly seen, its wonder shines in a marvellous way, and continues to shine when ideal systems vanish. But reason is not the flesh, any more than it is a Beethoven quartet or a mystical experience. The quartet or the experience isn't an "ideal", it's a fact. So is delight, so is the wisdom of a wise man, so is the exercise of the hand on a violin tailpiece or in cracking a nut on a stone.

In the same way, freedom is a fact while it is being experienced. Afterwards analysis in its familiar fashion will attempt to rationalize it, to find its determinants, but if the determinants are non-rational the attempt must fail, and accordingly any "explanation" will *appear* to explain away. One might say that as analysis destroys life in the amoeba so it destroys spontaneity in freedom. And if all this may look like an exercise in reason — I hope it does — at least it is directed towards indicating reason's sphere of action. For reason by its very nature will make an effort to work in all spheres, and though this is one of its most valuable urges it has got to be watched or presently it begins to develop the familiar arrogance of the dictator and pooh-poohs what is beyond its power to grasp, then inhibits or suppresses it, until finally whole fishing fleets of psychiatric rig, afloat on couches and other clinical barges, using archetypal and other weird hooks, are engaged, both on inshore and deep sea grounds, fishing up hysteric monsters, with names like obsessive neurosis or manic-depressive psychosis, in order to give them a breath of fresh air, the air that we take for granted in the strath of freedom.

All of which reason, in one or other of its guises, will again promptly pooh-pooh, for reason is extraordinarily cunning, particularly when it dresses up to play a part under the solemn and sincere impression that the part is the whole play. Thus freedom will mean little or nothing to the moralist unless it is moral freedom; to the psychologist, psychological freedom. Now we enter into the books, the libraries and the systems, the territory of the qualifying adjective: fascinating country, if only one didn't keep tripping over the adjectives. But I cannot begin to look at this territory here, beyond remarking that adjectives like solemn, sincere, moral, psychological (how they started to crop up!) have no relevance in the actual experience of freedom, in the child's spontaneity, the boy's nut-cracking, the mathematical physicist inside the atoms, the mystic apprehending Unity, the wise man realizing that wisdom widens beyond him, not to mention the experience of composers, poets, archers, cricketers, jumpers, and putters of the shot. Even in golfing the adjectives come afterwards.

This freedom is an experience of wholeness and in the wholeness is delight. This delight is being continuously filched from us. But we have had our moments. On such moments the second self feeds and is encouraged to go on towards experiencing similar moments of a richer nature. That the second self (essence or soul — no matter the name) acts or develops in a way that reason calls non-rational (when it is being polite) merely means that reason cannot explain how it acts. But it acts in its own way, in its own right and in its own freedom. The old schoolmen had the word intellect for this kind of action or apprehension. But reason has tended to collar intellect in our time, and inutition is the sort of word that reason boggles or goggles at in a squint that is always driving the poor thing underground, and, characteristically, not a rebellious but a disreputable underground. For reason knows that we all want to have reason on our side. But once we have seen reason plain, we can use it as the wonderful tool it is, and then get on with the real business of being alive along the way whose milestones are momentary or timeless experiences of being whole — mind, body and hand — in the delight that is memorable and breathe an immemorial air.

How ambiguous words are can be tested by directing reason upon a few of them in that last paragraph — or in any paragraph, for that matter. Endless analysis might give an infinite series of approximations towards "meaning", much as arithmetical subdivisions of space give an unending series of approximations in Achilles' race to overtake the tortoise. But a man who has never given a thought to any infinite series will go to a horse race, put his money on his fancy and get the full thrill of a photo finish. The writer, like the horses, does his best in a context wide enough to imply in any paragraph, he hopes, the nature of his steeplechase.

The poet has a way of mounting himself on a paradox or symbol when he comes to a hurdle, for his leap — to him, hopefully, always a new leap — is, as we say, into the unknown. The more hurdles of this sort the better. He lives for them, and a clean leap is his joy. "He's a grand lepper," said an Irishman to me with glory in his eye for the horse we had put our money on.

But how impossible to convey in rational terms the meaning even of the simple paradox! In his *Psychology and Alchemy*, C. J. Jung writes: ". . . the paradox is one of our most valued spiritual

possessions, while uniformity of meaning is a sign of weakness."
"Non-ambiguity and non-contradiction are one-sided and thus
unsuited to express the comprehensible." and he quotes
Tertullian: "And the Son of God is dead, which is worthy of
belief because it is absurd. And when buried He rose again which
is certain because it is impossible."

Immediately I read such words I have the usual urge to put
reason's gloss on some of them. Thus, any logical process is
incapable of expressing the incomprehensible, but the
incomprehensible would convey nothing at all on any level unless
it were apprehensible on the level of experience — for example,
within the non-rational region of the second self. I seem to get
some sense of design now and attempt to convey it — as a
statement of experience, not as a piece of logic.

The poet's paradoxes and symbols are statements of
experience. When his hurdle is between the first and the second
self his statement is a startling leap to those in the first self, even
an incomprehensible leap; hence critical adjectives like obscure,
ambiguous, absurd. Which is not to say that a poet cannot make
himself obscure or even absurd without having had any traffic
with his second self. Reason or intellect can use esoteric words or
terms in a design more difficult than any crossword puzzle.
Indeed he could drop the words or terms in a hat, then pick them
out at random and for a time flummox us. And the trick would
flummox because the esoteric words or terms, carrying with them
some vestige of real experience from an earlier or original usage,
would have a vague "something" for the second self of the reader.
But the trick does not last long. What does not come from the
poet's own experience is soon detected. There is always a second
self that knows. An experience by the second self is a unified
experience and never ambiguous.

Chapter 43

The Evil Eye

Reading in the same book by Jung, I come on this expression: "Human wholeness is the goal to which the psychotherapeutic process ultimately leads." I admit I first used the word wholeness here because at the moment I could not think of a better. It seemed to denote the tangible within a boy's experience, the rounded fullness of a football or a fruit. In a way difficult to explain I realize that I have been continuously prompted by this need to meet the boy's experience; to eschew abstract words not so much because they are vague as because they are sticky, as though tradition had condensed them into an aerated glue that raps the wings of delight, the boy's spontaneous delight; to apprehend the freshness, the newness, of the world, wherein an experience can be a wonder, and a memorable wonder when it pauses, and the boy comes upon himself in the heart of it almost shyly as upon a stranger; to be concerned with what happens, with the happening rather than with the meaning. Possibly an underlying prompter has been concerned to give even an autobiographic fragment some sort of design as though, haunted by the old feeling "this is not what matters", the prompter had to find from experience what did matter. But as the prompter is no longer the boy, though he includes the boy, what did matter will also tend to be what does matter. What mattered and what matters will be on the same way. The selective process, forever active in whatever man does or makes, will see to that, even though it be as non-rational as a coral polyp.

Possibly, too, there is a didactic process at work which may be a concealed communal process — our old need to communicate and thereby enjoy participation in the tribal warmth. This is a very ancient and a very deep need, as fundamental in politics as in psychotherapy. In philosophy as in love it is the recognition of the Other over against one's own aloneness or loneliness. In communal life it is quite simply the recognition of the others, the need to be one with them and to enjoy the work and games, to contribute what one can to increase the mutual delight. The didactic note could be found in the useful comment by any one to any other: Why cut off your nose to spite your face? Why destroy delight in so absurd a way? Why destroy the wholeness of your face, such as it is? When a whole community goes in for such destructiveness, then the elements of delight have to be found again: the therapeutic process back to wholeness, of which delight is the flower. Otherwise continuing destruction, disintegration, death, and, conceivably, if we may believe the scientists, universal death.

I hardly know of a problem in living, however discussed by the most brilliant intellects, that has not been a problem for the primitive or superstitious tribe. Let us look, for example, at that somewhat philosophic statement about the recognition of the Other beyond one's loneliness. It has been searched out in an unusually vivid way by Jean-Paul Sartre. It becomes so vivid indeed that the Other by looking at you drains your virtue away. It is as though you are yourself and whole in your fashion, until the other person's eye looks at you and you feel your coherence going. The power of the Look. The disintegrating force of the Eye. Many have experienced something of this look in an occasional human eye. It may even have made one stutter or stammer. But to Sartre every Other has this kind of eye. The Other is not thought of as a particular individual, not even as man, woman or child, but just the Other with the power of the Eye, the power that takes the substance out of you.

To the community in which the boy was brought up "the evil eye" was not some hypersensitive extension of a subtle apprehension into a philosophic universalism but something as real as rupture or influenza or delusions. It acted not only on the mind but on the body. And not only on a human body but on, say, a cow's body. It could either dry up the cow or take "the substance" out of her milk. And being as real as this, the folk proceeded empirically to find effective techniques against its maleficent exercise. They achieved ways of putting the substance back in the milk.

But perhaps here, once more, an experience should be given. And the boy remembers the experience quite vividly though he must have been very young at the time. One morning the skipper of a fishing boat on his way to the harbour to put to sea encountered "the witch", the one person in the district who had "the evil eye". He returned home and in low tones discussed the encounter with his wife. The boy cannot remember the actual words used, but he can remember their tone, their air of quiet mystery. To have gone to sea now would have been dangerous. Afterwards the boy discovered that there were skippers who would not have gone to sea *that day* and so have ensured themselves against any chance of disaster. But he knew nothing about such mysteries at the time for they were not readily discussed, just as the name of the Lord God was not taken in vain. However, what next happened was this. After the man and the woman had said their words to each other in a communion that was extraordinarily close, the man sat down on a wooden kitchen chair and lifted his feet off the flagstone floor, held them in the air for a short time, then, firmly planting them on the floor again, got up and proceeded to sea.

For some obscure reason the boy never mentioned this incident to anyone and so never discovered what underlay, if it was rationally known, the lifting of the feet. But clearly it had to do with severing one's connection with the earth and then finding it again in a fresh beginning.

So the power of the evil eye, the Eye that in looking dissipates "substance", has been known from the beginning. But the difference between what I may call the Parisian milieu and the primitive one is that in the latter the evil eye belonged as a rule only to one person. To the skipper his wife was the Other, and vice versa, but in their case the eye of the One enriched and reinforced the substance of the Other. This was shown in action: not in theory but in the act. And the act was effective. So the boy found it in his relations with other boys, with girls, with grownups. The communal warmth, with the "evil eye" completely absent. That happened, and even if it had happened only once, even if the skipper and his wife had enriched each other's substance only on that solitary occasion, still it would have been enough to fracture any Parisian theory about the Other and his

Eye. Indeed if it had been suggested that in a certain Parisian milieu everyone had the evil eye, the Highland community wouldn't have believed it on the basis that nature does not work in that way, not as a going concern. Any Parisian troubled with such a notion might have been advised to go home quietly, have a talk with his wife, and lift his feet off the kitchen floor. And if he hadn't a home of his own and a real wife, still he could go to his café and have a small affair with a chair there. One never knows! That would be the empirical approach.

However, as an exercise in the macabre the notion of every eye being an evil eye might have been conceivable. But the Parisian group or community would then have been seen as dark, backward and very primitive — fecklessly primitive in not having developed a technique for dealing with the evil. There would have been no surprise on finding that the leaders of such a group considered nature disgusting and the body vile, particularly in their writings, which would accordingly be records of cruelty, destruction, perversions. For taking the substance out of the milk of human kindness is a mere pastime compared with taking it out of the milk of a cow. As experts, the old primitives would not have been impressed by the new.

If this may seem a somewhat elaborate comparison between the two groups, at least its intention is to indicate how delight can get smothered by the extension of an "evil" in an introverted way. The intellectual brilliance that can not only examine but also express in words such extension is no doubt a vast development upon the dumbness of the primitive, but neither volubility nor dumbness as such qualifies the "reality" of the Eye in its baleful exercise of extracting substance. As before, high enough tribute cannot be paid to intellectual brilliance, to the modern exercise of reason as appreciated by us, but that very reason should also prevent our overlooking what actually happened when the "dumb" primitive encountered the evil eye. Presumably the primitive had reasons which our reason knows little of, because he not only in his own way observed and studied the evil, but then, unlike the Parisian tribesman, went on to develop successful techniques for countering it. He was empirical and inductive in a fashion that is still supposed to distinguish the British approach to philosophy or reality from the Continental. Anyhow, he kept the substance in the milk.

With the substance in the milk, there is warmth in life, delight in living. Without it there isn't. Without it there is the depressive phase in living, when words like substance, delight, elation, connubial bliss, goodness, happy endings, communal warmth, connote conditions of being so disgusting that an urge to jeer at and destroy them is strongly felt. An articulate person who has survived prolonged attacks of manic-depressive psychosis can describe — has described — the experience in detail. In the swing from elation to depression he can forecast when he will want to spit upon what so recently entranced him in goodness or in simple delight. Psychotherapy thereupon proceeds to do its best to mend the psychic split with the "substance" and so restore that "human wholeness" which Jung describes as "the goal", and which the manic-depressive himself realizes is the goal, the ultimately desirable state.

Lest such "explanation" should appear to have a complacent air, I touch wood. I lift my feet off the floor. Antaeus, the wrestler, by landing on his feet, renewed his contact with the earth mother and was refreshed with substance and invincible strength. I would hesitate here to offer a technique of the most primitive kind to anyone. Yet if depressed Parisians of a certain existentialist kind were to start lifting their feet off café floors, leaping in the air, cavorting down appropriate thoroughfares, I should be profoundly interested in the result. It would certainly stagger the Eye.

Not any explanation, not a technique, but perhaps for the moment the simple injunction — don't let them filch delight. Always come back to that, to: I have had delight; I know it; and when I speak of wholeness, I know what I mean. Sure, so far, one goes dogged against the disrupters, from the compulsive authoritarian to the depressive nagger, the squirter of malice, for always with luck there is further adventure ahead.

Chapter 44

The Contemporary Situation

Such apparent concentration on the "I", such inwardness towards a very elusive second self, may appear an escape from "the real world", from "the contemporary situation", but it will only so appear to the first self. It is impossible to escape from the contemporary situation because one is in it, but it is possible to question any particular or accepted assessment of it. Thus when Socrates had pondered the oracle: Know thyself, his assessment of the contemporary situation was so thorough that it led him to the poison bowl. It was not Christ's escape from the contemporary situation that led Him to the Cross, it was his assessment of it. Such profound assessments have affected every contemporary situation ever since. Than this no more can be said on the highest level.

But on the ordinary level much can be said in an ordinary way. Let the literary level be taken as a single example, seeing we have had some traffic there already. When the poet is accused of escaping to his ivory tower he is being condemned for deserting the contemporary situation and taking refuge in illusion. But by whom? If the accuser is held so fast in the contemporary situation that all outside of it is illusion, then he himself is in his own ivory tower or his steel-and-concrete one. There is no more rigid tower than that which a businessman or politician or führer can inhabit; any assessment of it other than his own is to him unreal. The rigidity of his tower is all but absolute. But whether an ivory or a steel-and-concrete tower, a new assessment of it can come only from outside, from beyond the everyday of the first self.

But even within the literary scene, where the second self is not unknown, the same capacity for assessment will inevitably be exercised. There is no escape from being *engagé*. M. Sartre may have found nature disgusting and the body loathsome, but D. H.

Lawrence had quite other findings. The Zen master, beginning
with the hand and the arrow, as the boy with the nut and the
stone, brought "It" to his assessment. The intellect, the body, the
hand. The trio enrich the capacity for assessment. Lawrence
endeavoured to give back its own delight to the body made
disgusting or impotent by intellect, so that even the very thought
of his effort is permeated by the sensation of the body's freedom,
as in the boy's I'm off! I'm away! The essence of what he was after
is selected and retained by the apprehension of wholeness. That
this essence knows itself is made clear by the way in which it at
once attempts to express itself in reply to any chance criticism or
assessment of Lawrence. It knows beforehand as it were what it
wants to say — if only it could find the words. And finding the
words is the old game of approximations.

Again, nature may have been found disgusting by some
modern writers but not by a writer like John Cowper Powys, for
whom it opens up a realm of inexhaustible adventure with his
senses attuned to the subtlest emanations and influences, from the
pre-human, the non-human, to the human eye beholding, to the
forehead on the cool lichened stone — and, preferably, a stone in
Stonehenge. The wind and the rain. The elements. The Zen
master? But what about the Druid, explaining over and over how
to look at a shaft of sunlight on a bedroom wall or a flower box
on a window ledge in a dreary street? Not vague optimisms, but
efforts in subtle skills. Not games with arrows and balls, but
techniques all the same for apprehensions of exquisite delights,
that are ancient and known in regions which, from causes given,
are all but smothered. How crude, how blind the word
"disgusting" now, an emanation of a grey puritanism in thought
that, by implication at least, holds the ideal of the non-disgusting,
an ideal that, analysed far enough, can hardly fail to appear as an
inverted sentimentality.

Indications of this kind can only be partial and may appear to
distort, but possibly they serve to show how what I have been
concerned with in these pages, far from being an escape from is a
commitment to (in this instance) the contemporary literary
situation; out of its essence it prompts assessment and exercises
choice among its writers. That it should have landed by the way
on John Cowper Powys may indicate how individual the choice

can be for his name was not found in books by eminent critics on the important writers of our time. But how unerringly he comes upon himself in the moment of delight!

Chapter 45

Tamám Shud

And so I am back at the beginning, at books and their "marked passages", even at the key for which memory can provide no lock. It is not so much that there is a door to which we can find no key as that we have an urge to find the door for which we fancy we have a skeleton key. But when the last metaphor or fancy has been stripped off, the urge is left in the psychic stuff and knows itself. Whether we like it or not, it is there, as the radioactive atom to the physicist. Knowing itself, it knows the direction towards gratification; and it knows it is truly on the way in that moment when the experience of wholeness provides its rare delight.

Metaphor, or analogy with the physical, may help, but vaguely and only up to a point. Thus the radioactive atom of material stuff may be said to fulfil itself in the moment of its disintegration, in the moment of its "death", but the radioactive atom of the psychic stuff fulfils itself in a moment of wholeness, which, though it may seem to be "an end", is presently apprehended as an intimation of a further experience of wholeness along the same way. To say that the way has "no end" is but to say that the adventure is open.

To pursue the adventure here would be to take it from the boy's world to the adult world, and this I confess I had intended to do, for in my mind were experiences which ordinary men and women had revealed in rare moments; for so intimate a revelation is made uncertainly, secretly, and always with a strangely glowing surprise at an understanding response. But I now realize that this would mean something like a fresh beginning after clearing one's feet from the digressions of boyhood (the digressions that seemed "by the way" until insensibly they became "on the way"). To examine these experiences and, if possible, re-evoke their elements might, it had seemed to me, have interest, not in support of some theory or system, but in recognition of what happens, what is, of the happening that in its wholeness has delight as its radioactive atom.

But doubtless that would not only lead into deeper consideration of the "second self", a "higher intelligence", but in particular, and on the basis that it is the experience, the empirical, that primarily matters, into an examination of those destructive or disintegrating forces that seem so wantonly to destroy delight in living; and beyond that, if possible, into suggestions of means for countering them. But that seems so large if not impossible a task that it would be more than has been earned at this point if the boy has given intimations of it.

Afterword: Highland Zen*
by Alan Spence

* A fuller version of this appeared in New Edinburgh Review, Summer 1982 as a review
of *A Highland Life* by F.R. Hart and J.B. Pick.

The last part of Gunn's life was when he turned from the writing
of books. J. B. Pick puts this down to a combination of
circumstances, among them "lack of enthusiasm from his
publishers, lack of attention from the critics, lack of
understanding from his readers . . . concern for matters which he
knew quite certainly were beyond the interest of his former
public."

The books which provoked this response, or lack of it, were the
later novels and the "spiritual autobiography", *The Atom of
Delight*. Of all Gunn's books, *The Atom of Delight* is the one I
have re-read most often, returning to it again and again for its
clarity, its lucidity, its depth. No ordinary autobiography, it is, as
Pick suggests, reflective philosophy, yet grounded firmly in what
he had seen for himself and knew to be true. The light it throws
back on the novels is considerable. In it he distils to an essence
what he had been saying in the novels all along, in behind the
narrative. And yet, saddened by the reception of *The Atom of
Delight*, he wrote no more books. He did write a few articles, in
the same vein, for the *Saltire Review*, but according to Pick, these
were received with "something like embarrassed bewilderment,
and the myth grew that Neil Gunn had retreated into esoteric
nonsense."

This of course is the all too familiar Scottish response, "Neil
Gunn a mystic? Awa wi ye man, ah kent his faither!" And there
is a pervading sense among critics that Gunn's later work was
somehow "tainted" by his interest in Zen. For instance, Maurice
Lindsay, in his *History of Scottish Literature* has it that Gunn's
"increasing preoccupation with . . . Zen Buddhism blurred his
practical sense of purpose", and talks of Gunn's "retreat into a
personal mysticism."

I'm suggesting that there's another view that can be taken; that in the later works, and particularly in *The Atom of Delight*, Gunn was coming closer than at any time to expressing the true essence of his profound vision, and that he himself was closer to the heart of it at this stage of his life, the work reflecting the insights, the flashes and glimpses of truth experienced in his "contemplation". His *true* sense of purpose, far from being blurred, was never sharper. As for his "retreat" into mysticism, I prefer to think of it as an ascent, pathfinding, showing the way. (The joke is of course, that Gunn didn't like being called a "mystic", and in this he displayed a true Zen spirit.)

In *The Atom of Delight* Gunn has a passing word for the critic who has not had what he calls "the glimpse". For Gunn, what such a critic has to say "can manifestly have no relevance in this region of experience. When the glimpse is the touchstone anything less is nothing."

And what does he mean by "the glimpse"? Perhaps one of the clearest examples in his writing is to be found in *The Well at the World's End*, in a passage which is directly autobiographical.

On holiday in France, Gunn, had almost drowned, been rescued by a friend, and woke the next morning with "a pleasant feeling of lightness." He crossed to the window and found himself looking out over an old Spanish garden. What he experienced next, he described as follows:

> *It was now that the odd feeling came over me that the stillness itself was holding something, much as the walls held the garden; and in a moment I realised that what it was holding was time. Time was stopped, not by any kind of magic or enchantment, but actually . . . Quite simply, then, I knew with an absolute conviction . . . that there exists an order of things outside our conception of time . . . There was nothing at all in the ordinary sense 'religious' about this experience; but what is astonishing, I think, is that there was nothing personal . . . as I sat down . . . I was overcome by a divine, a delicious sense of humour.*

Here, described with a beautiful simplicity and directness, is the "timeless moment", epiphany, what in Zen is termed *Satori*, a sudden awakening to reality, an intuition and a certainty, direct *seeing*, the "doors of perception cleansed."

Francis Hart points out that this passage contains all th elements of "what would become Neil's view of life." (Th incident described took place as early as 1934). And not the least of these elements was that "divine, delicious sense of humour." It was the quest for such moments, the striving to give them adequate expression, that informed the whole of Gunn's work as a writer. And yet balanced against this were the continuing demands of his publishers, his general readership, for the solid, mainstream Scottish novel. Gunn was always conscious of balancing the two elements, as it were rationing out his little moments of "self-indulgence." Hart quotes from a letter he received from Gunn, concerning the expression of his "unexpected insights."

"Sometimes I was a bit bothered by these insights, because I had a liking for them (like having a drink, a tot, on the way), but the internal thing that did the 'telling' would stand no nonsense . . . Sometimes when I got an insight (let the word pass) that might run to two sentences, the 'balance' frowned on what it obviously considered was self-indulgence if not worse . . . But if I had done a fair amount of straight action, I might have my own way for a whole small paragraph. It was sometimes amusing to look on at this happening . . ."

By the time he wrote *The Atom of Delight*, the need to express the "insights" and to expand upon them had become uppermost. He told Pick: "When I finished *The Atom of Delight*, I felt that was the end of my youth and now I'd really get down to it . . . I would start the real work and have a few years for it . . ."

But his readers on the whole were not willing to follow him. Pick expresses what he sensed was Gunn's feeling at this time: "Perhaps Neil now felt that for years he had been deceived into thinking that readers appreciated his books because they appreciated the nature of the mind that made them, only to find that the true 'inwardness' of the novels did not register at all — only the surface, the events, the emotional charge."

So it was goodbye to books, though not to that inner search.